W9-BQT-427

Across Boundaries:
The Book in Culture & Commerce

ACROSS BOUNDARIES
THE BOOK IN CULTURE & COMMERCE

Edited by
Bill Bell, Philip Bennett & Jonquil Bevan

ST PAUL'S BIBLIOGRAPHIES

OAK KNOLL PRESS

First published 2000
by St Paul's Bibliographies
West End House
1 Step Terrace
Winchester
Hampshire SO20 5BW
UK

and

Oak Knoll Press
310 Delaware Street
New Castle
DE 19720
USA

ISBN 1-873040-47-4 (St Paul's Bibliographies)
ISBN 1-58456-006-1 (Oak Knoll Press)

Library of Congress Cataloguing-in-Publication Data

Across boundaries: the book in culture & commerce/edited by
Bill Bell, Jonquil Bevan & Philip Benett.
   p. cm.
  Includes bibliographical references and index.
  ISBN 1-58456-006-1
  1. Book industries and trade—Europe, Western—History—
Congresses.   2. Book industries and trade—North America—
History —Congresses.   3. Books and reading—Europe,
Western—History—Congresses.   4. Books and reading—North
America—History— Congresses.   5. Written communication—
Europe, Western—History—Congresses. I. Bell, Bill.
II. Bevan, Jonquil, 1941– III. Bennett, Philip.
Z280 .A26   2000
002—dc21   99-056404

Typeset by Cambridge Photosetting Services, Cambridge
Printed in England by St Edmundsbury Press, Bury St Edmunds

CONTENTS

LIST OF CONTRIBUTORS

Alan Bell has been Librarian of The London Library since 1993, having previously held library appointments in Edinburgh and Oxford. He is a member of the Saintsbury Club.

Bill Bell is co-director of the Centre for the History of the Book at the University of Edinburgh. He is a general editor of *A History of the Book in Scotland,* to be published in 4 volumes, and has written widely on nineteenth century literature and culture.

Philip E. Bennett, Reader in French at the University of Edinburgh, has published widely on medieval French literature, particularly on the epic and the Tristan legend. His latest publications are *The 'Chanson de Guillaume' and the 'Prise d'Orange'* and an edition of the *Chanson de Guillaume.*

Jonquil Bevan, Reader in English Literature, is a co-director of the Centre for the History of the Book at the University of Edinburgh and a general editor of *A History of the Book in Scotland.* She is working on an edition of Izaak Walton's *Lives* for the Clarendon Press, Oxford.

Fiona A. Black, a librarian, is co-editor of volume 2 of *The History of the Book in Canada.* Her research includes Scottish-Canadian book history and the applications of geographic information systems for print culture studies.

Roger Chartier is Directeur d'Études at the École des Hautes Études en Sciences Sociales at Paris. He writes on the history of the book, education, and reading. His recent publications include *On the Edge of the Cliff: History, Language, Practices* (Baltimore, 1997) and as co-editor *A History of Reading in the West* (Cambridge, 1999).

Sylvia Huot is University Lecturer in French and a Fellow of Pembroke College, Cambridge. She has written widely in the field of medieval French literature and manuscript studies and is the author of *The Romance of the Rose and its Medieval Readers* (1993) and *Allegorical Play in the Old French Motet* (1997).

Lisa Jardine is Professor of Renaissance Studies at Queen Mary and Westfield College, University of London, and an honorary fellow of King's College, Cambridge. She is the author of a number of scholarly books on the

Renaissance, including *Erasmus, Man of Letters* and (with Dr Alan Stewart) *Hostage to Fortune: The Troubled Life of Francis Bacon.*

Wallace Kirsop is Honorary Professorial Fellow in French Studies and Director of the Centre for the Book at Monash University. He has edited the *Australian Journal of French Studies* since 1968.

James Raven is University Lecturer in Modern History at the University of Oxford and Tutorial Fellow of Mansfield College. He has written widely on the history of printing, publishing and reading practices in eighteenth-century Britain, Europe and the colonies. His most recent book is *London Booksellers and American Customers.*

Ian Willison is a senior research fellow of the University of London Institute for English Studies and one of the general editors of the Cambridge *History of the Book in Britain.*

PREFACE

'The Paratext constitutes a zone between text and off-text, a zone not
only of transition but of transaction.'

Gerard Genette, *Paratexts*

This volume is about the crossing of boundaries, both literal and figurative.
Self-evidently broad in its historical scope (there are essays here on topics as
diverse as the book as symbol in medieval allegorical and moral thought, and
the position of the text in relation to contemporary post-colonial critique)
the thematic integrity of *Across Boundaries* is to be found in its pursuit of a
material culture that, in its broadest sense, fundamentally challenges existing
disciplinary and national affiliation. In 1993, the *Chronicle of Higher
Education* announced that 'after several decades of growth book history is
now at a point of transition. Researchers are beginning to cross disciplinary
and national borders to establish new journals, book projects, centers, and
academic programs'. Since then, the field has continued to grow exponen-
tially. By the middle of the decade several large-scale national histories of the
book were underway, dedicated research centres had been established at the
Universities of London and of Edinburgh, and throughout North America
and there was even talk in some quarters of a possible 'World History of the
Book'. Consequently, it was felt that the time to explore in its broadest sense
the space between national, as well as disciplinary, boundaries had come. The
occasion from which this volume emerged was a conference in 1996 at the
University of Edinburgh, whose chief aim was to explore a set of often difficult
questions arising from a much-vaunted, though seldom demonstrated, interdisciplinarity.

Our volume opens with a consideration of the kinds of transformation that
texts can be seen to undergo as they cross and recross ontological boundaries.
In 'Orality Lost', Roger Chartier explores the complex manoeuvres involved
in the movement between orality, manuscript, and print, paying particular
attention to material aspects of textual presentation in the interpretation of
enunciations. Drawing on a range of reference, from Petronius to Borges,
Professor Chartier shows how modern critics ignore at their peril the materiality of the text and the historicity of its composition and transmission, providing a highly nuanced account of the way in which texts resist universal and
even generic categorisation. A similar theme is pursued by Sylvia Huot in
'The Writer's Mirror: Watriquet de Couvin and the Development of the
Author-Centred Book', in which she explores the transition of the manuscript
from being a reader-centred item, frequently a collection of works of disparate origins, to an author-centred presentation. An important aspect of this

development is shown to be the evolution in religious and moral thought of the self as book, writing itself or being written by another, with eschatological significance.

Several of these essays remind us of the way in which a sociological regard for the production of texts can reveal another kind of boundary-crossing, namely between the categories of 'commerce' and 'culture'. All in some senses might be said to explore, to a greater or lesser extent, the deep and mutually implicating relationship that has existed for centuries between economics and literary culture. In her essay 'Book Ventures, Cultural Capital and Enduring Reputation in the Italian Renaissance', Lisa Jardine examines the role of the book as '*objet d'art*' and '*objet de vertù*' in addition to its function as repository for text. The investigation of prefatory and dedicatory images alongside words, of illustration and marginal decoration, of binding and finishing, all contribute to an understanding of the importance of books in fifteenth-century Florentine society, for rulers in particular, as icons of power and prestige. For these banker-princes the physical manifestation of culture was as significant as the culture itself, being a symbol of the wealth that sustained both. Wallace Kirsop extends the concern with intellectual and commercial exchange into the area of subscription publishing. Taking account of the many factors affecting the distribution of this important print medium, 'Patronage across Frontiers' traces the dissemination of French literature across the globe in the eighteenth and early nineteenth centuries, showing the extent to which communications networks, methods of credit extension, and political disruption, all helped to shape the intellectual life of the period.

Whether in earlier forms of direct patronage, through the collective economic support typical of the subscription publishing that reached its zenith in the eighteenth century, or in the formation of a 'symbolic capital', the material text has represented not only an important factor within international commerce, but has acted in profound ways as a carrier of culture across frontiers. Taken together, these essays show how economic infrastructures were made to serve cultural networks that in turn informed the exchange of texts as commodities over several centuries. These factors are more than apparent in James Raven's 'Commodification and Value: Interactions in Book Traffic to North America, *c.* 1750–1820', which offers an account of the sometimes difficult, and often eventful, book-trade links between Britain and America. Fiona Black's detailed reconstruction of the reading habits of Hudson's Bay employees demonstrates how books, as well as following colonial networks, served in important ways to create and sustain new international routes. In the same vein Bill Bell's account of nineteenth-century Scottish emigrants reveals how cultural values were often reproduced, and even sometimes modified, through the use of books and reading in exile. Such geo-political relations are set in a broader context by I.R. Willison in a *tour d'horizon* of the many factors involved in the creation of such colonial print cultures. Going on to explore some of the cross-fertilisations that are now taking place between traditional institutional taxonomies, Willison offers an illuminating survey of the many places where today the history of the book can be seen to meet other intellectual fields. At a moment when new forms of enquiry are emerging, these essays, taken together, remind us of the extent to which a regard for the material culture of the text has already begun to offer a new understanding of what might be called 'the geography of communications'.

The symposium on which this volume is based would not have been possible without the generous support of the Saintsbury Winery of Napa, California, and so it is appropriate that this volume should conclude with a writer whose long career was dedicated to boundary crossings of many kinds. George Saintsbury's manoeuvres between journalism and *belles lettres*, between literary cultures – French, English, German – between genres – criticism, drama, fiction – make him the ideal reason for such a collection. Alan Bell shows how, throughout his career as writer and academic, Saintsbury crossed and recrossed the boundaries between classical and contemporary learning, between commerce and the art of the 'bon vivant'.

Debts of gratitude are also owed to those other members of the Saintsbury Series organising committee who helped to make the original concept a reality, particularly to Peter France and to Roger Savage, and, in her capacity as Saintsbury Professor, Elizabeth Ermarth. Finally, we would like to thank Robert Cross and David Way, whose patience and good will throughout the production of this book is ample demonstration of the humane understanding that can sometimes still exist between 'commerce and culture'.

Bill Bell
Philip Bennett
Jonquil Bevan

ORALITY LOST:
TEXT AND VOICE IN THE SIXTEENTH AND SEVENTEENTH CENTURIES

ROGER CHARTIER

THIS PAPER IS devoted to the nexus of relations formed during the sixteenth and seventeenth centuries between the forms of transmission of texts or, to put it another way, the different modalities of their 'performance', and their possible reception by different audiences. Our inquiry has two objectives: on the one hand, to identify the modes of circulation and appropriation of works and genres whose original status, function, and usages were not those exclusively implied either by printed inscription or by silent, individual reading habits; and on the other hand, to study the relationships which two accepted versions of the category of genre entertain: the one discursive and literary, the other material and editorial.

I would like to show that the contemporary relationship to works and to genres cannot be considered either invariable or universal. Against the temptations of an 'ethnocentrism of reading', it is necessary to recall how numerous are the ancient texts which in no way implied, as addressee, a solitary and silent reader, in search of meaning. Composed to be spoken or to be read out loud and shared before a listening audience, invested with a ritual function, thought of as machines designated to produce certain effects, they obey the laws proper to 'performance' or to oral and communal transmission. I will situate this question within my own field of interest, one which strives to link the study of texts, whether they be canonical or ordinary, 'literary' or not, the analysis of their material forms and their modes of circulation, and their interpretations, usages, and appropriations by their different reading and listening audiences.

This point of departure is an attempt to break with the uncritical posture which assumes that all texts, all works, all genres must reasonably be read, identified, and received according to criteria which characterise our own relation to the written word. It is thus a question of historicising criteria of classification between genres, ways of reading, and representations of the structure of address and the addressee of texts as they have been bequeathed to us by the 'literary institution'. Confronted with works dating from the sixteenth and seventeenth centuries (and *a fortiori* from earlier periods or from non-Western cultures), categories which we have used unreflectingly begin to lose their assumed self-evidence and universality.

Let us consider, to illustrate the above, the reading of a 'tale' – a '*cuento*' as its author Borges writes. It is a 'fiction' entitled *El espejo y la máscara* (*The Mirror and the Mask*), published in the collection *El libro de arena* (*The Book of Sand*) (Borges, 1975a). In it, Borges tells a story about a king and a bard. After having conquered his Norwegian enemy, the High King of Ireland asks the poet Ollan to write an ode that will celebrate his triumph and establish his glory for all eternity. 'Las proezas más claras pierden su lustre si no se las amoneda en palabras [. . .] Yo seré Eneas; tu serás mi Virgilio.' ('The greatest deeds lose their lustre if they are not coined in words. [. . .] I will be Aeneas; you will be my Virgil.') Three times, at one-year intervals, the bard returns to the king with a different poem. And, each time, the poetic writing, the aesthetic which governs it, the form of publication of the text, and the figure of its addressee find themselves modified.

The bard composed his first ode according to the rules of his art, mobilising all the knowledge which is his: a knowledge of words, images, verse, examples, genres, tradition. The poem is declaimed by its author 'con lenta seguridad, sin una ojeada al manuscrito' ('slowly, confidently, without a glance at the manuscripts') before the king, the court, the 'School of Bards' and crowds of those who 'agolpados en las puertas, no descifraban una palabra' ('thronging at the doorways, were unable to make out a single word'). This first panegyric is a 'monument': it respects rules and conventions, it summarises all of Ireland's literature, it is set down in writing. Inscribed within the order of representation, it leads one to believe in the exploits of the sovereign. It should thus be conserved and disseminated: the king commands 30 scribes to copy it twelve times each. The bard has been a good artisan who has faithfully reproduced the teachings of the ancients: 'has attribuido a cada vocablo su genuina acepción y a cada nombre sustantivo el epíteto que le dieron los primeros poetas. No hay en toda la loa una sola imagen que no hayan los clásicos. [. . .] Has manejado con destreza la rima, la aliteración, la asonancia, las cantidades, los artificios de la docta retórica, la sabia alteración de los metros.' ('You have given each word its true meaning, and each substantive the epithet given it by the poets of old. In your whole panegyric there is not a single image unknown to the classics. [. . .] You have skilfully handled rhyme, alliteration, assonance, quantities, the artifices of learned rhetoric, the wise variations of metres.') In recompense, the bard is given a mirror, the work of an artisan like himself which, like the ode of praise, reflects what is already there.

The king, however, remains dissatisfied. Although it is perfect, the poem remains lifeless. It does not produce effect either on the soul or on the body:

'Todo está bien y sin embargo nada ha pasado. En los pulsos no corre más a prisa la sangre. Las manos no han buscado los arcos. Nadie ha palidecido. Nadie profirió un grito de batalla, nadie opuso el pecho a los vikings.' ('All is well and yet nothing has happened. In our veins the blood runs no faster. Our hands have not sought the bow. No one has turned pale. No one uttered a battle cry or set his breast against the Vikings.') The bard deserves a reward, but in order to qualify he must compose another work: 'Dentro del término de un año aplaudiremos otra loa, poeta' ('Before the year is out, poet, we shall applaud another ode').

One year later, the poet is back before the king. His new poem is quite different from the preceding one. On the one hand, it breaks all existing rules, whether they be grammatical ('Un sustantivo singular podía regir un verbo plural. Las preposiciones eran ajenas a las normas communes' – 'A singular noun could govern a plural verb. The prepositions were alien to common usage'), poetic ('La aspereza alternaba con la dulzura' – 'Harshness alternated with sweetness'), or rhetorical ('Las metáforas eran arbirarias o así lo parecían' – 'Metaphors were arbitrary or so they seemed'). The work in no way conforms to the conventions of literary art; it is no longer imitation but invention.

As the poet reads his work, he no longer recites it with the mastery which was demonstrated one year earlier. He reads with uneasiness, hesitation, uncertainty – 'lo leyó con visible inseguridad, omitiendo ciertos pasajes, como si él mismo no los entendiera del todo o no quisiera profanarlos'. ('He read with a visible lack of self-confidence, omitting certain passages, as if he did not completely understand them himself or did not wish to profane them.') This reading again takes place before the king and the circle of men of letters, but this time the public has disappeared. This new text, strange, surprising, no longer belongs to the order of representation but, through its invention, to that of illusion. It does not lead one to believe in the exploits of the king. It *is* these exploits, shown to the listening audience. 'No era una descripción de la batalla, era la batalla.' ('It was not a description of the battle, it was the battle.') The poem gives rise to the event itself, in its original force. *Ekphrasis* has been substituted for representation.

The poem captures and captivates its audience: 'Suspende, maravilla y deslumbra' ('It astounds, it dazzles, it causes wonderment.') It exerts an effect which the first ode failed to accomplish in spite of its formal perfection. Borges goes back, in order to characterise these effects, to the very vocabulary of the Spanish 'Golden Age' literature: 'embelesar', 'maravillar', 'encantar', a time when fiction was thought of and described as a dangerous enchantment that annuls the gap between the world of the text and the world of the reader (Ife, 1985). The poet's second ode is to be preserved, though not destined for the illiterate but, rather, only for a small company of the learned: 'Un cofre de marfil será la custodia del único ejemplar' ('An ivory casket will be the resting place of its single copy'). In return for his creation, which has the force of theatrical illusion, the poet receives a theatrical object, a golden mask, a sign of his inventiveness. Yet the king requires a work still more sublime.

Upon his return one year later, the bard brings with him an ode which is no longer written, consisting only of a single line. The bard and the king are alone. The bard utters the ode a first time, after which 'el poeta y su Rey la paladearon, como si fuera una plegaria o una blasfemia' ('the poet and his king savoured it as if it were a secret prayer or a blasphemy'). Turning everything upside down, the poem is inscribed within the order of the sacred, a prayer or a blasphemy, inhabiting the poet like an inspired word. The poet has not respected the rules; nor has he transgressed them but has been overwhelmed like the Homeric bard or the lyric poet by an inspired word: 'En el alba, me recordé diciendo unas palabras que al principio no comprendí. Esas palabras son un poema.' ('In the dawn I woke up speaking words I did not at first understand. Those words were a poem.') Thus inhabited by a language other than his own, the poet becomes other. 'Casi era otro. Algo, que no era el tiempo, había surcado y transformado sus rasgos. Los ojos parecían mirar muy lejos o haber quedado ciegos.' ('He was like another man. Something other than time had furrowed and transformed his features. His eyes seemed to stare into the distance or to be blind.')

Ollan is thus inscribed in the line of blind poets, dear to Borges. In a lecture given in 1977, *La ceguera* (*Blindness*), he reminds us that it was at the very moment when he was named Director of the National Library in Buenos Aires, in 1955, that he became aware that he had lost his sight (Borges, 1980). The *Poema de los dones* (the *Poem of gifts*) begins as follows: 'Nadie rebaje a lágrimas / Esta declaración de la maestria / De Dios que con magnífica ironía / Me dio a la vez los libros y la noche' ('Let no one debase with pity or reprove / This declaration of God's mastery, / Who with magníficent irony / Gave me at once books and the night.') A librarian and blind, Borges is doubly heir: of the blind librarians who preceded him in his position at the National Library, Paul Groussac and José Marmól, and of the blind poets, inspired in their dark night – Homer, Milton, Joyce.

Murmured, the third ode is an event and not a monument. It was not written; it will not be repeated. It constitutes a unique experience, and no reading of it is possible. Its mystery leads those who utter it to forbidden contemplation. 'Sentí que había cometido un pecado, quizá el que no perdona el Espíritu'. ('I felt I had committed a sin, perhaps one the Holy Ghost does not forgive') says the poet. And the king replies: 'El que ahora compartimos los dos. El de haber conocido la Belleza, que es un don vedado a los hombres. Ahora nos toca expiarlo.' ('The one we two now share. The sin of having known Beauty, which is a gift forbidden to men. Now it behoves us to

4

expiate it.') The king's third gift is thus an instrument of death: a dagger with which the poet commits suicide. The king's expiation takes another form, one appropriate for the 'great theatre of the world' where roles are ephemeral and interchangeable: 'es un mendigo que recorre los caminos de Irlanda, que fue su reino, y no ha repetido nunca el poema' ('he is a beggar wandering the length and breadth of Ireland – which was once his kingdom and he has never repeated the poem').

Borges's fable takes us from the monument to the event, from inscription to 'performance'. It designates, with the acuteness of a Cervantes, the different registers of opposition that span written culture. These have to do with aesthetic norms (imitation, invention, inspiration), modes of transmission of the text (recitation, reading aloud, saying it to oneself), the nature of the addressee (the public at large, the learned, the prince or, finally, the poet himself), and the relationship between words and things (inscribed within the order of representation, that of illusion, or that of mystery). The 'tale' of the mirror and the mask, of the poet and the king, thus provides points of reference which allow the historian to enter into the analysis of forms of production, circulation and appropriation of texts, considering as essential their variations across time, place, and community. The lesson does not fully account for the poetic optimism of Borges's text but it is perhaps faithful to what Borges wrote in a preface to *Macbeth*: '*Art happens* (El arte ocurre) declaró Whistler, pero la conciencia de que no acabaremos nunca de descifrar el misterio estético no se opone al examen de los hechos que lo hicieron posible.' ('*Art happens* declared Whistler, but the idea that we will never have done with deciphering the aesthetic mystery does not stand in the way of our examination of the facts which made it possible.') (Borges, 1975b).

The opposition I made between the text 'monument' and the text 'event' was proposed by a historian of classical literature, Florence Dupont, in a book entitled *The Invention of literature. From Greek intoxication to the Latin book* (Dupont, 1994). Dupont's book serves to underscore the insufficiency of categories traditionally associated with the idea of literature as a means of accounting for the production and circulation of texts in Antiquity. What are, in fact, the fundamental notions which constitute the 'literary institution'? First of all, the identification of the text with a writing that is fixed, stabilised, and manipulable owing to its permanence. Second, the idea that the work is produced for a reader – and a reader who reads in silence, for himself and alone, even where he happens to be in a public space. Finally, the characterisation of reading as a quest for meaning, a work of interpretation, a search for signification. The fundamental genres of Greek or Roman literature show that we must distance ourselves from these three suppositions in order to

5

understand the reasons for their production, the modalities of their performance, and the forms of their appropriation.

The ode, for example, should not be thought of as a 'literary' genre, but as
a ritual speech act which takes place in a form of religious sociability that is
essential to ancient Greece, the *symposión*, or banquet of Dionysiac drunken-
ness. The ode is a song addressed to the gods of the banquet, and above all to
Dionysius, as well as a song inspired by the Muses, of which the singer is but
the instrument. Far from being the result of an individual creation, the product
of a poetic art, the banquet song manifests the overpowering of the speaker by
sacred inspiration. The meaning of the text depends entirely on its ritual effectiveness. It cannot be separated from the circumstances in which the poetry is
sung since, by invoking the gods, it requires their participation in the banquet.
Irreducibly singular, the text can be neither written down nor repeated. It is a
moment of surging forth, it is mystery, it is event.

It is in Greek antiquity itself that this poetic, ritual, and singular word was
progressively transformed into 'literature'. During the festivals and competi-
tions accompanying the cults of the city-states or the great panhellenic sanc-
tuaries (such as Delphi or Epidaurus), the song inspired by the Muses
becomes a genre which has its rules and whose productions can be classified
and hierarchised.

This transformation of a ritual event into a poetic monument has considerable consequences. The most fundamental is the gap introduced between the
circumstances of actual enunciation – namely, the poetic competition which
seeks to crown literary excellence – and the fictional scene of enunciation in
the poem itself which refers back to an already vanished situation – that of the
banquet where the ode was sung for its ritual function. The primeval enunciation has become a literary fiction. The banquet which it evokes is no longer a
Dionysiac *symposión* but an imagined feast. A second effect of the transformation from ritual word into literary monument is the necessity to assign it to
an author. For this mythical authors were required and each genre became
associated with one author considered as its founder: Homer for the epic,
Anacreon for lyric poetry. The primordial author becomes as it were the guar-
antor for the genre in which new creations are inscribed. A third consequence
is the possibility (or the necessity) of elaborating a poetics that codifies the
rules. The inspired word that overwhelms the poet who conveys it, is substituted by the idea of the work as creation and as labour. That is why it is only
with lyrical poetry, Pindar or Baccylides, that the poem can for the first time
be compared to a woven textile, and art to a craft. Never in the *Iliad* or the
Odyssey is the metaphor of verbal weaving, which is used to designate con-
tests in eloquence, ever applied to the song of the poet which, after all, is not
his but the Muses' (Scheid and Svenbro, 1994).

When the production of the text is no longer attributed to the wild and spontaneous irruption of the sacred word, it comes to depend on the correct application and imitation of rules. This is why, according to Aristotle's *Poetics*, or at least his commentators, a tragedy ought to be judged, not on the basis of its theatrical performance, but through a reading which measures its conformity to the norm. The opposition between rules and performance as the fundamental criterion for the evaluation of works (as established in the classical *ars poetica*) provides the foundation for polemical arguments mobilised during the literary *querelles* of the seventeenth century, for example those concerning plays by Corneille (Merlin, 1994) or Lope de Vega (Lope de Vega, 1609). They oppose, in fact, the learned, who judge plays on the basis of rules and reading, and those (not least the authors themselves) who consider the effects produced on the audience during the theatrical representation to be of prime importance. Recalling in 1609 in his *Arte nuevo de hacer comedias en este tiempo*, addressed to an Academy of Men of Letters assembled in Madrid by the count of Saldaña, that he is the author of 483 'comedies', Lope de Vega adds: 'Fuera de seis, las demás todas / pecaron contra el arte gravamente. / Sustento, en fin, lo que escribí, y conozco / que, aunque fueran mejor de otra manera, / no tuvieran el gusto que han obtenido / porque a veces lo que es contra lo justo / por la misma razón deleita al gusto.' ('Except for six in fact, all without exception / have gravely sinned against the laws of the art. / No matter, I uphold what I have written and I know / that, if done otherwise, they would have been better, / but they would not have enjoyed such favour / for sometimes that which runs counter to what is right, for that very reason is what pleases the most.')

From these three features (the disjunction between the actual circumstances of the enunciation and the fictive enunciation inscribed in the text; the invention of founding authors; the formulation of an *ars poetica* stating what the rules ought to be) there follows another: the written inscription of texts which thus constitutes, by this very fact, a scholarly canon, an object of apprenticeship, and a repertoire from which to draw citations, examples, and models necessary for composing new texts. The trajectory of the Greek world thus takes us from a poetry fundamentally linked to its performance, one governed by the forms of sociability and religious rituals in which it is sung, to a poetry that is governed by the rules of the 'literary institution'. The endpoint of such a trajectory occurs during the Hellenistic period, with the constitution of the Library and the Museum of Alexandria in the third century A.D. It is at that time that the fundamental categories which structure the order of modern literary discourse, as characterised by Foucault in two famous texts, *Qu'est-ce qu'un auteur?* (*What is an Author?*) and *L'ordre du discours* (*The Order of Discourse*) (Foucault, 1969 and 1970, Chartier, 1992), were crystallised in the concept of work, with its criteria of unity, coherence, fixity; the category of author which assigns the work to a proper name; finally the commentary, identified with the work of interpretation, which brings meaning to light. The three fundamental disciplines of the 'literary institution' (philology, literary history, hermeneutics) are thus set in place at the close of a trajectory leading from 'event' to 'monument' and they find their formulation in the dream of a universal library.

Dupont offers two other examples from the Roman world. First of all, the poetic and erotic games linked to another form of banquet, not the sacred banquet which convokes the presence of the gods, but the banquet of conversations and cultivated pleasures: the *commissatio*. The evolution of poems recited during these feasts is similar to that of the lyric ode. It transforms into literature a form of entertainment whose meaning was fully linked to its circumstances. The ephemeral nature of the poetic event is substituted by written inscription, by the constitution of a repertoire, by the development of commentaries, by the reuse of citations.

The second example is to be found in the novel: *The Golden Ass* of Apuleius or *The Satyricon* by Petronius. In both cases, the question is the same: why were these collections of loosely structured stories composed for recitation fixed in writing? There is in every form of oral transmission of tales or stories a certain mobility of the text which comes from the singularity of each of its performances. The gap thus appears irreducible between written inscription which, by definition, sets things down in a fixed form and the practice of recitation which is invention, variation, movement. These features, which are valid for all Latin 'tales', are also valid for those of the modern age. Take, for example, chapter XX of the First Part of *Don Quixote* in which Sancho recounts a tale to Don Quixote (Cervantes 1605). The description shows with extraordinary acuteness, which one might define as 'ethno-sociological', the gap that separates Sancho's way of telling a story and the expectations of the reader which are those of Don Quixote's. Sancho tells his story by multiplying the repetitions, the relative clauses, the broken clauses. He constantly interrupts his story with references to the situation in which he finds himself with Don Quixote. Don Quixote, however, expects a linear narrative, without repetition, without digression. Cervantes thus stages the absolute gap which differentiates between ways of speaking and manners of reading (or of listening to a reading). Sancho tells his story the way one tells a story (*consejas*) in his village. But Don Quixote becomes impatient upon hearing this manner of telling so foreign to a reader accustomed to a text that is written, stable, fixed, linear (Moner, 1989).

The resulting tale does not belong to the canonical repertoire of literature, its cultural disqualification militating against its becoming a 'monument' like the lyric ode or the poetry of the banquets. Why then its written inscription? The question leads one to reflect on the type of reading involved and the use that can be made of collections of stories and tales. It seems that, in the case of *The Golden Ass* or *The Satyricon*, the hypothesis of individual acts of reading is implausible in relation to a genre linked so explicitly to sociability, public occasions, and the sharing of texts, as is the hypothesis of reading aloud for an audience of listeners. In Antiquity, reading out loud serves, basically, two purposes. On the one hand, a pedagogical function: demonstrating that one is a good reader by reading out loud constitutes an obligatory rite of passage for young men who thus display their mastery of rhetoric and public speaking. On the other hand, a literary purpose: to read aloud is, for an author, to put a work into circulation, to 'publish' it. This form of publication, incidentally, will survive well into the modern period, insofar as it will function, between the sixteenth and eighteenth centuries, as a primary form of circulation, before the appearance of the printed edition.

The reading of the stories from *The Golden Ass* or *The Satyricon* does not belong to either of these two categories. Stories are not part of the academic repertoire and are not considered legitimate texts. It may thus be thought that they constitute above all collections of models and *exempla* destined to produce other stories, good for the telling. To read them is to understand the rules and recipes which allow one to invent new narratives. By recording some of the stories circulating in the oral tradition, novels constitute the matrix of a new orality which is based on a series of examples which they gather together. They are like machines for producing discourses whose reading serves for the mobilisation of resources which they make available to makers of tales and stories.

This detour through Antiquity suggests several fundamental principles which might also be seen to apply to early modern times. The first defines the 'literary institution' starting with the objectification of literary expressions separated from their ritual functions and made available for pedagogy, citation, commentary. The second cautions against all forms of anachronism, that is to say, all forms of projecting as universal what are individual experiences, localised in time and space – not least, our own. Readers of Antiquity did not read an ode by Anacreon, a poem by Catullus, or the *Satyricon* as we read them. Their relationship to texts was governed by the ritual or practical efficacy of works read or heard. They were not necessarily silent or solitary readers, characterised by a hermeneutic position. Their reading remained strictly linked to orality and to ritual. Whence the importance of a history of reading devoted to recording the historicity of fundamental morphological differences: for example, between reading in silence and reading aloud, reading in solitude and reading in public, reading for oneself and reading for others, etc. (Cavallo and Chartier, 1995). The third principle reveals a trajectory from the inspired word to controlled imitation, from the singularity of the speech act to its inscription in writing, from the ephemeral of the poetic performance to the repetitiveness of reading. These displacements which characterise ancient literature are not without parallel in modernity. By going through the same itinerary in reverse, Ollan, Borges's Irish poet, attests to the lasting nostalgia for an orality lost.

Let us consider two major poetic genres of the sixteenth and seventeenth centuries studied from the perspective of the same question: how should one understand the relationship between their oral performance and their written inscription, whether written by hand or printed? The ballads will take us to Elizabethan England; the *romances* to the Castille of the Golden Age.

Ballads are a basic poetic and editorial genre in England from the mid-sixteenth to the mid-seventeenth century, the number of titles in circulation having been estimated at about three thousand. They are texts with a very wide diffusion owing to a low price which put them within reach of the most modest of buyers. Ballads were generally printed on a single side of a sheet, according to a regular disposition with, from top to bottom of the sheet, the title, directions for the tune to which the ballad ought to be sung, a woodcut, and the text set in two columns. These broadside ballads (the term *broadside* designating a sheet of paper printed on one side) could be pasted on a wall, in the interior of the house or in a public place, and could also circulate from hand to hand (Watt, 1991).

Broadside ballads constituted a large market, progressively won by specialised publishers, which established a quasi-monopoly on the genre. From 1624 onward, in fact, five publishers of the Stationers' Company, the *ballad partners*, take over the large-scale diffusion of printed ballads. It is during the course of the very history of the genre that its characteristics were established: the image, in the form of woodcuts, became more frequent after 1600 (we find it in five ballads out of six); the lay-out of the text also found its canonical form in the 'two-part folio sheet' in which directions for the tune to which the text is to be sung are present more often than not. On the other hand, between the mid-sixteenth and the mid-seventeenth century, a preference arises for secular at the expense of religious ballads, as if the songs found themselves progressively excluded from a legitimate religious culture, tending toward other poetic forms: psalms, for example, chanted at home or in church. Linked to a more popular and more communal culture, the ballad is excluded from the religious domain and becomes, thereby, a fundamentally secular genre.

One must begin with the very materiality of the broadside ballads in order to attempt to reconstitute how they were 'read' in the England of the sixteenth and seventeenth centuries. It is clear that the object itself provides an indication of something other than solitary and silent reading. It suggests, first of all, a reading that is done in common – posted on a wall, the ballad can be read aloud by those who, better educated, can serve as reading mediators for the less learned. The directions for the melody which figure on many of these broadsides also indicate that the text is written in order to be sung, with or without instrumental accompaniment.

According to Tessa Watt, oral performances of the ballads, when they were executed by 'professionals', might be seen to have applied within different contexts. The first was that of the professional musicians, minstrels or waits, who are often accompanied by an instrument (violin, lute, harp) and played during fairs, at markets, in taverns, on the occasion of urban festivals or in aristocratic houses. A second more theatricalised form, was provided by companies of actors, more or less professional, who inscribed the songs in 'interludes' (dramas, morality plays or histories) at country fairs and markets or in the houses of the nobility. Finally, a third mode of the oral circulation of ballads was provided by the peddlers who not only sold them, but sung them as well. Such peddlers were not professional singers but merchants who, in order to attract a clientele, sang either the text of the ballads they were peddling, or the list of goods they were selling.

In *The Winter's Tale*, Shakespeare creates a vending and ballad-singing peddler – Autolycus – who intervenes on numerous occasions during the fourth and fifth acts of the play (Shakespeare, 1611). Several features characterise him, not least his name which is that of the son of Hermes (Mercury for the Romans), a rakish and deceitful god. And, in fact, Autolycus is not simply a vendor and singer of ballads. He is also a sheet thief ('My traffic is sheets') and a pickpocket ('My revenue is the silly cheat'). In scene III of the fourth Act, he works with wiliness to steal the Clown's purse by feigning the man of property who was himself robbed by a 'rogue', about whom he sketches a funny biography – which is supposedly his own: 'he hath been since an ape-bearer, then a process-server, then he compassed a motion of the Prodigal Son, and married a tinker's wife: Some call him Autolycus'. A crafty thief, expert in the ruses of the intellect, Autolycus is also a cunning peddler whose figure Shakespeare construes out of different features which characterise the craft in Elizabethan England.

The first of these features makes of Autolycus a character of the performance, one who not only sings the ballads he sells because, as he says, 'I can bear my part; you must know 'tis my occupation' but one who also sings out the inventory of his pack as found in the two songs *Lawn as while* and *Will you buy*. The fiction here works through reference to the peddler's songs, present in other contemporary plays and later collected by folklorists. Announced by the Servant as one who peddles ballads ('he sings several tunes, faster than you'll tell money; he utters them as he had eaten ballads') and merchandise ('he sings 'em over as they were gods or goddesses'), Autolycus is a close relative of all the itinerant merchants who, like the blind peddlers of printed materials in Castille or *colporteurs* of pamphlets in Paris (those whom

Pierre de L'Estoile calls *porte-paniers* or *contre-porteux*) cry out, utter, or sing the titles and the texts they proffer.

A second feature that characterises Autolycus's trade is the link between songs and haberdashery. If all that he sells as far as printed texts go are ballads, he tries to sell to the imaginary Bohemian peasants of the last two acts of *The Winter's Tale* all the objects which are to be found in the packs of the English peddlers of the seventeenth century: woven fabrics, everything necessary for sewing and embroidery, vestimentary ornaments, pieces of jewelry, perfume, as well as writing notebooks (the 'table books') (Spufford, 1984). A relation is thus established, in the plots that are knotted around Autolycus, between the ballads, which for the most part are songs of love, and all the objects which are so many presents offered by young men to young maidens in order to seduce them. The link between the ballads which speak of love and the objects which are love-tokens is at the heart of the dispute between the Clown and the peasant girl Mopsa to whom he has promised perfumed gloves and a silk ribbon ('a tawdry-lace and a pair of sweet gloves').

Autolycus 'hath songs for man or woman, of all sizes' and, among them, 'the prettiest love-songs for maids' whose proclaimed innocence is ironically given the lie by the words of the Servant, words which allude to their double meaning, rendering them licentious and ribald. Of the 'ballads in print' sold by Autolycus, Shakespeare indicates three titles, which comically play upon the genre's repertoire. The first, 'to a very doleful tune', recounts 'how a usurer's wife was brought to bed of twenty money-bags at a burden, and how she longed to eat adder's heads and toads carbonated'. The second tells the fantastic story about a young girl transformed into a fish because she refused the advances of her lover. The third is a 'merry ballad', a love song which 'goes to the tune of "Two maids wooing a man"' and in which two maidens pay court to the same young man – which, in the play, finds a parallel in the situation of the Clown who is coveted by Mopsa and Dorcas, who, in addition, sing the ballad along with Autolycus. The titles of the staged ballads are in the case of the first two at least parodic inventions, but inventions that are based on the repertoire of ballads produced at the time by London publishers, exploiting, like their French counterparts, the register of monstrous births, fantastic creatures, terrifying and exemplary punishments.

The Shakespearean text ironically dismantles the strategies employed in the ballads in order to guarantee the truth of the extraordinary narratives put forth in the songs. Autolycus multiplies, in fact, the details which lead the audience to take as true the hard-to-believe facts they narrate. The monstrous birth is attested to in writing by the midwife ('Here's the midwife's name to 't') and 'five or six honest wives that were present'. The story of the maiden transformed into a fish has 'five justices' hands at it, and witnesses more than my pack will hold'. The attraction of the genre thus appears to lie in the reader's belief in the narratives that he or she sings or hears. On a number of occasions, Mopsa and Dorcas interrogate Autolycus in order to be reassured about the truth of the stories that he is selling: 'Is it true, think you?', 'Is it true too, think you?'. The pleasure experienced during the reading or the hearing supposes that the ballads can be taken as true. But, at the same time, this desire for authenticity, just like the marks of authentification, are always parodically contradicted. The midwife who is supposed to have delivered the wife of the usurer is named 'Mistress Taleporter'. The date of the metamorphosis into a 'cold fish' of the frigid maiden is 'Wednesday the forescore of April'.

How are we to interpret this tension between the expectation of truth on the part of the buyers of ballads and the parody (which is not only Shakespearean but is also present in contemporary texts produced by London publishers) serving to situate the narratives within the order of the unbelievable? Does this tension point out the credulity of the fictional peasants on the stage who take as truth the implausible (something the clever and forewarned learned spectator refuses to do)? Or does it describe a 'popular' relation (in the sense of shared or common) to literary fiction; a relation which, at one and the same time, persuades and dissuades, makes one believe and not believe, linking together adhesion and distance?

This model of intelligibility, both subtle and complex, is one that Richard Hoggart proposes in *The Uses of Literacy* (Hoggart, 1957) in which he describes, based on his own experience, the relations working-class readers and listeners entertain in the England of the 1950s with mass circulation newspapers, magazines, horoscopes, serials, love songs. He characterises this relation by the ambiguity of attitudes, as if the necessity and the pleasure of believing shared common ground with the greatest lucidity concerning the falseness of what is believed. Logically contradictory categories are thus paradoxically associated, as if belief experienced moments of eclipse, as if the 'suspension of disbelief' did not efface clairvoyance. A similar perspective is brought into play in Paul Veyne's *Did the Greeks Believe in their Myths?*: 'Among the learned, critical credulity, so to speak, alternated with a global skepticism and it rubbed elbows with the rash credulity of the less learned – these three attitudes tolerated one another and popular credulity was not culturally devalorised. This peaceful coexistence of contradictory beliefs had an effect that was sociologically curious: each individual would interiorise the contradiction and would think concerning the myths irreconcilable things, 'irreconcilable' according to a logician at least: the particular individual, however, did not suffer from these contradictions, quite on the contrary: they each served different purposes' (Veyne, 1983). Before Hoggart, before Veyne, Shakespeare staged – with his shepherds and shepherdesses of Polixenes's Bohemia – the inseparable duality of adhesion and distance.

13

There is perhaps here, as well, a way of characterising the relationship between the spectators and the play. What it recounts, in fact, is a 'winter's tale' as the title says, restated on several occasions throughout the text. Take for example the first scene of the second Act, when Hermione asks her son Mamilius to tell her a story. He replies that 'a sad tale's best for winter' and begins the narrative of the story about a man who used to live close to a cemetery – which will be the fate of Leontes after the death of Hermione, unjustly accused of adultery. Another example occurs in scene II of the last Act, when the marvellous story about the child who was lost and found again and about the dead queen who came back to life is compared, at one and the same time, to 'an old tale' whose truth is suspect and to a series of prodigies such that 'ballad-makers cannot be able to express it'. The play, just as implausible as the tales or the songs, is nevertheless, just like them, supposed to captivate the listener, to persuade him of its plausibility, to make him or her believe in the unbelievable. With paramount skilfulness, *The Winter's Tale* explicitly designates, by assimilating the plot to an old tale, the ambivalence that any reader or spectator feels when confronted with a work of fiction: he knows about the imposture and, yet, he believes in it, for the duration of a ballad or a theatrical play. The relation of Mopsa and Dorcas to the songs by Autolycus ('Is it true, think you?') is thus transformed into a metaphor for the central theme of a play that deals with the tension between nature and art, between truth and artifice (or, better, the truth of artifice) and that also deals with the *jouissance* of those who give way to the pleasure of believing without however being duped by their belief.

The literary text can thus allow us, on condition that its 'literariness' be respected, to reconstruct something of the oral circulation of printed genres and to comprehend the relationship with texts that this particular form of communication and reception of works implies. In the case of the ballads, a supplementary step is possible, which is much rarer, to move no longer from the printed text to its oral performance, but from the editorial genre to its popular production. A large number of ballads, in fact, were not written in order to be printed, if indeed they were written; and they were composed, not by professional authors working for the publishers of the Stationers' Company, but within the confined world of the rural community (Fox, 1994). An examination of them has been possible thanks to the archives of the Star Chamber which was charged with judging all defamation lawsuits. Plaintiffs brought their cases to the tribunal if they felt that they had been slandered or insulted. In the case where an insult had taken the form of a song, the plaintiffs had either to provide evidence in the law courts of the manuscript ballad as it had been posted on walls, or produce a *verbatim* copy of the text that had been sung or recited.

Adam Fox has worked on these 'popular' ballads, defined as 'libellous', 'scandalous', 'infamous', or 'lascivious'. He has thus been able to compare, for the same genre, printed forms with spontaneous forms, either written by hand or simply oral, which are their contemporaries. We have here a fascinating piece of work which has very few equivalents owing to the fact that such popular forms (which is not to imply unlearned) have left few written traces, having been collected quite late. Consider, for example, the fairy tales whose printed versions used to circulate during the seventeenth and eighteenth centuries in the *colportage* repertoire, but whose oral versions were not knowable until after a point in time when folklorists undertook to collect them. What is unique about the case of the English ballads is the contemporaneity which exists between the printed ballads and those, simply written by hand or sung, which are conserved in the archives of the Star Chamber. The only comparable body of documents (though in a genre not codified in the same way as the ballad) is furnished by manuscript placards such as those conserved by the Archives of the *Tribunale del Governatore* (Antonucci, 1989), posted in Rome on doors as a means of ridicule or insult. As in the case of the later ballads, we encounter here the expression of a popular literature of denunciation. And, in both cases, the preoccupation of justice is to identify the authors of the defamatory texts – presupposing, in the Roman case, an expertise allowing one to trace from the written text the hand that wrote it.

Popular and spontaneous ballads were born in tavern culture. Their written inscription often required the intervention of someone who knew how to write. In their own defence, a number of the accused pointed out that they were incapable of writing, often more explicitly declaring that they were incapable of reading or writing 'the written hand'. This notation in the form of an excuse points out the difference, fundamental in the societies of the *Ancien Régime*, between the capacity to read and perhaps to form characters of printed writing (since the acquisition of reading is done with printed texts) and a more complete mastery of writing, which allows one to read handwriting and to write by hand. This dichotomy opposes, in the French language of the seventeenth century, the '*lettre moulée*' that is to say typographical characters, and 'writing' (*l'écriture*) which is handwriting. Since the school curriculum of children from the working classes often terminated with the acquisition of reading, one can suppose that the majority of them were incapable of writing and reading hand-written script. The opposition between reading and writing does not simply distinguish between two competencies; it also distinguishes between what is possible (or impossible) to read when one only knows how to read. The defence of the accused before the Star Chamber is thus not simply a skilful attempt to have the indictment dismissed. It implies a recourse to those who know how to write for the transcription of ballads that have been collectively composed – for example, itinerant merchants, schoolmasters, students returning to their villages, clerics – that is, intermediary 'learned men' who write for others. The delegation of writing here occurs, not within the confines of a single social rank, as is the case in contemporary Rome (Petrucci, 1989), but within a network of social practices that reunites the members of a village community.

The ballads born of tavern culture knew several forms of 'publication'. Some are linked to the oral tradition (texts are declaimed, sung by their authors or sung by professional musicians hired for this purpose); others to the placarding tradition (on the doors of churches, the walls of inns, on crosses, the pillory, etc.). Just as there was mediation in writing, so there was in reading: some people read for the others assembled around a placarded text. In both cases, the oral performance is essential for the dissemination process.

Between the accusers and the accused, the social difference is striking. The accusers belong to the world of authority and the élite: they are officers of the Crown, tax collectors, landowners, pastors, millers, tradesmen, etc. Among the accused, about half come from the lower or middle strata of English society. Consequently, the ballads give vent to a popular mode of protest which takes a poetic form and which is neither revolt nor submission to order. The ballads are inscribed within another register, that of 'local poetic mockery', as Adam Fox puts it, which points to the private existence of those who are 'balladed' and ridiculed for the unfaithfulness of their wives, their illegitimate children, or their sexual misconduct, as well as to the 'local knowledge' which is necessary to appreciate such mockery. 'Popular' ballads are thus entirely caught up within the network of tensions and conflicts characterising the communities in which they are placarded and sung.

They nevertheless also entertain relationships with the editorial genre of ballads printed for the marketplace. These relations have a double face. On the one hand, as rarely happened, London publishers had manuscript ballads retouched by a professional prior to publication. On the other hand, and in reverse manner, some manuscript ballads can be seen to adopt aspects of the printed version (thus, the layout of the text in two columns or the inclusion of directions for the tune to be played) or else adapt the text of a broadside ballad to local circumstances. But, in spite of these few borrowings, emphasis ought rather to be placed on the heterogeneity of the two repertoires – printed and spontaneous – and on the autonomy of popular poetic protest with respect to printed production. The irregularity of forms, local circulation, the particularising of the text strongly differentiate oral and manuscript ballads from the mass of texts produced by London publishers. A similar difference is to be found in the case of tales in the French tradition where significant gaps separate the oral versions, such as have been collected by folklorists, and the printed versions which, even in the repertoire of *colportage*, come out of the learned tradition (Velay-Vallantin, 1992).

The second example that I would like to propose is that of the Castillian *romances*, which also provided a highly codified poetic genre. *Romances* are poems composed in octosyllabic verse, whose even-numbered lines are assonanced, and whose origin is linked either to medieval epic poetry, that is to say, to the *chansons de geste* (of which they are fragments which had later become autonomous) or to traditional lyric poetry. Composed in order to be sung, like all epico-lyric poetry, set down in writing and then in print, the *romances* were destined to have a double circulation in the Hispanic world of the sixteenth and seventeenth centuries. Their oral circulation is attested to, at one and the same time, by their transcription both in the song-books and in music books, and by their presence in the modern tradition. Collected, then recorded by folklorists, *romances* are sung with or without accompaniment, by one singer or by several, sometimes alternating between singer and chorus, and, most frequently, using feminine voices (Romancero, 1994).

Starting from the beginning of the sixteenth century, *romances* circulated also in print, but in two very different forms. The first of these was in anthologies, collections, compilations which take the form of *cancioneros* (or collections of songs) and which comprise several scores or even hundreds of *romances*. One can say that these collections, whose series began with the *Cancionero general* of Hernando del Castillo in 1511 and which rather often carried the title of *Silva de romances*, are addressed to well-to-do readers, who belong to the world of the literate. A second form of circulation was made possible by the *pliegos sueltos*. A *pliego* is a sheet of paper, folded twice, resulting in a printed object in an in-quarto format, composed of four leaves, in eight pages. The oldest conserved *pliego* carrying a *romance* dates from 1510 and was printed in Saragosa by Jorge Cocí. The *pliego* is thus a very inexpensive form of printed material, lending itself to a very wide diffusion. In the *pliego* we thus find associated a concise poetic genre and an editorial genre wholly adapted to the possibilities of Spanish printing in the sixteenth and seventeenth centuries, characterised by small workshops with a capacity for limited production but which can, with a single printing press, print between 1,250 and 1,500 copies of a sheet in one day (Cátedra and Infantes, 1983; Infantes, 1986). The success of the formula is attested to by the number of titles published in the sixteenth century (of which at least one copy of each survives): about 1,250 titles have been counted (Rodríguez Moñino, 1970).

If, in its first stage, the printed formula adjusted itself to the poetic form, one finds subsequently a reverse movement. The first repertoire of printed *romances*, that of the *romances viejos*, resulted from the choice made by publishers during the first half of the sixteenth century within the corpus of the oral and manuscript tradition in which a certain number of texts were fixed and reproduced without wide variation from one edition to another. The *romances nuevos*, which were then composed by lettered poets (Góngora, Lope de Vega) for learned readers, reused the traditional metrics of the *romancero viejo*, playing with archaisms of the language and conforming to the dimensions of the *pliego*. A similar observation can be made regarding the seventeenth century *romances de ciego*, or *de cordel*, composed for a popular public by specialised and anonymous authors, presented by those responsible for their itinerant sale – namely, blind peddlers of print (García de Enterría, 1973, Marco, 1977).

The relationship between these two generic definitions (poetic and material) is often forgotten by a literary criticism which rarely turns its attention to those forms and objects, which are the very vehicles of texts. The printed form of the *pliego* gained authority because of its correspondence to the poetic format of the *romances* drawn from medieval tradition. This form was subsequently responsible for certain constraints on the *romances nuevos* and the *romances de ciego*. With the blind *colporteurs* one once again encounters Hispanic culture's obsession with blindness. A Castillian Autolycus would surely have been blind since it was a fraternity of blindmen who held in Castile the monopoly on the sale of 'papeles públicos' defined by a late royal decree of 1739 as 'Gacetas, Almanaques, Coplas y otros papeles de devoción y diversión que no excedan de cuatro hojas' ('Gazettes, almanacs, songs and other books of devotion or diversion which do not exceed four leaves') – 'cuatro hojas', that is to say the very definition of the *pliego* in the in-quarto format (Botrel, 1993).

The social usages with which the *romances* were invested were wide-ranging, deeply penetrating the culture of the everyday thanks to their printed circulation in the form of the *pliego*. Recited or sung, they accompanied work, dances, festivals. Read, they served as manuals for the acquisition of reading. Learned by heart, they provided a repertoire of formulas and clichés that could be deployed in ordinary oral tradition. The circulation of poetic *pliegos* (caught between oral transmission, printed inscription, and a return to orality) illustrates how the same genre could, in diverse forms, be addressed to completely different publics serving a variety of uses.

Singling out the effects specific to the different modes of representation, transmission, and reception of texts allows for the anthropological, sociological, and historical understanding of works. Here it is necessary to follow the programme traced out by Pierre Bourdieu: 'S'interroger sur les conditions de possibilité de la lecture, c'est s'interroger sur les conditions sociales de possibilité des situations dans lesquelles on lit [. . .] et aussi sur les conditions sociales de production des *lectores*. Une des illusions du *lector* est celle qui consiste à oublier ses propres conditions sociales de production, à universaliser inconsciemment les conditions de possibilité de sa lecture.' (Bourdieu, 1987) ('Inquiring into the conditions of possibility of reading means inquiring into the social conditions which make possible the situations in which one reads [. . .] and inquiring also into the social conditions of production of *lectores*. One of the illusions of the *lector* is that which consists in forgetting one's own social conditions of production, and unconsciously universalising the conditions of possibility of one's own reading.') The fundamental aim of this remark consists in opposing the logic of practice – that of the performance of myths or rites – to the logic of the interpretation, and commentary, which is a logic of the order of discourse. Imposing a textual logic on rite or myth is submitting it to categories that are foreign to them. On a smaller scale and one more compatible with my own research, this remark leads one to distinguish between the oral, communal and ritual performance of texts, that obeys its own laws, and a reading of these same texts as practised by a reader who is in the position of a *lector* in search of meaning. Here we have a pertinent warning against any temptation to project our own relationship with classical texts onto that of the ancients – which would be an error similar to the one that projects 'into practices what is the function of practices for someone who studies them as something to be deciphered' (Bourdieu, 1987).

Whence, for the historian, a problem of method: how to reconstruct situations proper to the *oral* appropriation of ancient texts when these are for us, by definition, mute forms of orality? There are, it seems to me, several strategies which allow us to confront this difficulty. The first seeks to decipher in literary representations the practices of orality: recitation, song, reading aloud, etc. It is therefore a question of constituting the corpus of these silent forms of orality which certain texts represent through the fiction of writing. This is the case with the tale told by Sancho or the ballads sung by Autolycus. It is also the case with other texts – for example, in chapter V of the *Rustical Sayings* (*Propos rustiques*) of Noël du Fail that stage the way in which a rich peasant, Robin Chevet, recounts some old folk tales before his assembled household (Du Fail, 1548). The features that Du Fail retains in order to characterise this recitation are the very ones that Cervantes uses in order to qualify the manner with which Sancho tells his *consejas* – thus the appeals to the audience, the digressions, the parenthetical remarks, the repetitions, etc. This first path of inquiry is in no way to be understood as reducing the text to a documentary status, but it does take into account the fact that the literary representations of the practices of orality designate (while displacing them onto the register of fiction) the specific procedures that govern them (Chartier, 1980).

The second mode of inquiry seeks to collect in the works themselves the 'indicators of orality' such as they have been defined by Paul Zumthor: 'By indicator of orality, I mean anything that, within the text, informs us about the intervention of the human voice in its *publication*, I mean in the mutations through which the text passed, once or many times, from a virtual state to its current form and henceforth existed in the mind and the memory of a certain number of individuals' (Zumthor, 1987). These indicators of orality, deposited within texts, are not representations of oral practices, but implicit or explicit devices that destine texts to addressees who read aloud or listen to a text being read. They may be indisputable, just as when a musical notation indicates that a text is to be sung. They may be simply probable, as in the case of texts that are addressed to a double audience: those who will read and those who will listen to the text being read to them. In all European languages, a couple of verb pairs mark this double reception: *to read* and *to hear*, *ver* and *oír* or *leer* and *escuchar*, *voir* and *écouter*. Prologues, notices to the reader, and chapter titles very frequently indicate this double nature of address and double circulation of the text (Frenk, 1981).

Other indicators, inscribed within the formal structure of works, may equally suggest the oral destination of texts. A number of works, starting with the greatest, such as *Don Quixote*, are organised in short chapters, perfectly adapted to the necessities of 'oral performance', assuming a limited time of delivery in order not to tire the audience and to account for the audience's inability to memorise an overly complex plot. Brief chapters, which are so many textual units, can be considered units of reading, closed in upon themselves and separate. William Nelson has thus demonstrated how the rewriting of certain works (the *Amadigi* by Bernardo Tasso or the *Arcadia* by Spenser) can be understood as the adjustment of the work to the constraints of reading aloud at a time when this practice was a major form of lettered sociability (Nelson, 1976/77). The division of the text into shorter units, the multiplication of autonomous episodes, and the simplification of the plot are all indicators of the adaptation of the work to a modality essential to its transmission. This is doubtless the case for a number of older verse or prose works – in particular, the collections of short stories where a staged fictive enunciation (which imagines the reunion of several storytellers within an enclosed space) possibly coincides with the real conditions of its circulation (through reading out loud).

A last line of inquiry is more technical and more specific. It is devoted to the transformations of punctuation beginning with the hypothesis of the passage from a punctuation of oralisation to a grammatical punctuation or, as William Nelson writes, from mutation (which according to him dates from the end of 'the late seventeenth century') such that elocutionary punctuation indicative of pauses and pitches was then largely supplanted by syntactic punctuation. Verifying such a hypothesis poses a preliminary difficulty: to whom should one attribute the orthographic and graphic forms of ancient editions? According to diverse traditions of study, the answer varies widely.

In the context of analytical bibliography, graphic and orthographic choices are the doing of compositors. The compositors of ancient printing workshops did not share a consensus in matters of spelling and punctuation. Whence the regular recurrence of the same forms in the various quires of a book, according to preferences of orthography, punctuation, or layout of the compositor who set the pages of the different formes. It is the reason why 'spelling analysis' and 'compositor studies' which allows one to attribute the composition of such and such a sheet or a forme to such and such a compositor constitutes, with the analysis of damaged types and ornaments, one of the surest means to reconstruct the very process of the making of a book, by formes or *seriatim* (McKenzie, 1959, Hinman, 1963, Flores, 1975, Tanselle, 1981, Veyrin-Forrer, 1989). In this line of inquiry, based on the study of the materiality of printed works, punctuation is considered, in the manner of graphic or orthographic variations, as the result, not of the will of the author who wrote the text, but of the habits of the compositors who composed the printed book.

From another perspective, that of the philological history of language, the essential role is played out elsewhere: in the preparation of the manuscript for composition as practiced by the '*corrector*', that is to say the copy editor who adds capitals, accents, and punctuation marks and who thus standardises the spelling and establishes graphic conventions. If they remain the result of a work linked with the printing house, choices relative to punctuation are no longer here assigned to the compositors, but to the humanists (clerics, university graduates, schoolmasters, etc.) employed by publishers and printers in order to assure the greatest possible correctness of their editions. Paolo Trovato has reminded us how important it was, for the advertising of a new book in *cinquecento* Italy to emphasise the exactitude of its 'correctness' (Trovato, 1991). Whence the decisive role of the copy editors whose interventions are spread out over several stages of the publishing process: the preparation of the manuscript, the stop-press corrections made during the printing process, the proofreading, the compilation of *errata* in their diverse forms (corrections made in ink on each printed copy, loose leaves which encourage the reader to make the corrections himself on his own copy, or pages of *errata* added at the end of the book).

The role of copy editors and proofreaders in the graphic and orthographic fixation of the vernacular tongues was far more decisive than the propositions for the reform of orthography advanced by those writers who wanted to impose an 'oral writing', entirely governed by pronunciation (Catach, 1968). There is, for example, a wide gap between the moderation of the solutions chosen for the printed editions and the boldness of the 'reforms' suggested by the authors of the Pléiade. Ronsard, for example, in his *Short History of French Poetic Art (Abrégé de l'Art poétique françois)*, proposes doing away with 'all superfluous orthography' (that is to say, all the letters that are not pronounced), transforming the written appearance of words so that they would be closer to the manner in which they are spoken (as is the case with 'roze', 'kalité', 'Franse', 'langaje' etc. – thus rendering the q and the c useless), and introducing letters in imitation of the Spanish like ll or ñ so as to correctly pronounce 'orgueilleux' or 'Monseigneur' (Ronsard, 1565). In the advice that he addresses to the reader as a preface to the first four books of the *Franciade*, Ronsard directly links punctuation marks and reading: 'Je te supliray seulement d'une chose, Lecteur: de vouloir bien prononcer mes vers et accomoder ta voix à leur passion, et non comme quelques uns les lisent, plutost à la façon d'une missive, ou de quelques lettres Royaux, que d'un Poëme bien prononcé; et te suplie encore derechef, où tu verras cette marque *!* vouloir un peu eslever ta voix pour donner grace à ce que tu liras' ('I will ask of you but one thing, Reader: to pronounce carefully my poetry and to accommodate your voice to its passion, and not as some read them, more in the manner of a letter or some Royal missive than of a well-read poem- and I also ask you once again that where you see this mark ! to raise your voice a little so as to give grace to what you are reading') (Ronsard, 1572).

Far from such radical propositions, the practice of publishers and printers, if they preserve some link with oralisation, tends to limit innovation in regard to the determination of the length of pauses. Here, the fundamental text is that of the printer (and author) Etienne Dolet, entitled *La Punctuation de la langue françoise* (reproduced in Catach, 1968). He defines in 1540 the new typographical conventions which were to distinguish, according to the length of the interruption or its position in the sentence, the '*point à queue* or comma', the 'comma' (or semi-colon), 'which is placed in a suspended sentence and not at all at the endpoint', and the 'round point' (or period) which 'is always placed at the end of the sentence'. Language dictionaries at the end of the seventeenth century record both the efficiency of the system proposed by Dolet (enriched by the colon which indicates a pause of intermediate duration between that of the comma and the semi-colon) and the distance established between the reader's voice and punctuation, considered heretofore, according to the terminology of Furetière's dictionary, to be a 'grammatical observation' marking the logical divisions of discourse. Exemplary passages from the same dictionary by Furetière, published in 1690, include: 'Ce Correcteur d'Imprïmerie entend fort bien la ponctuation' ('This copy editor understands punctuation perfectly well') and 'L'exactitude de cet Auteur va jusques là qu'il prend soin des points et des virgules' ('This author is exact to the point of paying attention to periods and commas'). If the first example normally assigns punctuation to the technical skills proper to the copy editors and proofreaders employed by the printers, the second example implicitly refers back to a common lack of interest on the part of authors concerning punctuation.

Furetière points out, nevertheless, that there are authors who are attentive to the punctuation of their texts. Is it possible to find traces of this '*exactitude*' in the printed editions of their works? Let us take the case of Molière. It would be very risky to attribute to him in too direct a manner the punctuation choices such as are to be found in the original editions of his plays, since, as has been shown for the 1660 edition of *Les Précieuses Ridicules*, punctuation varies from sheet to sheet, even from forme to forme, according to the preferences of different compositors (Veyrin-Ferrer, 1987). And yet, the different usages of punctuation that exist between the first editions of the plays, published shortly after their first Parisian productions, and the later editions allow one to reconstruct, if not the author's 'intention', at least the circumstances of the implied destination of the printed text.

Molière's reticence concerning the printed publication of his plays is well-known (Zanger, 1988). Before *Les Précieuses Ridicules* and the necessity of acquiring an advance on the publication of the text by Somaize and Ribou, a text made from a pirated copy and under cover of a privilege obtained by surprise, never had Molière sent any of his plays to the printers. There were financial reasons for this fact since, once published, a play could be staged by any theatrical troupe; but there were aesthetic reasons also. For Molière, in fact, the theatrical effects of the play depend entirely on the 'action', that is to say on performance. The address to the reader which opens the edition of *L'Amour médecin*, produced at Versailles, then at the Theatre of the Palais Royal in 1665, and published the following year, underscores the gap that exists between the spectacle and the reading: 'Il n'est pas nécessaire de vous avertir qu'il y a beaucoup de choses qui dépendent de l'action: on sait bien que les comédies ne sont faites que pour être jouées; et je ne conseille de lire celle-ci qu'aux personnes qui ont des yeux pour découvrir dans la lecture tout le jeu du théâtre'. ('There's no need to tell you that there are several Things in it which depend upon the Action. 'Tis generally known that Comedies are only writ to be Acted; and I won't have no Body read this but such as have Eyes to discover the Acting in the Reading of it.') (Molière, 1666). Punctuation is one of the possible devices (along with the image and stage directions) that allow for the restoration of something of the '*action*' to the printed text and its reading.

Systematically compared to the punctuation adopted in the later editions (not only in the nineteenth century but also as early as the eighteenth and late seventeenth centuries), the punctuation of the first editions of Molière's plays clearly attests to its link with orality, either insofar as it destines the printed text for reading aloud or for recitation, or in that it permits the readers who will read it in silence to reconstruct, for themselves, the timing and the pauses in the play of the actors. The passage from one form of punctuation to another has more than a little effect on the very meaning of the works (Hall, 1983). On the one hand, the original punctuation marks, always more numerous, portray the characters in different ways – thus the comma, present in the 1669 edition yet suppressed thereafter, following the first word ('Fat') in this line of verse from *Tartuffe*: 'Gros, et gras, le teint frais, et la bouche vermeille' ('Stout, and fat, with blooming cheeks and ruddy lips') (Act I, scene 4, line 233), or the accumulation of commas and capitals in order to distinguish the Master of Philosophy's way of speaking from that of the Master of Danse in *Le Bourgeois Gentilhomme* (Act II, scene 3). On the other hand, the punctuation marks of the original editions give the reader the time needed for reconstituting or imagining the play of the actors. For example, in the scene of the portraits from *Le Misanthrope* (Act II, scene 4, lines 586–594), the 1667 edition contains six commas more than modern editions, which allows Célimène to emphasise some words, to introduce pauses, and to elaborate upon the mimicry. Finally, these original punctuation marks throw into relief those words which are charged with a particular signification. While the last two verses of *Tartuffe* do not contain any comma in the modern editions, this is not so in the edition of 1669: 'Et par un doux hymen, couronner en Valère, / La flamme d'un Amant généreux, & sincère' ('And, with my daughter's hand, reward Valère / For this, a love both generous, and sincere'). The last word of the play, 'sincere', is thus clearly designated as the antonym of the word who figures in the title, *Le Tartuffe, ou l'Imposteur* (The Impostor). These abundant punctuation marks, which point out certain pauses that are more numerous and, generally, longer than those retained in later editions, inform readers how they should say (or read) the lines of verse and give emphasis to a certain number of words, endowed with capital printed letters which have generally been suppressed with the commas in the later printed editions.

The inquiry which I have sketched here raises several problems of a general nature. The first is that of dating the passage from rhetorical punctuation to grammatical punctuation. Is this passage organised around a single chronological trajectory wherein a decisive moment would be constituted by the end of the seventeenth century? Does it obey different rhythms depending on the genre? Or even, according to the hypothesis formulated by Philip Gaskell with regard to the 'maske' of Milton's *Comus* (Gaskell, 1978), should we not trace these variations back to the diverse destinations, contemporary to one another, of the same text?

A second problem: that of the reasons and mechanisms that convey attempts at the restoration of the punctuation marks of oralisation during the eighteenth century. The case of Benjamin Franklin would be, from this point of view, exemplary. By imagining the diverse devices that would allow one to uphold the role of the public orator in the midst of a dispersed population, Franklin strives to reconcile the new definition of public and political space, which has the dimensions of a vast republic, with the traditional forcefulness of a live speech, addressed to an assembled citizenry (Melish, 1992). On the one hand, Franklin invites authors of 'public discourses', in their writings, to make use of genres most directly linked to orality: proverbs, dialogues, and letters (which belong to the oratory genre). On the other hand, the apprenticeship of reading aloud, which points out the duration of pauses and voice pitches, should become a fundamental element of the school curriculum. Finally, a reform of typographical conventions should make the oralisation of texts easier thanks to an 'expressive typography' that plays with italics, capital letters added to certain words, or new punctuation marks (for example, with the introduction into English of the inverted exclamation point or inverted question mark, proper to Spanish and which, placed at the beginning of a sentence, point out from the outset how one is to pitch one's voice). By mobilising these resources which he knew quite well from his own experience as a printer, Franklin brings printed discourse as closely as possible in line with oratorical performance and, by the same token, allows different orators to reproduce in identical fashion, and in different places, the original discourse. Thanks to reading out loud, thanks to 'expressive typography', the discourse of the 'publick Orator' will be reproduced as if it was 'present' in its very absence. In a manner contrary to Condorcet or Malesherbes, who were distrustful of the passions and emotions engendered by oratory rhetoric, and, because of this, full of praise for Gutenberg's invention, Franklin thinks it possible to surmount an apparently insoluble contradiction: how is one to organise around speech a public space which would not necessarily be enclosed within the confines of Antiquity's city-state?

'If we offend, it is with our good will. / That you should think, we come not to offend, / But with good will. To show our simple skill, / That is the true beginning of our end' (Shakespeare, 1600). The faulty pronunciation followed by Quince makes him say, in the prologue of the 'Comedy of Pyramus and Thisbe', the very opposite of what he would like to say – and what it would have been suitable to say. The play of faulty punctuation, which reverses the very meaning of the text, is played out on several occasions in Elizabethan literature. It indicates that the construction of meaning of texts depends on the forms which govern their inscription and their transmission (Chartier, 1994 and 1995). Against every critical approach that considers the materiality of texts and the circumstances of their performance to be without importance, Quince the clumsy reminds us that identifying the effects of meaning produced by forms (whether they be written, printed, or oral) is a necessity in order to understand, in their full historicity, the diverse appropriations of texts, whether literary or otherwise.

BIBLIOGRAPHICAL REFERENCES

Antonucci, Laura, 1989, 'La Scrittura giudicata. Perizie grafiche in processi romani del primo Seicento', *Scrittura e Civiltà* 13, pp. 491–534.

Borges, Jorge Luis, 1975a, 'El espejo y la máscara', *El Libro de arena*, Buenos Aires, Emecé Editores.

Borges, Jorge Luis, 1975b, 'William Shakespeare, Macbeth', *Prólogos con un prólogo de los prólogos*, Buenos Aires, Torres Aguero Editor, 1975, pp. 142–147.

Borges, Jorge Luis, 1980, 'La Ceguera', *Siete Noches*, México, Fundo de Cultura Económica.

Bourdieu, Pierre, 'Lecture, lecteurs, lettrés, littérature', *Choses dites*, Paris, Editions de Minuit, pp. 132–143.

Botrel, Jean-François, 1993, *Libros, prensa y lectura en la España del siglo XIX*, Madrid, Fundación Germán Sánchez Ruipérez.

Catach, Nina, 1968, *L'Orthographe française à l'époque de la Renaissance (auteurs, imprimeurs, ateliers d'imprimerie)*, Genève, Librairie Droz.

Catedra, Pedro et Infantes, Victor, 1983, 'Estudio', *Los pliegos sueltos de Thomas Croft (siglo XVI)*, Valencia, Primus Calamus, Albatros ediciones, pp. 11–48.

Cavallo, Guglielmo et Chartier, Roger (ed.), 1995, *Storia della lettura nel mondo occidentale*, Roma-Bari, Editori Laterza.

Cervantes, Miguel de, 1605, *El Ingenioso Hidalgo Don Quijote de la Mancha*, Edición de John Jay Allen, Madrid, Cátedra, 1984.

Chartier, Roger, 1980, '*Loisir et sociabilité : lire à haute voix dans l'Europe moderne*', *Littératures classiques*, 'La voix au XVIIe siècle', Patrick Dandrey (ed.), 12, pp. 127–147.

Chartier, Roger, 1992, *L'Ordre des livres. Lecteurs, auteurs, bibliothèques en Europe entre le XIVe et le XVIIIe siècle*, Aix-en-Provence, Alinéa.

Chartier, Roger, 1994, 'George Dandin, ou le social en représentation', *Annales. Histoire, Sciences Sociales*, mars-avril, no 2, pp. 277–309.

Chartier, Roger, 1995, *Forms and Meanings. Texts, Performances, and Audiences from Codex to Computer*, Philadelphia, The University of Pennsylvania Press.

Du Fail, Noël, 1548, *Propos rustiques,* in *Conteurs français du XVIe siècle*, Paris, N.R.F., Bibliothèque de la Pléiade, 1965.

Dupont, Florence, 1994, *L'Invention de la littérature. De l'ivresse grecque au livre latin*, Paris, La Découverte.

Flores, R.M., 1975, *The Composition of the First and Second Madrid Editions of Don Quixote, Part I*, London, The Modern Humanities Research Association.

Foucault, Michel, 1969, 'Qu'est-ce qu'un auteur?', *Bulletin de la Société française de Philosophie*, t. LXIV, juillet-septembre, pp. 73–104 (reprinted in *Dits et Ecrits 1954–1988*, Edition établie sous la direction de Daniel Defert et François Ewald avec la collaboration de Jacques Lagrange, Paris, Gallimard, 1994, *Tome I, 1954–1969*, pp. 789–821).

Foucault, Michel, 1970, *L'Ordre du discours*, Paris, Gallimard.

Fox, Adam, 1994, 'Ballads, Libels and Popular Ridicule in Jacobean England', *Past and Present*, 145, pp. 47–83.

Frenk, Margit, 1981, '"Lectores y oídores". La difusión oral de la literatura en el Siglo de Oro', *Actas del Septimo Congreso de la Asociación Internacional de Hispanistas*, celebrado en Venecia del 25 al 30 de agosto de 1980, Giuseppe Bellini ed., Roma, Bulzoni Editore, Vol. I, pp. 101–123.

García de Enterría, María Cruz, 1973, *Sociedad y poesía de cordel en el Barroco*, Madrid, Taurus.

Hall, Gaston H., 1983, 'Ponctuation et dramaturgic chez Molière', *La Bibliographie matérielle*, présentée par Roger Laufer, table ronde organisée pour le CNRS par Jacques Petit, Paris, Editions du CNRS, pp. 125–141.

HINMAN, Charlton, 1963, *The Printing and Proof-Reading of the First Folio of Shakespeare*, Oxford, Clarendon Press.

HOGGART, Richard, 1957, *The Uses of Literacy: Aspects of Working-Class Life with Special Reference to Publications and Entertainments*, London, Chatto and Windus.

IFE, B.W., 1985, *Reading and Fiction in Golden-Age Spain. A Platonist critique and some picaresque replies*, Cambridge, Cambridge University Press.

INFANTES, Víctor, 1992, 'Los pliegos sueltos poéticos : constitución tipográfica y contenido literario (1482–1600)', *En el Siglo de Oro. Estudios y textos de literatura aurea*, Potomac, Maryland, Scripta humanistica, pp. 47–58.

LOPE DE VEGA, 1609, *Arte nuevo de hacer comedias en este tiempo*, in *Lope de Vega Esencial*, Edición de Felipe Pedraza, Madrid, Esenciales Taurus, 1990, pp. 124–134.

MCKENZIE, D.F., 1959, 'Compositor B's Role in the "Merchant of Venice" Q2 (1619)', *Studies in Bibliography*, 12, pp. 75–89.

MARCO, Joaquín, 1977, *Literatura popular en España en los siglos XVIII y XIX. Una aproximación a los pliegos de cordel)*, Madrid, Taurus.

MELISH, Jacob, 1992, *As Your Newspaper was Reading. La culture de la voix, la sphère publique et la politique de l'alphabétisation : le monde de la construction de limprimé de Benjamin Franklin*, mémoire de D.E.A., Paris, Ecole des Hautes Etudes en Sciences Sociales, dact.

MERLIN, Hélène, 1994, *Public et littérature en France au XVIIe siècle*, Paris, Les Belles Lettres.

MOLIERE, *L'Amour Médecin*, in *Oeuvres complètes,* Paris, N.R.F., Bibliothèque de la Pléiade, 1971, tome II, pp. 87–120.

MONER, Michel, *Cervantès conteur. Ecrits et paroles*, Madrid, Bibliothèque de la Casa de Velazquez, 1989.

NELSON, William, 1976/77, 'From «Listen, Lording» to «Dear Readers»', *University of Toronto Quarterly. A Canadian Journal of the Humanities*, Volume XLVI, Number 2, pp. 110–124.

PETRUCCI, Armando, 1989, 'Scrivere per gli altri', *Scrittura e Civiltá*, 13, pp. 475–487.

RODRIGUEZ MOÑINO, Antonio, 1970, *Diccionario bibliogriáfico de pliegos sueltos poéticos (siglo XVI)*, Madrid, Castalia.

Romancero, 1994, Edición, prólogo y notas de Paloma Díaz-Mas, con un estudio preliminar de Samuel G. Armistead, Barcelona, Crítica.

RONSARD, 1565, *Abrégé de l'Art poétique françois*, in *Oeuvres complètes*, Paris, N.R.F., Bibliothèque de la Pléiade, tome II, pp. 995–1009.

RONSARD, 1572, *Les Quatre premiers livres de la Franciade. Au lecteur*, in *Oeuvres complètes, op. cit.*, tome II, pp. 1009–1013.

SCHEID, John, and SVENBRO, Jesper, 1994, *Le métier de Zeus. Mythe du tissage et du tissu dans le monde gréco-romain*, Paris, Editions La Découverte.

SHAKESPEARE, William, 1600, *A Midsummer Night's Dream*, Edited by Harold F. Brooks, London and New York, Routledge, The Arden Edition of the Works of William Shakespeare, 1979, reprinted 1993.

SHAKESPEARE, William, 1611, *The Winter's Tale*, Edited by J.H.P. Pafford, London and New York, Routledge, The Arden Edition of the Works of William Shakespeare, 1963, reprinted 1994.

SPUFFORD, Margaret, 1984, *The Great Reclothing of Rural England: Petty Chapmen and their Wares in the Seventeenth Century*, London, The Hambledon Press.

TANSELLE, Thomas G., 1981, 'Analytical Bibliography and Renaissance Printing History', *Printing History,* Volume 3, Number 1, pp. 24–33.

TROVATO, Paolo, 1991, *Con ogni diligenza corretto. La stampa e le revisioni editoriali dei testi letterari italiani (1470–1570)*, Bologna, Il Mulino.

VELAY-VALLANTIN, Catherine, 1992, *Histoire des contes*, Paris, Fayard.

VEYRIN-FORRER, Jeanne, 'A la recherche des Précieuses', in *La lettre et le texte. Trente années de recherches sur l'histoire du livre*, Paris, Collection de l'Ecole Normale Supérieure de Jeunes Filles, pp. 338–366.

VEYRIN-FORRER, Jeanne, 1989, 'Fabriquer un livre au XVIe siècle', *Histoire de l'Edition française, Roger Chartier and Henri-Jean Martin (ed.), tome 1, Le Livre conquérant Du Moyen Age au milieu du XVIIe siècle*, Paris, Fayard/Cercle de la Librairie, pp. 336–369.

VEYNE, Paul, 1983, *Les Grecs ont-ils cru à leurs mythes ? Essai sur l'imagination constituante*, Paris, Editions du Seuil.

WATT, Tessa, 1991, *Cheap Print and Popular Piety. 1550–1640*, Cambridge, Cambridge University Press.

ZANGER, Abby E., 1988, 'Paralyzing Performance : Sacrificing Theater on the Altar of Publication' *Stanford French Review*, Fall–Winter, pp. 169–185.

ZUMTHOR, Paul, 1987, *La Lettre et la voix. De la 'littérature médiévale'*, Paris, Editions du Seuil.

THE WRITER'S MIRROR: WATRIQUET DE COUVIN AND THE DEVELOPMENT OF THE AUTHOR-CENTRED BOOK

Sylvia Huot

W HAT I WISH to explore in this paper is a way of approaching the medieval concept of the book by means of the allegories and metaphors of the book that occur so frequently in medieval writings. These metaphors bespeak different concepts of the book and its relationship to both reader and author, and can in turn help lead to a way of analysing and categorising actual medieval books. I want to emphasise that I do not see this as an absolute typology, nor am I claiming that medieval authors, compilers, and readers consciously used these metaphors as a basis for the production or consumption of books. However, it is a useful way for us to approach the topic and can help in distinguishing different kinds of books and their cultural significance – in particular, the ways in which the medieval book is designed to foreground either the reader or the author as subject. First, therefore, I will sketch out some of the more predominant metaphors of the book, and the important role of these metaphors in the construction of subjectivity and identity. I will then suggest ways that this discourse of the book might be correlated with actual practices in the design and reception of books in the Middle Ages. And finally, I will examine ways in which this frame of reference can prove useful in reading the poetic compilations of the fourteenth-century poet Watriquet de Couvin.

THE SELF AS BOOK

One pervasive metaphor in medieval writings is the book of the conscience. This is, by definition, a private sort of book of which the individual subject is both author and reader. One of the many vernacular texts that uses this trope is the early fourteenth-century *Ovide moralisé*, a translation of Ovid's *Metamorphoses* with extensive moral and allegorical commentary.[1] The anonymous Franciscan author of this work recommends constant reading of the book of the conscience, saying:

> Encor se doit estudier
> Cil qui veult philozophier

29

An example of such a book is Paris, BNF, fr. 24429, a devotional anthology made around 1300 for a French queen, perhaps Marie de Brabant.[10] The queen is a dominant figure, appearing visually in several miniatures and also addressed as a female reader – though not by name – in some of the texts. In addition to the images of her as a figure of humility and piety, there are also images of female saints and sinners and of female personifications of both virtues and vices. She must decide as she reads that book together with the book of her conscience, which images mirror her most closely; she must attempt to conform herself to the ones that she wishes to see herself in. When the same anthology appears in another manuscript (Vatican Library, Vat. Reg. 1756), the reader is again constructed as subject within the book; this time, textual signals and miniatures alike indicate a male reader. And when one of its texts, a treatise describing a method of contemplative prayer to the Virgin, appears in still another manuscript (London, BL, Egerton 745), we find the representation of that book's owner, whom we can recognise from his heraldic garb as the Count of St-Pol.[11] Similarly, Books of Hours commonly depict the owner of the book in a posture of prayer before the images of Christ and the Virgin. Such books not only mirror the reader, constructing him or her as an exemplar of piety and humility and as a willing pupil of clerical authority; they actually function as imaginary spaces into which the reader can be projected, encountering and communicating with authoritative figures and sacred beings.

Reading the bodily book of Christ or the human body, in turn, teaches us about the author of that book – about the spirit that inhabits the body and animates it. After the Final Judgment all individuals will be open books, and we will all be able to read one another.[12] Likewise, books can be designed to provide a sort of *exposé* of an authorial figure. Such books may recount episodes in the life of the authorial persona or, having constructed the persona of the author, proceed to explore the workings of his mind, his imagination, his access to the allegorical, the poetic. Rather than a unity of destination, like the reader-centred book, these author-centred books present a unity and coherence of origin. It is almost as though the author is opening the book of his conscience and letting us read it, or even letting us watch him as he writes, reads, and revises it. Just as, at the end of Time, our bodies become the open book of our conscience; and just as Christ's body is the book displaying the text of his divinity; so these books are the metaphorical bodies of their authors. Of course, these books are literary constructs, and thus fictional, unlike the book that is Christ or the book that each of us will become on Judgment Day. The important point, however, is that they are constructed on a similar model.

In the domain of French literature, this type of book appears particularly from the early fourteenth century, and is associated most strongly with the genre of the *dit*: both the didactic *dit*, as practised by such poets as Baudouin de Condé, Jean de Condé, and Watriquet de Couvin; and the *dit amoureux*, as practised by such poets as Guillaume de Machaut and Jean Froissart.[13] The *dit*, like courtly lyric, is very commonly transmitted in the format of author corpora, among which are the earliest examples of manuscripts devoted exclusively to the collected works of a single vernacular poet. The first-person voice of the *dit* is to be distinguished from that of the lyric, which has a more universal quality to it.[14] The voice of the song is easily appropriated by anyone who cares to sing it. It purports to express a sort of anonymous and universal experience, exemplary, perhaps more pure or more intensely felt than that of others, but essentially one with which the public can identify. The use of lyric insertions in romances illustrates how easily these songs can be assigned to a persona other than the author, even though the first-person focus simultaneously encourages the construction of an author persona. The lyric 'I' can be said to function as a mirror for the reader/listener, who attempts to conform himself to the courtly ideals reflected therein.

It is really in the genre of the *dit* that the authorial persona, while remaining the first-person subject of the text, emerges as a unique entity, distinct from his audience, not a voice that we can appropriate or a persona with whom we identify. The first-person figure of the author is certainly no less fictional than that of the singer; but it is differently construed. The poet-protagonist of the *dit* is a clerkly figure, able to impart knowledge. He has access to allegorical realms and privileged experiences; he has the gift of poetry. Sometimes, as in certain of Machaut's *dits*, the authorial persona may be a comic or melancholic figure; but either way, he is something other than a mirror of the reader. Unlike courtly lyric, the *dit* very commonly bears the name of its author inscribed within it. It may also contain information concerning aristocratic patronage, and the date and circumstances of composition. In reading such texts, we learn about the life of a court poet, not the life of Everyman. Of course, what he writes about is still relevant to the lives of his readers, to the moral choices they face, to political events, to social comportment. But the images and lessons thus presented are all filtered through him.

THE BOOKS OF WATRIQUET DE COUVIN

The manuscripts of Watriquet de Couvin are among the earliest known examples in French of this kind of author-centred book.[15] Watriquet was a minstrel at the court of Gui de Châtillon, Count of Blois, and his poetic career spans the early decades of the fourteenth century. Several manuscript copies of his collected *dits* survive today, and his presence in these books is pervasive. In one, for example, the opening miniature depicts Watriquet presenting his book to the Count, while the rubric states:

Veschi comment Watriqués sires de Verjoli baille et presente touz ses meilleurs diz en escrit a monseigneur de Blois son maistre. Premierement le mireor aus dames.

(Paris, BNF, fr. 14968, fol. 1v)

[See here how Watriquet, lord of Prettyverse, gives and presents all his best poems in writing to my Lord of Blois, his master. First the *Mirror of Ladies*.]

The book does not derive its unity from the figure of the reader, since the Count of Blois is not the only patron to appear in the collection. Some of the individual poems are announced as having been written for the Count or are set at one of his castles, but others are addressed to different figures: we are told that the Duke of Bourbon commissioned Watriquet's elegy for the Constable of France, for example, while certain other poems are addressed to the King, or to noble ladies. What we see unfolding is Watriquet's poetic career; his privileged experience of the abstract and the allegorical; his access to the nobility and to the values that govern their lives. We see him in attendance at different courts; witness to various events; writing or performing for one or another aristocratic patron; and freely moving between the realm of imagination and that of common experience. We also literally see his image in a great many of the miniatures with which each new poem is headed; he is always recognisable through the distinctive parti-coloured outfit that he wears in the opening presentation miniature and throughout the book.

Some of Watriquet's poems are simply discourses on moral or political virtues, but in many the lesson is embedded in a frame narrative that details Watriquet's personal experience of allegory, and the imaginative processes that produced the poem. In the *Dit de l'arbre royal*, for example, Watriquet first refers to his daily prayer for material with which to compose a new poem. God then answers his prayer by granting him a dream, in which he enters an orchard of trees bearing the fleur-de-lis and guarded by a set of allegorical personifications. As he watches, a large, crowned tree falls over dead; of its four offshoots, two also die, as does an additional small sprout. A third is crowned, while the fourth is surrounded by leopards. The scenario is clearly an allegory for the crisis of the Capetian dynasty. The large dead tree represents Philip IV; the two dead offshoots are his sons Louis X and Philip V, each of whom died after reigning for only a few years, while the little sprout is the John I, posthumous son of Louis X, who died in infancy. The remaining trees are Philip's daughter Isabelle, queen of England, and his third son Charles IV, who had just ascended to the throne when the poem was written in 1322. All of this is in fact explained within the poem, though not by the narrator himself: the commentary is provided by one of the allegorical figures, in response to Watriquet's questions. The dream concludes with Watriquet's visit to the royal court, where he recites his new poem before the king; he then wakes up and dutifully writes it all down. If Watriquet had wanted to compose a poem in honour of Charles IV's accession to the throne, he could simply have expressed his lamentations for the recent demise of so many French kings and his hopes for the new king's success. But instead, he chose to embed this political message within a story of poetic inspiration and composition, outlining the processes by which an author receives his material through divine intervention, and also stressing the ways in which this material should be received by the public.

The *dit* opens with the figure of the reader, stressing the wisdom of amending one's life in accordance with the teachings and the *biaus dis* that one hears. Watriquet then describes his recent desire for poetic inspiration as he lay in bed one Thursday morning:

> Si fis ma priere en latin
> A Dieu et à sa douce mere,
> Que il me moustrassent matere,
> Par aucuns signes ou par letre,
> Que je peüsse en rime metre
> Et conter devant les haus hommes.
> *(DAR*, vv. 8–13)

[I made my prayer in Latin to God and his sweet mother, asking that they might show me some material, through signs or letters, that I could set in rhyme and recount before noblemen.]

From the figure of the reader in need of instruction, we have passed to that of the poet in need of material with which to provide such instruction, and the poem that follows tells the story of the dream that God granted him so that he would have something to write about. We see the allegorical orchard entirely through his eyes, hearing about his joy at its beauty, his sorrow at the tragic events and his puzzlement over the meaning of the vision. We receive the explication of the allegory not so much from him as through him, for it is the figure of Hardement who supplies the commentary, in response to the narrator's questions:

> Si demandai con des premiers
> Qu'il me deïst par charité
> De touz ces moustres vérité:
> Que senefioit li vergiers
> Où tant d'arbres ot arrengiés,
> Et li vens qui a abatu
> L'arbre où tant ot force et vertu.
> *(DAR*, vv. 332–38)

[Thus I asked him straightaway to tell me, out of charity, the truth of all these spectacles: what was signified by the orchard, where so many trees were lined up, and the wind that felled the tree that had so much strength and virtue.]

The entire process of inspired vision, interpretation, oral recitation, and transcription is recorded in the poem, which then assumes its place in the book that is the ongoing representation of Watriquet's poetic career.

Watriquet, as author, emerges as a privileged figure whose life is a staging area for the stuff of books. As poet he has access to the world of imagination, encountering potent images; he is granted intellectual and moral insight, so that he can use these images both to entertain and to instruct his aristocratic audience. He has a special and intimate relationship with allegorical figures, who speak to him and in some cases practically abduct him, leading him away to witness things that he can then write about. In the *Mireoirs as dames*, Dame Aventure accosts him while he is out riding and offers to lead him to the allegorical castle of feminine beauty, explaining that once he has understood the system of virtues that make up the ideal woman, he will be able to incorporate that into his ongoing project of literary portraits of aristocratic ladies:

> Puis dist: 'Bien veigniez vous, amis,
> Desormais vous veul estre amie;
> . . . . .
> Escouté vous ai grant pieça,
> Comment vous estes gramentez
> Et debatus pour les biautez
> Des roynes et des contesses,
> Des dauffines et des duchesces,
> Des dames de pluseurs pays.
> Or n'en soiés pas esbahis,
> Je vous menrai o moi veoir
> De biauté le vrai mireoir,
> Le droit compas, le parfait monstre;
> Se je fais tant con le vous monstre,
> Faire en devriez aucun biau dit.'
> (*MD*, vv. 96–97, 110–21)

[Then she said, 'Welcome, friend, from now on I wish to befriend you. . . I have listened to you for quite some time, how you have worked on the beauty of queens and countesses, dauphines and duchesses, ladies of many lands. Now don't be frightened, I will take you to see the true mirror of beauty, the absolute measure, the perfect demonstration; if I go so far as to show you this, then you should make a beautiful poem about it.']

In the *Dit de l'iraigne et du crapot*, Dame Raison, distraught over her poor treatment at the hands of Envy and Slander, seeks out Watriquet's company as that of an old friend:

> Mais elle à moi tantost acourt,
> Ambedeus les iex lermoiant;
> Et sus le siege verdoiant,

Sous une ente de fruit chargie,
S'assist lez moi par compagnie
Comme dame de bonne affaire,
Et je empris grant joie a faire,
Car sa compaignie oi moult chiere.
(*DIC*, vv. 28–35)

[But she came right up to me, tears streaming from both eyes; and on the green seat, under a fruit tree, she sat beside me for companionship, like a proper lady, and I took great joy in it, for I was very glad of her company.]

And indeed Watriquet does not hesitate to take advantage of his friendship with no less a personage than Lady Reason: witnessing some unusual behaviour involving a toad and a spider, he asks her for an explanation, and she proceeds to gloss the event as political allegory, representing the malevolent effects of wicked courtiers and the need for princes to protect the common people. And in the *Tournois des dames*, to offer a third example, it is Dame Vérité who approaches the poet as he is puzzling over the significance of a stained glass window. She first explains the allegory represented in the window, and then takes him on a long walk, during which she points out various strange occurrences and explains them as social and political allegories.

Watriquet's imaginative, intellectual, and linguistic powers are all very much a matter of public service: he is not a Romantic poet seeking an outlet for his yearning heart or teeming brain, but rather one whose aim is to entertain and to instruct the nobility. In his formulation, the poet mediates between the world of common experience – the world of the court – and the realm of the imagination. It is his task, and his special gift, to recast the lives and experiences of his aristocratic audience, and the values that they live by, in the guise of striking or exotic images. This is perhaps especially clear in the *Dit des .iiii. sieges*. In this poem, Watriquet describes his vision of four thrones in Heaven. Each throne is guarded by a fanciful creature. In each case the creature says that the throne is waiting to be occupied by a famous literary or historical character: King Arthur, Alexander the Great, and two figures from the epic cycle of Charlemagne, Duke Naimes and Girart de Fraite. In response to Watriquet's questions, it is then revealed that although one might think that all of these characters are dead, that is not so. Each lives on in the person of a contemporary nobleman: Charles de Valois, Guillaume de Hainaut, Gauchier de Châtillon, and Robert de Béthune respectively. Each fanciful creature then also explains itself as an allegory for moral or political qualities of the sort embodied by the character in question. A female personage who, like a set of Siamese twins, has two bodies from the waist up, but only one from the waist down, represents the fusion of Arms and Love in Arthur and the Count of Valois; a crowned lion with the head of a man represents the Largesse of Alexander and the Count of Hainaut; an eagle with the head of a queen

41

figures the Loyalty found in Duke Naimes and in Gauchier, Constable of France; and a fox with the head of a boar incarnates the Prowess of Girart du Fraite and the Count of Flanders, both valiant warriors who became tragically embroiled in conflicts with their king.

In this complicated poem, then, Watriquet matches up several different literary registers: a fictional or fictionalised character from literary tradition, an exotic grotesque figure, a set of noble attributes, and a contemporary nobleman. In so doing he not only succeeds in praising several important members of the court circle for whom he wrote, but also provides a lesson in the interpretation of texts and images, showing how romances, histories, and *chansons de geste* can be read as commentaries on contemporary society and how visual drolleries, resembling the figures so commonly found in the decoration of medieval manuscripts, can be decoded into a set of moral teachings. By writing his poem in this way, rather than simply producing a panegyric of the noblemen in question, Watriquet shows us the poet's craft as maker of images and manipulator of literary codes. Thus although Watriquet does not portray himself as a courtly lover, or as a hero in the ordinary sense of the term, he does portray in considerable detail his own intellectual and imaginative work. In that sense, one could say that in the books he compiled, the poet is the central character and the hero in an ongoing exposition of literary creation.

CONCLUSIONS

I have now presented two bodies of material: first an outline of the metaphor of the book in medieval moral and devotional treatises, then a description of the collected works of Watriquet de Couvin. In closing, I wish to make some suggestions concerning the ways in which we can approach the manuscripts of Watriquet's collected poems as literary artifacts, the ways that these manuscripts can be related to the elaborate metaphorics of the book, and the implications that all of this might have for the history of the book in general.

First, let us consider the fact that the books containing Watriquet's *dits* are designed for a public trained to think of a book as a mirror of the soul, and indeed of their own inner self as a book. In Watriquet's book they can see themselves or the image of what they should be; they can read the images it presents in terms of their own lives. This is particularly true for his immediate circle of intended readers, who appear as characters in the poems or are addressed directly; but it also holds for other members of the aristocratic world for whom Watriquet wrote. The format of the poems encourages the reader to think about the allegorical images they present and to formulate his or her own interpretation. Watriquet does not begin by stating, for example, that he will show how an evil courtier is like a spider, nor even by alerting us that his poem will be about courtiers in any way. He begins by describing the unusual behaviour of a spider in the garden, then puzzles over what its actions might mean, and only then proceeds to the explanation of how this spidery behaviour mirrors that of humans. Thus the reader has ample opportunity to exercise his or her own interpretative skills, which are then corrected or confirmed as the case may be.

In the course of the collection, Watriquet teaches his public to read different kinds of texts and images. We learn to read literary texts as mirrors of contemporary events; we learn to read the natural world as a book reflecting human vices and virtues; we learn to equate inner virtue with bodily beauty; we learn to interpret drolleries and other visual images as allegorical figures. The truly attentive reader can put these techniques to use in subsequent encounters with stained glass windows, books of hours, romances, even spiders. Because each poem not only presents a lesson, but also takes us through the whole process of seeing it, pondering it, and having it explained, the collection as a whole serves an important pedagogical function beyond that of simply imparting moral precepts about social and political conduct.

In effect, Watriquet's book can function as an external prop for the Book of Memory. It is explicitly a storehouse of edifying memories, each crystallised in a meaningful image. Committing these images to memory enables one better to remember the historical events and the moral teachings associated with them. As one gazes at the pages of the book, in turn, the mere sight of the illustrations that head each poem can trigger the memory of that particular lesson. Again, it is not at all difficult to imagine the appeal of such books for a public that had been trained to remember important teachings by associating them with elaborate visual constructs, and to conceive of meditation and introspection as a process of reading an internal book. Watriquet's book would well serve a reader in search of an authoritative guide book that could be read in tandem with the book of the conscience, a technique recommended in some medieval devotional writings.

But Watriquet's manuscripts also have an added dimension: the pervasive presence of the authorial figure throughout the collection. The book not only mirrors the preoccupations of the reader, but also embodies its author. It is his thoughts that are transcribed and given material, visual form: as the author of the *Livre de vie* put it, Watriquet's thoughts are incorporated in the book. When we read it, we not only learn how to see ourselves and our society in images and in texts, but we also learn about him – or at any rate, about the persona he has created and set forth in the book. One could draw an analogy here with the book that is Christ, sent as reading material for the further education of the human race, and written down so that we could see and understand him. Watriquet has committed his poems, and indeed himself, to parchment. His poetic persona, his imaginary self, is bodied forth in the pages of the book and can be read and interpreted by all who see it.

Thus Watriquet's books not only present an image of the reader and a lesson in the art of reading; they also present an image of the poet, and map out an art of exposition. This ongoing representation of poetic production and the literary imagination could still, in a sense, reflect on the reader, who is after all similarly engaged in the ongoing process of writing, compiling, and editing the metaphorical books of conscience and memory. But more importantly, I would argue, it serves to foreground the figure of the author and his presence in, and responsibility for, the book. In this respect Watriquet is representative of an important development in the history of the book. During the later Middle Ages, other vernacular authors also played an increasing role in the design and production of books, and foreground these processes in their writings. In some of the *dits amoureux* of Guillaume de Machaut and Jean Froissart, for example, the love story is virtually eclipsed by the elaborate account of poetic composition, allegorical explication, and textual transcription and compilation. In the anthology manuscripts produced by such authors as Machaut, Froissart, and Christine de Pizan, individual poems are dedicated to a variety of patrons; and, especially in the case of Christine, there can be considerable diversity of genre and subject matter. But the figure of the author – represented in miniatures and named in texts and rubrics – pervades the collection and is an important source of unity.

This development has consequences, though perhaps unintended ones, for the marketing and distribution of books. When a book must be crafted as the individualised mirror of a specific reader, it requires custom design and production. The devotional anthology of Paris, BNF, fr. 24429, for example, remains forever a mirror and construction of a royal female persona; the other copy of that same anthology remains forever a construction of a different persona, that of the man for whom it was made. Obviously these books can still be read by anyone who wishes, and undoubtedly each has had numerous readers and owners. Still, something is lost in the experience of all readers other than the one figured in the book. The effort that went into crafting the book as a mirror of that particular reader will no longer serve any purpose once the book passes from its original owner.

But when a book is constructed around the figure of the author, it can be mass-produced. To revert to the allegorical language with which I began, the book of the conscience is unique for each individual; there are as many conscience books as there are human beings. But the book that is Christ is ever and always the same for all who read it. As poets began increasingly to conceive of themselves as authors of books, and of the book as an incarnation of their authorial persona, there resulted a type of book that was endlessly susceptible to reproduction. Instead of a proliferation of individual books, each unique and existing in a single copy designed for a particular reader, one can now imagine the proliferation of identical copies of a single book. Such a book is still founded on the construction of a literary subject, indeed pervaded by the explication of this subjectivity. The authorial presence imparts unity to the collection and allows the disparate poems, with their different frame-works and different inscribed readers or dedicatees, to coalesce into a unified book, one equally accessible and equally relevant to all who read it.

REFERENCES

1. *Ovide moralisé, poème du commencement du quatorzième siècle*, ed. by Cornelis De Boer, vol. 2, *Verhandelingen der Koninklijke Akademie van Wetenschappen te Amsterdam, Afdeeling Letterkunde*, NS 21 (Amsterdam: Müller, 1920; rpt. Wiesbaden: Martin Sändig, 1966).

2. *Venerabilis Baedae Opera Historica*, ed. by Charles Plummer, vol. 1 (Oxford: Clarendon Press, 1896; rpt. Oxford University Press, 1961), chapter 13.

3. 'Memorare nouissima tua', *Sermo in die cinerum*, in Alain de Lille, *Textes inédits*, ed. by Marie-Thérèse d'Alverny (Paris: J. Vrin, 1965), pp. 267–74.

4. The text is unedited. It appears, in different redactions, in MSS Paris, BNF 24432 and 1317. A related text appears in Paris, BNF 12786.

5. As is stated in the *Livre de vie*: 'Et ceste consideration dou jugement nostre seigneur nous doit esmouver a corriger et a oster de noz consciences l'escripture de pechié. Car aussi comme vous veez que l'escripture est arse qui contient erreur, especiaument encontre foy; tout aussi au jour dou jugement sera il ou feu d'enfer jeté en qui conscience sera trouvee l'escripture de pechié, qui contient erreur encontre foy' (BNF, n. a. fr. 4338, fol. 165r–v).

6. See Mary Carruthers, *The Book of Memory: A Study of Memory in Medieval Culture*, Cambridge Studies in Medieval Literature, 10 (Cambridge: Cambridge University Press, 1990).

7. As is stated in *Li Livres des enfans Israel*: 'Et sachiez que leçons n'apartient pas tant seulement aus clers, mais autressi aus lais. Car diex a fait .i. livre commun ou tout puent lire: c'est l'espece des creatures' (BNF, fr. 1802, fol. 202r).

8. 'Le tiers livre est le livre de sapience, qui nous donne congnoissance de toute beneurté. Et cest livre est escript de leittres d'or, car ceste sapience est le souverain don dou saint esperit' (BNF, n. a. fr. 4338, fol. 142v).

9. For discussion of this passage and reproduction of miniatures illustrating it, see Susan Hagen, *Allegorical Remembrance: A Study of 'The Pilgrimage of the Life of Man' as a Medieval Treatise on Seeing and Remembering* (Athens, GA: University of Georgia Press, 1990).

10. See my discussion of this manuscript in 'A Book Made for a Queen: Text and Illustration in a Medieval French Devotional Manuscript (Bibl. Nat. fr. 24429)', in *The Whole Book: Cultural Perspectives on the Medieval Miscellany*, ed. Stephen G. Nichols and Siegfried Wenzel (Ann Arbor: University of Michigan Press, 1996), pp. 123–43.

11. See Paul Meyer, 'Notice du MS Egerton 745 du Musée Britannique', *Romania*, 39 (1910), 532–69. The miniature depicting the Count is reproduced opposite p. 537.

12. As the *Livre de vie* explains with regard to the Day of Judgment: 'Et ce est touchié en ce que Saint Jehan vit que chascun sera jugié selon ses propres euvres escriptes ou livre de sa propre conscience. Et la seront les livres des consciences de touz ceus et celes de la lignie Adam ouvers et apers touz ainssi que chascun lira et congnoistra et ses pechiez et les autrui' (BNF, n. a. fr. 4338, fol. 165r).

advantage of his book-selling business. If we look a little more closely at Medici book acquisition the place and significance of book-collecting in their family history looks rather more problematic.

For the remainder of this paper I shall argue that the detailed evidence reveals a variety of motives governing Medici practice in the matter of commissioning books, and the practice of professional humanist scholars in presenting them to members of the household.

Taking individual volumes as my starting point, I have identified at least four distinct strands of contemporary understanding as to what constitutes the 'memorial effectiveness' of a library (its impact on the family's public reputation) – none of which involves the book as straightforward written record, either of a particular intellectual tradition, or of particular scholarly interests. Each strand is represented by a different type of book in the Medici library:

(1) books establishing a family reputation for patronage of the humanistically arcane (rare texts, sometimes in copies dedicated to a family member);

(2) books establishing a family aura of probity and social 'good practice' (modern works dedicated to or inspired by individual members of the Medici family);

(3) classical tradition books which are 'precious' (acquired on the open market in luxury, lavishly illuminated copies);

(4) books establishing a traceable genealogy or pedigree of book acquisition itself, that genealogy lastingly inscribed in the paraphernalia of dedicatory material.[10]

What all this adds up to, I shall argue, is a recognisable programme of self-promotion and public commemoration of a family name, in which books simply happen to be the artefacts used for such classic conspicuous consumption.[11]

I have picked out a selection of surviving works known to derive from this period of Medici book-collecting:

(1) a recently recovered work of Cicero's, which Poggio Bracciolini copied in 1408, and which was in Cosimo 'Il Vecchio''s library in 1425;

(2) a treatise on conduct specially written for Cosimo's brother Lorenzo in 1416;

(3) a copy of the *Natural History* of Pliny the elder, which Vespasiano records as being commissioned for Piero in 1458;

(4) a collection of Aristotle's works, translated into Latin by Johannes Argyropoulos for Cosimo and his son Piero, in a copy probably made for Piero's son, Lorenzo il Magnifico.[12]

In the early decades of the fifteenth century the humanist scholar and papal secretary Poggio Bracciolini made a series of scholarly expeditions to monastic libraries across Europe in search of rare classical works, and unmutilated copies of works known only in corrupt form. A significant part of the funding for these trips was provided by Cosimo de' Medici.

In April 1425, Poggio wrote to his fellow scholar, and fellow scholar-servant of Cosimo's, Niccolò Niccoli, from the papal curia in Rome:

I am copying the *De oratore*, filching free time for myself though with difficulty; but still I have begun and shall finish. Then it is my intention to copy the *Orator* and the *Brutus*. And so send me as soon as possible . . . your volume, if you have it. . . . Besides I need Cicero's *Letters to Atticus*, which I copied and which our friend Cosimo now has; for the scribe is writing them pretty inaccurately because of the model [he is following]. I shall quickly correct them if I have this book of Cosimo's and so send it to me. Ask Cosimo for me to let me have the book for a little while; I shall send it safely back to him.[13]

The copy of Cicero's *Letters to Atticus* in question – one derived from the unmutilated manuscript discovered in the cathedral library at Vercelli in 1393 by Coluccio Salutati – is probably the one currently in Berlin, inscribed, 'Scripsit Poggius anno domini MCCCCVIII'.[14] It is recorded as in Cosimo's possession in the inventory of his library taken in 1418. In this case an extremely rare work, of scholarly importance, gives academic humanistic *kudos* to Cosimo's collection. Poggio seeks access to it again in order to correct the copy or copies currently being made in the papal curia. And Cosimo is clearly accustomed to responding to such requests – two months later Poggio writes to Niccolò to ask him to send a consignment of folio size parchment so that he can make a further copy of Cosimo's unmutilated *Letters to Atticus* for his own use.[15] This is the kind of intellectually nurturing role played by the Medici library in the revival of classical learning to which scholars have liked to give attention. We have Cosimo funding manuscript-recovering expeditions, providing rare exemplars from his private collection to facilitate collation of exemplars, providing materials (parchment) to subsidise skilled reproduction of key originals, and finally securely housing the finished work (with arrangements for loaning it on occasion for scholarly purposes).

There is no indication, however, that the head of the Medici house *himself* is involved in any of these scholarly transactions, which takes place between two of his learned advisors. In Poggio's dialogue *De nobilitate* (written in 1440) Cosimo's brother Lorenzo de' Medici appears as a discussant, along with Poggio's old friend Niccolò Niccoli. There Lorenzo is depicted above all as a connoisseur – an enthusiastic collector of antiquities and of manuscripts. Another contemporary account describes Lorenzo as devoting his life to gathering together 'the richest pasture, the richest gold, the most precious garments' and the most remarkable 'furniture, statues, sacred paintings, vases, gems, pearls and books'.[16] In accounts such as these books simply belong alongside the other types of fine objects which define the Medicis as 'magnificent'.

My second example is one to which Professor de la Mare draws attention as an anomaly in her survey of Cosimo de' Medici's early, personal library holdings, as itemised in an inventory of March 1417/18 when he was not quite 30 years old. The inventory includes two apparently identical copies of Francesco Barbaro's *De re uxoria* (*On Matrimony*), a text composed for Cosimo's brother Lorenzo on the occasion of his wedding in 1416.[17] One of these is the presentation copy, presented to Lorenzo; the other was made for Cosimo by Giovanni Aretino shortly thereafter. Professor de la Mare suggests that the presence of these two copies of the same work together 'nello scriptoio di Cosimo' [in Cosimo's study] is evidence that this private library was a 'joint' collection, representing a shared interest of the two brothers.

If we read Barbaro's text itself, however, it seems more likely that Cosimo thought of the two copies as distinct items in his personal collection, fulfilling different (though related) functions. The *De re uxoria* is (on its author's own admission) a fairly banal little treatise on the exemplary conduct of wives, fulsomely dedicated to Lorenzo, and formally offered (the text tells us) as a wedding gift. Like Politian's dedication with which I opened, this one too converts the written text into a material object, to be set alongside such precious items as gems and brocades, presented on the occasion of a prestigious marriage:

Beloved Master Lorenzo, our great ancestors used the occasion of the marriages of relatives and of friends to acknowledge their indebtedness to them, or to commemorate the affection in which they held them, by presenting some kind of gift. . . . Leaving aside the necessities of life, you already possess an abundance of precious garments and fabrics, gems, and other magnificent belongings. But turning over in my mind the memory of the many familiar conversations we had together, I judged it more to your taste to give your something from myself, your Francesco, than something costly to me. On which account I have decided to write in your name some brief comments concerning matrimony, which I believe may prove useful to you at this time of your marriage.[18]

In a strong sense, then, the specially scribally prepared version of the treatise offered to Lorenzo is a personal gift from scholar to possible patron (or at least, important figure in a community which he had visited the previous year, and in which he ultimately settled) – an attempt like Politian's to trade a place in the household for a specially concocted gift-book. However, the preface also makes careful complimentary gestures towards Cosimo:

Nor do I want anyone to think that I have chosen to write on this subject to teach you [Lorenzo] what you do not already know, but rather so that through you others among our contemporaries, taking their example from you, can learn proper matrimonial conduct more readily. . . . And I am aware that you already imitate the example of that most highly regarded man, your father Giovanni, and your most distinguished brother Cosimo. You are richly endowed with their qualities of authority, prudence, and political good sense.[19]

The closing section of the *De re uxoria*, entitled 'De liberorum educatione' ['On raising sons'], shifts the treatise's discussion from appropriately chaste and modest wives to the broader family topic of raising sons worthy of the Medici family name. So aside from the physical gift of the presentation copy, Barbaro's text celebrates the house of Medici as the foremost in Florence – as a dynastic model to whose example humbler families might aspire. The two copies in the library thus perform two distinct functions: one (personalised) marks the occasion of an important dynastic marriage; the other (taken from it) immortalises the Medici family (invoking Cosimo by name). Both suggest that the memorial significance of the two copies is rather like the inscriptions in folio Bibles of the period – they mark an important moment in family history, remembering it in conjunction with a book-object, in a form particularly well-suited to the family's claim to civilised values.

My next example is more straightforward. By the 1450s every respectable collector was required to own a copy of Pliny's *Natural History* – a compilation of remedies, botanical and biological facts, myths and folklore, which was much studied during the middle ages, but restored to textual integrity by early Renaissance humanistic scholarship. Poggio Bracciolini went to considerable lengths to borrow a corrected version of the text from Leonardo Bruni, in order to make a copy for Cosimo de' Medici.[20] The copy which Vespasiano mentions in letters as having been copied for Cosimo's son Piero in 1458 is a veritable trophy. Its exquisite illumination contains a possible pair of portraits of Piero and his wife, as well as repeated ornamental recapitulations of the Medici arms.[21] Once again, the importance of this volume seems to have less to do with its content (familiar, encyclopaedic; to be browsed rather than read through) than its symbolic status as a desirable (almost, obligatory) work for any respectable collector to own, in a copy calculated to fill with respectful awe the privileged visitor allowed to handle it.

Finally, Lorenzo il Magnifico's copy of a collection of scientific works by Aristotle is also a volume with carefully incorporated dynastic implications. Three of the works it contains are dedicated by the translator, Johannes Argyropoulos, to Lorenzo's grandfather, Cosimo (before 1464) while others are dedicated to Cosimo's son Piero di Cosimo (Lorenzo's father, d. 1469). Argyropoulos had first visited Florence for the Council of Florence in 1439 (an event heavily funded, and hosted, by the Medici family), and settled there in 1456. So the translated ancient works plus their dedications commemorate Medici involvement with key Church business, and provide a lasting celebration of their long-standing public prominence in civic affairs in Florence. The volume is lavishly embellished. It is richly illuminated, with portraits of Argyropoulos, and Cosimo and Piero de' Medici, and the recurring marginal ornament of the Medici arms. Here is a memorial to three generations of a great dynasty, exquisitely constructed around the figure of the ancient author, ornamenting the difficult texts themselves so that even an ill-educated viewer (indeed, even a semi-literate one) immediately takes the sense of occasion from the rare and precious object.

Books often feature in *quattrocento* paintings as markers of eloquence and erudition in the hands of a saint or scribe. Tendered towards the figure of a patron, the book bestows upon its *recipient* the intellectual qualities it notionally contains. Inner reverie is made visible and material as the precious volume in the hands of a recognisable individual – the Virgin Mary, Saint Jerome, Pope Nicholas V – as a tangible substitute for what we would be inclined to call 'mind' or 'consciousness'.

I have tried to suggest, with these few, select examples from the Medici collection of *quattrocento* books, that such graphic representations may be closer to a Renaissance understanding of the book as cultural capital than we suspect. Handled, admired, studied, scrutinised for its paraphernalia of dedication and donation, the early Florentine book has more stories to tell than the one announced on its titlepage. That story is inscribed in material which the modern scholar treats as largely redundant – prefatory gestures of service and gift-exchange, illuminated frontispiece and marginal decoration, carefully selected compilations of works whose significance is particular to the recipient, rarities or translations of works in arcane languages, offered as compliments to a particular patron, by a renowned donor. It is to these supplementary stories that early owners expected posterity to give sustained, lasting attention. For a Renaissance audience it was on all of these that the lasting reputation of a library and its benefactor depended.

REFERENCES

1 Alan Stewart, *The Bounds of Sodomy: Textual Relations in Early Modern England* (unpublished University of London PhD thesis, 1993), p. 22.
2 cit. Stewart, *Bounds of Sodomy*, p. 25.
3 Stewart, *Bounds of Sodomy*, p. 22. The two books of the *Iliad* which Politian translated for Lorenzo are a nice balance of a buccaneering martial book (2), and a sensual book, which closes with a bedroom scene between Paris and Helen.
4 On Cosimo de' Medici's and his son Piero's libraries see A. C. de la Mare, 'Cosimo and his books', in F. Ames-Lewis (ed.), *Cosimo 'il Vecchio' de' Medici, 1389–1464* (Oxford: Clarendon Press, 1992), pp. 115–56; F. Ames-Lewis, *The Library and Manuscripts of Piero di Cosimo de' Medici* (New York: 1984)
5 For a broad account of this tendency see L. Jardine, *Worldly Goods: A New History of the Renaissance* (London: Macmillan, 1996).

6 The model for this kind of benefaction was Pope Nicholas V's collection of books, which formed the cornerstone of the Vatican Library in Rome. See Antony Grafton, *Rome Reborn*, ( ).

7 Caroline Elam, 'Cosimo de' Medici and San Lorenzo', in F. Ames-Lewis (ed.), *Cosimo 'il Vecchio' de' Medici, 1389–1464* (Oxford: Clarendon Press, 1992), pp. 157–80; 157.

8 On Cosimo's donations to the San Marco library see B. L. Ullman and P. A. Stadter, 'The Public Library of Renaissance Florence' (*Medioevo e umanismo*, 10; Padua, 1982), pp. 12–27, 310–13, cited by de la Mare, 'Cosimo and his books', p. 115.

9 Vespasiano has the same kinds of thing to say about Niccolò Niccoli, whose library Piero de' Medici later incorporated in the Medici library, thus, by implication, magnifying its 'humanity'. Less laudable, perhaps, are the strenuous efforts the Medici made to purchase Pope Nicholas V's library when they were tentatively put on the market by his successor – who regarded Nicholas's books as representing the kind of inappropriately ostentatious expenditure of Papal funds as Paul II later lavished on gems and cameos.

10 This represents only a beginning of such a study. I have simply taken advantage of scholarly material already readily available in printed form, notably in the work of Ames-Lewis and de la Mare. A systematic study would undoubtedly uncover some further 'family memory' strategies at work in the library.

11 A further obvious category of book in the Medici collection which I have not had time to deal with here is the presentation copy of a work of devotion, to honour a particular family occasion. See for example the two copies of Books of Hours made for Medici daughters' weddings in Alexander, *The Painted Page* (see note 12 below).

12 For the first of these I have used de la Mare, 'Cosimo and his books', and P. W. Goodhart Gordan, *Two Renaissance Book Hunters: The Letters of Poggius Bracciolini to Nicolaus de Niccolis* (New York: Columbia University Press, 1974, 1991); for the second, de la Mare and E. Garin (ed.), *Prosatori Latini del Quattrocento* (Milan and Naples: Riccardo Ricciardi, n.d.); for the third and fourth I have used J. J. G. Alexander (ed.), *The Painted Page: Italian Renaissance Book Illumination 1450–1550* (Munich and NY: Prestel, 1994).

13 Goodhart Gordan, *Two Renaissance Book Hunters*, pp. 88–9.

14 de la Mare, 'Cosimo and his books', p. 149.

15 Gordan, *Two Renaissance Book Hunters*, p. 93. Ullman identifies Cod. Laur. 49.24 as the copy of Cicero's Letters to Atticus which Poggio made for his own use in 1525. A MS of this work was in Poggio's library at the time of his death. See B. L. Ullman, *The Origin and Development of Humanistic Script* (Padua: Antenore, 1963), pp. 43–5, cit. Gordan, p. 282.

16 Unedited manuscript by Antonio Pacini, transcribed by Angelo Fabroni in his life of Cosimo, *Magni Cosimi Medicei vita* (Pisa, 1789), ii, pp. 155–6 n. 78: 'erat enim ditissimus agri, ditissimusque auri, atque pretiosae vestis, et universae supellectilis, signis, tabulis pietis, vasis caelatis, margaritis, libris mirum in modum affluit &c. et prope calcem.' Cit. John Paoletti, 'Fraternal piety and family poer: the artistic patronage of Cosimo and Lorenzo de' Medici', Ames-Lewis, *Cosimo*, pp. 195–219; 198.

17 de la Mare, 'Cosimo and his books', pp. 118–19.

18 'Maiores nostri, Laurenti carissime, benevolentia vel necessitate sibi coniunctos in nuptiis donare consueverunt, ut apud illos amoris et officii sui monumentum etiam ornamentum esset. . . . Nam, ut omittam ea quae vitae necessaria sunt, tibi pretiosa vestis multa, et lauta suppellex et magnifica multis in locis est. Mihi praeterea recordanti multos in nostra familiaritate sermones gratius atque iucundius tibi munus fore visum est, si potius a Francisco tuo quam a fortuna sua donareris. Quam ob rem tuo nomine de re uxoria brevis commentarios scribere institui, quos huic nuptiarum tempori accommodatos arbitror non inutiles futuros' (Garin, *Prosatori latini*, p. 104).

19 'Nec vero haec scribere aggredior ut ipse te, sed ut per te nonnullos id aetatis instituam, et cum quid agendum sit eos commonefacio, tu quod per te fecisti, facis et facturus es, in te

recognoscas. . . . Imitaris profecto spectatissimum virum Ioannem patrem tuum et ornatissimum Cosmum fratrem, quorum auctoritate, prudentia, consiliis abunde munitus es' (Garin, *Prosatori latini*, p. 106).

20 Goodhart Gordon, *Two Renaissanc Book Hunters.*, pp. 165, 175.
21 Alexander, *The Painted Page*, pp. 120–1.

PATRONAGE ACROSS FRONTIERS: SUBSCRIPTION PUBLISHING IN FRENCH IN ENLIGHTENMENT EUROPE

Wallace Kirsop

L'histoire du livre, the history of books – call the discipline what you will – has not escaped the tyranny of fashion. When it is possible, in 2008, say, when Lucien Febvre and Henri-Jean Martin's *L'Apparition du livre* will be half-a-century old, to look back with some serenity at the long-term impact of a remarkable work, shifts in emphasis and swings in mood will be easier to identify and to situate.[1] Not that we shall ever be able to reduce the mass of academic and semi-popular writing on this subject to a simple and beautifully coherent narrative. Scholarship, in our time above all, cannot be so neatly pigeon-holed. Antiquarians of all sorts continue imperturbably on their way far from the battles and preoccupations of theorists or of devotees of what I shall call the *Annales* tendency. Even those of us who look for synthesis, for the ability to make meaningful and apt comparisons, and for awareness of wider issues, cannot fail to recognize the worth and the solidity of much of the painstaking research done on printing, papermaking, binding and all the other crafts and trades that are part of the world of books, not neglecting those that pertain to scribal publication. Over recent decades there has been not only some doubt – perhaps even dissension – about the role that codicologists and physical bibliographers should play in the *histoire du livre* project,[2] but also a certain wavering about the priorities to be attached to the study of production, distribution or reception.[3] The last of the three, in the guise of the history of reading or of audiences, has enjoyed particular favour in the last decade or so.[4] My own view is – perhaps unfashionably – that there is not just one way to go, that all three aspects are equally important and significant and that the complete historian of books does not and should not neglect any of the techniques and auxiliary sciences available for the exploration of print or scribal culture.[5] However, it would be foolish to ignore the demands made on individual researchers by insistence on such a range of skills and interests.

Rightly or wrongly I suspect that questions relating to book distribution are coming back into prominence after a period of at least partial eclipse. The reasons may not need to be sought further afield than in the late twentieth century's passion for shopping. In the age of the mall, of the hypermarket and of the revitalized arcade it can seem more legitimate to be concerned with the history of consumption and of advertising.[6] Certainly there is in this trend a strong excuse for looking again at book subscriptions, a phenomenon that came to the notice of the scholarly world, especially in English-speaking countries, more than two decades ago. At that time the talking point, based on the work of Peter Wallis and Frank Robinson in particular, was the subscriber list, something that in Great Britain at least accompanied very many books produced and financed in this manner.[7] I must admit that my own curiosity was stimulated by the various Wallis-Robinson publications and that I have not abandoned a quest I have pursued in various ways and with recourse to several methods of investigation since the mid-1970s. Indeed, in collaboration with Patricia Gray, whose Ph.D. thesis 'From *prospectus* to *belle édition*: Investigations in the luxury booktrade in eighteenth- and nineteenth-century France' was accepted by Monash University in 1991, I am working on a general account of subscription publishing in France before the Revolution. It is this experience, reported in a number of case studies in various places and summed up provisionally in a paper at Viterbo in 1985, that I want to review now in the light of some new evidence and of recent discussions on the European dimension of the eighteenth-century French trade.[8]

My title suggests a definite approach and emphasis. Without wanting to call these into question, I must also draw attention to a paradox that resides in the fact that, alongside enterprises directed to a European market, there were others whose whole *raison d'être* was their appeal to a strictly localized area. This suggests a way of proceeding. We shall move from a brief account of this venture as introduced into France in the second decade of the eighteenth century to consideration of the international and transnational aspects of this form of publishing and finally to evocation of the parochial character it often assumed in practice. Along the way we shall have to take account of the sometimes contradictory and conflicting stances taken by authors, distributors, i.e. booksellers, and buyers or readers.

* * *

The specifically French history of subscription publishing began in 1716. In that year Dom Bernard de Montfaucon, the great scholar of the Congrégation de Saint-Maur and of the Abbey of Saint-Germain-des-Prés, came to an arrangement with seven Paris booksellers for the publication of his *Antiquité expliquée et représentée en figures* by subscription 'à la manière d'Angleterre'. The folio prospectus presented this as an unusual solution to the problem of financing a multi-volume set with a large number of copperplate illustrations. It was noted that this way of proceeding was both English and Dutch and that there were already many potential subscribers in France and England. In addition it was hoped that there would be interest in Flanders, Holland, Germany, Spain and Italy.[9] In the event, the predictions were proved correct and the work had enough success to encourage other Benedictines to issue various massive scholarly publications in the same manner in the course of the 1720s.[10]

The priority of Montfaucon was sufficiently notorious to pass into the reference works of the second half of the century. Both the *Encyclopédie* and the 1771 edition of the *Dictionnaire de Trévoux* give explanations of the general phenomenon and of its antecedents that are in conformity with the 1716 prospectus.[11] However, their information about the English and Dutch prehistory of this way of financing publication was both vague and erroneous. Even if Walton's Polyglot Bible was well known on the Continent, it was not Montfaucon's earliest precursor. One has to go half a century before Walton to find Minsheu's *Ductor in linguas* of 1617 as the authentic pioneering venture.[12] There is no doubt, though, that the innovation became much more common in the second half of the seventeenth century and that it was imitated in Holland and Germany as early as the 1660s.[13] By the second decade of the eighteenth century it was, therefore, well established in places that had become closer to the French trade as a paradoxical consequence of the Revocation of the Edict of Nantes.

The new development was not altogether to the taste of the authorities nor ultimately, one suspects, of the booksellers' guild. At all events, regulations were brought in in the 1720s ostensibly to protect the public against any abuses. Subscriptions, according to the provisions included in the *Code de la librairie et imprimerie de Paris* in 1744, were to be organized by booksellers and printers only – not authors – and these trade members were to be responsible for the proper administration of any such venture. This contrasted with the role played by Montfaucon, who had undertaken to place all the money collected for *L'Antiquité expliquée* in the safekeeping of the Procurator General of his Order. More important, perhaps, was the obligation to get official permission to print after examination of at least half the work proposed for subscription. No prospectus was to be issued without the authorization of the Garde des Sceaux. Each prospectus was to include a sample sheet of the whole work showing the types and paper to be employed. The time limits set out in the subscription proposal were to be respected.[14] Surviving guild and official registers suggest that these restrictions were followed more or less strictly in the decades up to the major book-trade reforms of 1777.[15] As always, the very existence of prohibitions hints at breaches and some disorder. Not for the first or last time government had been taken by surprise by changes in the media.

Things seem to have gone swimmingly at first for subscriptions. Georg Wallin's book – in Latin, then in German – on the scholarly world of Paris as he observed it in the 1720s devotes a chapter to the works being published in this way.[16] However, it was soon discovered that such ventures do not always succeed, far from it. Montfaucon's own second attempt, at the end of the 1720s, was in some ways a commercial failure.[17] Thus it is hardly astonishing that, after the initial enthusiasm, there was a noticeable slackening off of subscriptions in the 1730s and 1740s. A point to be borne constantly in mind is the trade's capacity to underwrite expensive works from its own capital resources. Although, as I have written elsewhere, we do not know nearly enough about the financial arrangements of guild members and other shadowier participants in the book business, it is obvious that fortunes waxed and waned in the course of the last century of the Ancien Régime.[18]

After 1750, in other words at the time of the *Encyclopédie*, subscriptions seem to have come back strongly into favour. The evidence, which is essentially that of surviving prospectuses and of advertisements placed in the journals, not to mention the *Catalogue hebdomadaire* from the early 1760s on,[19] shows that this formula was now being used more frequently. Significantly it was not confined to the large scholarly works characteristic of the 1720s. In the 1770s and 1780s one begins to see elegantly got-up small-format books – like the translation of the German poetical works of the supposed 'Merthghen'[20] – that belong to the category of what Cissie Fairchilds has called 'populuxe' objects.[21] In all sorts of ways we are in a new consumer age, and the book trade was uniquely equipped to exploit its possibilities. More than ever the 'discourse' – if I dare call it that – of the prospectus is about different paper qualities, the finest being, of course, the newly invented wove kind (*papier vélin*), about exquisite illustrations, fine bindings, gilt edges, and all the other paraphernalia of contemporary bibliophilic taste. This seems to have been a market that it was peculiarly appropriate to tap through subscriptions, with their illusion of exclusivity – witness the insistence on limited numbers of copies available in large paper or fine paper – and with their solid appeal to canniness via the discounts offered to those paying in advance.

None of this ended in 1789. Despite the changes analysed in Carla Hesse's *Publishing and Cultural Politics in Revolutionary Paris, 1789–1810*,[22] notably the abolition of the guild and the consequent deregulation of the trade, subscriptions remained part of the commercial arsenal of the bookseller/publisher or of the author, freed from total dependence in 1777 and never again shackled in the old way.[23] There is, then, a continuity across the Revolutionary decade and the First Empire into the Restoration. Better documented now in the pages of the *Bibliographie de la France*, the subscription enterprise lived on for the benefit of the heirs of the Enlightenment. It is not inappropriate, I believe, to draw on this later period for occasional examples of the behaviour of subscribers.

Certain characteristics of this century of bookselling and publishing practice need to be pinpointed. The *Encyclopédie* had noted that the very frequency of subscriptions in England had led to abuses that were beginning to discredit the formula. There are in France examples of works that appeared many years after the preannounced date, notably Dom Devienne's *Histoire de la ville de Bordeaux* of 1771. However, the prospectus of 1761 had required no more than a promise to pay within two months of the definitive announcement of publication.[24] The author had been more prudent about his ability to deliver quickly than most of us are. In the later part of the century authors or booksellers sometimes justify their decision to do no more than collect the names of interested parties by referring to bad experiences subscribers may have had with money lost in enterprises that never materialized. In French *souscription* tends to cover both sorts of situation, whereas German distinguishes *Pränumeration* (prepayment) from *Subskription* (a promise to pay on publication).[25] However, one finds the term *soumission* in the prospectus for Claude-Joseph Lévrier's *Mémoires chronologiques pour servir à l'histoire du Vexin et du Pincerais* in 1781. 5000 copies of this document were printed; 1190 were distributed; 231 *soumissions* or promises to pay were received, and the work was apparently abandoned.[26] Three years later a prospectus was issued for a two-volume octavo *Dictionnaire alchymique*. This too called for *soumissions* to be sent to Didot *l'aîné* in the form of promises to pay 36 *livres* when the work appeared. The edition was to be limited to the number of *soumissionnaires* registered by May 1785. As it happened, this work also disappeared leaving no further trace.[27] It is clear that the prospectus for a possible subscription edition had become for publishers a means of testing the water.

Half-failures or attempts at salvage are revealed by their prospectuses. One now in Monash University Library shows how Pierre-François Didot took over the remnants of the 1734–1742 edition of Réaumur's *Mémoires pour servir à l'histoire des insectes* and proposed to issue first mixed sets of original and newly recomposed quarto volumes from the six, then what amounted to a completely new edition disguised under the first imprint.[28] It is, in fact, an instance of what Ralph Leigh called the 'tap edition', notably in his Sandars Lectures on Rousseau.[29] A similarly complex case is to be found in the fate of Montenault's great edition of La Fontaine's *Fables* with Oudry's illustrations. The original four folio volumes appeared between 1755 and 1759 and were preceded by a prospectus that laid out both the conditions of the subscription and the different paper qualities available. By 1774 one finds amongst other later prospectuses dealing with the remainders of the work one from Mérande of Avignon offering 300 copies only at a discount rate.[30] An additional complication is thus unveiled: we enter a zone of undercutting and bargain-boosting that is only just beginning to be studied as it deserves. No one will be surprised to learn that the great entrepreneur Panckoucke is not far away from these commercial manoeuvres.

Another feature of French subscriptions – which were very numerous overall by 1789, as is clear from the number of *surviving* prospectuses in libraries across the world and, even more so, from the advertisements – is the paucity of printed lists of subscribers in the resulting volumes. I have tried to tackle this problem elsewhere and to give a reasonably comprehensive catalogue of the relevant works. There is certainly a contrast with normal London practice and, as Reinhard Wittmann has pointed out, with that of German-speaking Europe outside Berlin and Leipzig.[31] My hypotheses about this disparity have been challenged, so I propose to return to them and to their implications in the later sections of this paper. For the moment the essential thing is to note the fact that sets France somewhat apart from the rest of Europe at this time.

* * *

My exposition of the development of subscription publishing in France may well have seemed to emphasize commercial factors. This was done in a deliberate attempt to keep the realities of the book business clearly in view. Insofar as subscriptions were initiated and controlled by the trade – and until 1777 this was in theory the guild's exclusive territory – it is unwise to ignore cynicism, opportunism and greed as motives for certain ventures. However, the phenomenon does have other dimensions and it is important for us to explore these.

In the flurry of discussion of lists of subscribers in the English-speaking world in the early 1970s, the point was properly made that a subscription could be seen as an act of collective patronage. Where individual patrons prepared to underwrite an expensive work single-handedly had virtually disappeared, a large – but not necessarily anonymous – public had to take their place. In France, of course, there was the King or the State as munificent patron. The Imprimerie royale was at the service of many vast and prohibitively expensive works of scholarship.[32] Once again 1789 was in no sense a dividing line: the Republic and especially the Empire of Napoleon I continued the tradition with a reconstituted State printing house. Alongside this, the King was a generous subscriber – for up to 100 copies of some works – and thus a participant in the general movement of support for literary and scholarly endeavour. Despite the English evidence that multiple subscribers did not always claim their due, there was quite literally a 'Dépôt du Roi' from which complimentary copies were dispersed to members of the Royal Family, ministers and others who intrigued to be included in a not altogether stable 'free list'.[33] Support for publishing in the Fifth Republic a few years ago had uncanny similarities with this system, such is the power of tradition across regimes.

A State that was not infested with economic rationalists – how many physiocrats were there on the 'free list'? – could allow itself to deal with these things in a thoroughly unbusinesslike way. The fate of Rossel's official account in 1808 of Bruny d'Entrecasteaux's expedition in search of La Pérouse is probably not untypical of what happened before and after the Revolution. In 1814, 556 sets of the two-volume quarto remained unsold. Of the 444 others 252 had been given away.[34] As late as the 1970s one could buy – as new – productions of the Imprimerie royale of Charles X. Here we step outside normal commercial constraints into an unreal world where accountants and auditors held no sway. Similar attitudes and practices were not absent from those ventures supposedly controlled and directed by professional bookseller-publishers. Where authors alone were in charge, as in the later volumes of Antoine Court de Gébelin's *Monde primitif*, even greater financial disasters could be anticipated and indeed happened, as his creditors discovered when they met soon after his death in May 1784.[35]

The context of all this was not simply French, of course. It is hardly necessary after decades of research by Giles Barber, Robert Darnton, Jean-Daniel Candaux, Christiane Berkvens-Stevelinck, Jeroom Vercruysse, Jeremy Popkin and others to stress the role of foreign bookselling and printing businesses – in Geneva, Neuchâtel, Amsterdam, The Hague, Leiden, even Avignon – in the spread of the writings of the Huguenot diaspora and of the Enlightenment.[36] Indeed, because of the better preservation of these firms' archives, we are often at risk of having our view of the whole French-language trade skewed towards nests of dissidence in Switzerland, Holland and Germany and away from Paris. These are complex and contentious issues, and we have to take heed of a variety of more recent general approaches, for example Elizabeth Eisenstein's Lyell Lectures of 1989–1990, *Grub Street Abroad. Aspects of the French Cosmopolitan Press from the Age of Louis XIV to the French Revolution*[37] and Anne Goldgar's *Impolite Learning. Conduct and Community in the Republic of Letters 1680–1750*.[38] By and large, however, the subscription business has remained outside the debate.

One exception is Dena Goodman's *The Republic of Letters. A Cultural History of the French Enlightenment* of 1994. She includes a section on 'Public Subscription' at the end of her fourth chapter and is inclined to see the act of subscribing – to a periodical or to a book – as a gesture of solidarity, participation in an intellectual or literary community, ideological commitment. In proposing this way of looking at the phenomenon, she takes issue – explicitly – with points I made in a contribution to volume II of the *Histoire de l'édition française*:[39]

To focus on the material base of subscription while ignoring the ideological commitment it implied is to miss half the import of the practice.[40]

Am I guilty as charged? Not altogether, I think, as I look at the extended paper on the general topic I gave in Viterbo.[41] Alas, the proceedings of specialist conferences do not always attract much attention, so I shall try to sum up a point of view that is certainly not black and white.

There is no doubt that in publishing there is a fundamental and at times painful ambiguity. Ideological considerations – philosophical, political, religious – *are* important. Too many printers and booksellers, not to mention their customers, went to the Bastille, the stake or the guillotine for any argument to be possible on this. Various subscription enterprises – not least the multiple editions of the *Encyclopédie* – clearly belonged in a dubious if not sulphurous category. Just as obviously prudence dictated that no subscribers' names be published. For this sort of material Dena Goodman's characterization of subscriptions as 'collective and anonymous' is quite apposite.[42] The same has to be true of the periodicals that served the Enlightenment cause across the whole of Europe.

Similarly it is not difficult to accept the notion that subscriptions could involve not only a community of readers affirming their allegiances, but also a real complicity between author and purchaser. This is a theme that runs through Gébelin's correspondence with his subscribers. The *Monde primitif*, essentially philological in character, did not in itself mobilize the various ideological groupings with which its author had connexions: Freemasonry, Protestantism, the physiocrats, the cause of reform. However, support from all those tendencies is evident in the published subscriber lists. Gébelin was always anxious to have his correspondents, especially those as remote as Massachusetts, contribute material on unusual languages.[43] Subscription thus became potential collaboration. Two generations earlier, and without clear ideological overtones, Montfaucon's letters to learned Europe also circled round his subscription enterprises. In his vast surviving collection of inwards correspondence business matters and scholarly interchange sit side by side.[44]

We noted earlier that Montfaucon and the bookseller promoters of *L'Antiquité expliquée* were looking for an audience across political frontiers. The manuscript lists of subscribers that have survived in Montfaucon's papers demonstrate how effectively people were recruited from London and Cambridge in the West to Vienna in the East.[45] The booksellers will have had their part in this, particularly in attracting the carriage trade: the noblemen who would put sumptuously bound large-paper sets in their bookcases to be admired – from outside – by visitors and, in later generations, by tourists gawking from behind ropes. Nonetheless the effectiveness of the operation depended ultimately on Montfaucon's own contacts in the Republic of Letters. His agents and his confidants in widely scattered countries ensured that his personal approaches were reinforced in as many spheres and markets as possible. The author's European reputation guaranteed the permeability of borders. Gébelin, in scholarly terms, was an unknown when he launched into the *Monde primitif* adventure in the early 1770s. Despite this he had had even more experience than Montfaucon in negotiating on a European scale. As amanuensis to his father Antoine Court, the celebrated pastor of the Désert, he had worked long years on the correspondence that went out from the French Protestant seminary in Lausanne to communities in France itself and in the countries of the diaspora. As a publisher and distributor of clandestine books, as a smuggler of refugees, he had had unusual training in the marketing and advertising skills appropriate for subscriptions.[46] In both these exceptionally well documented cases the European and even extra-European dimension of the enterprises flowed naturally from the personality of strongly committed and involved authors. It is not hard to detect here the flavour of which Dena Goodman speaks.

And yet . . . There is ambiguity, contradiction, conflict between sentiment and belief on the one hand and astute business sense on the other. Authors were not always in command, and some booksellers could look remarkably like sharks. La Mottraye retired badly hurt from his experience with his *Voyages [. . .] en Europe, Asie & Afrique* in 1727. The full title of his protest says it all: *Relation en forme de factum. Ou exposition de l'indigne procedé de Th. Johnson & J. van Duren, bourgeois & Libraires de La Haye, envers A. de La Motraye, dont ils ont imprimé les Voyages; avec son Apologie (sur ce qu'ils ont fait tant attendre, après un ouvrage si mal executé) les personnes qui lui ont fait l'honneur d'y souscrire, & un ample Errata, à inserer immédiatement après la liste des souscrivans.*[47] Here is an example, by no means unique, of a French-language subscription launched in another country – and with a subscriber list. The bookseller Du Sauzet of The Hague and Amsterdam was urging Joly de Fleury in Paris as early as 1718 to emulate the noble English subscribers to large-paper copies of Dutch speculations on the names and reputations of classical French authors. The cautious customer usually settled for the small paper.[48] There is manifestly no ideology here, no innovation. The trade was catering for a taste for luxury and for showiness. More important, it was recognizing that it needed an international clientele to cover the costs of ventures that were too burdensome for one country alone.

There is not a long road to travel from such blatant opportunism to the art-book packages of the late twentieth century: same plates accompanied by introductory textual matter in a range of leading European languages. The difference is that the market is wider, genuinely 'populuxe', in our age. In addition we have been through the door-to-door subscription sales, often originating in Hartford, Connecticut, that flourished so spectacularly in the U.S.A. in the second half of the nineteenth century and had some currency at least in other countries.[49] Such developments lay in the future in the eighteenth century, but there can be no doubt that part of the vogue for subscriptions pointed in that direction. The researcher will look at each case on its merits, but he or she will be wary of simplistic conclusions. A cautionary tale – well told by Geraldine Sheridan – concerns Voltaire's somewhat dubious role in the history of the 'subscriber' edition of *La Henriade*.[50] Authorial involvement and commercial sharp practice came together in one of the most important publications of this sort in the early eighteenth century. It is a salutary reminder of the unpredictability of writers faced with their transnational audience and with imperatives of diverse kinds that can be taken back to local and parochial as well as personal issues.

* * *

Why are subscriber lists so rare in France? The question is worth asking again. My provisional conclusion nearly two decades ago – following Reinhard Wittmann's observations about German practice – was that capital-city audiences may have found them vulgar and provincial. Dena Goodman countered this with the suggestion:

It seems more plausible, however, that the reluctance of the French to have their names displayed in the works to which they subscribed was rooted in the need to keep private (that is, secret) one's ideological commitment.[51]

I am hesitant about accepting the counter-argument in this particular form for the simple reason that the great mass of French and French-language sub-scriptions involved no perceptible ideological commitment. They were typi-cally expensive but anodyne works, unlikely to attract any further attention from censors who had already passed them. Even in the case of suspect texts, people's documentable reasons for subscribing could be bibliophilic rather than philosophical.[52] But this does not help us over the initial difficulty.

In London, the most populous city in Europe by the late eighteenth century, lists of subscribers were perfectly acceptable. This was a recognized form of advertising: a sort of mass testimonial often arranged in hierarchical order within each letter of the alphabet, in the same way as the list of bed-and-breakfast houses in Cambridge in 1968 began with the 'Hon. Mrs X' leading the way from the untitled mob. So why did Parisian authors and booksellers not want to follow suit? Not because they had problems with their agents' transcription of names, even though this specific complaint occurs in more than one place throughout the century.[53] Is it just possible that they reacted normally as the Germans did? In the absence of commentary at the time specifically on this issue, the question probably has to be left open.

What is clear, however, is that many of the works including lists were pub-lished in the provinces, by provincials resident in Paris and somewhat on the margins of established society, or by people who had spent long years abroad in places where the subscriber list was normal practice. Few cases can be shown to be exceptions to this. In other words the local factor is strong, and the lists themselves tend to back this up.

The greatest mistake – one made a number of times in recent decades by incautious scholars – is to imagine that subscribers are readers. The graphs of readership by town and country sometimes produced for these publications are all different in quite striking ways. Naturally, there are genuine reader-subscribers, but they are usually in the minority, being swamped by relations, friends, associates, acquaintances and others who feel it their duty to support the author's work. In other cases a bookseller appointed as agent in a town inside or outside France has been particularly zealous in chasing subscriptions. The result is that lists can be and are vital sources for building up biographical databases, but they do not tell us very much about the intellectual and literary tastes of localities strongly represented in them for quite different reasons. Twentieth-century academics, reflecting on why they subscribe – *must* subscribe – to such and such a Festschrift, ought to be able to appreciate the point made. Books can sit unused on shelves whether they go to uncles and cousins in some small hometown or cross frontiers to the great metropolises of the Western world.

If one leaves aside the subscriptions where the trade took all the initiatives – typically to produce a deluxe edition of some classic work – the involvement and the interference of authors were often to be expected. Vanity could run counter to financial interest. Since the research done – and not yet published, unfortunately – by Bruce Eames on 'The Subscribers to Abbé Expilly's *Dictionnaire géographique, historique et politique des Gaules et de la France* (1762–1770)',[54] it has become obvious that a major cause for that work remaining incomplete was the burden of humouring the author's desire to give away free copies to foreign notabilities. Joan Lindblad Kirsop had long suspected that Antoine Court de Gébelin was doing the same thing with the *Monde primitif* and inflating the subscriber list. Last year I found unequivocal evidence – not yet published – that that was how Harvard College got into one of the later lists.[55] After 1777, if not before, Gébelin had to accept entire responsibility for the mismanagement of his affairs.

Personal commitment to a project meant much more than business success. For Gébelin and many others, no doubt, the work was the thing, and everything else had to be subordinate to it. When, as appears in a prospectus recently acquired by Monash University Library, Sylvain Maréchal put a personal *envoi* on the proposal for *soumissions* to *Les Voyages de Pythagore*: 'pour le Citoyen Duchesne De la part de Sylvain', he was playing the part expected of him.[56] In the end the rationale of many a grandiose outreaching project has to be sought in the individual and local tastes, habits and connexions of the initiating writer.

✻ ✻ ✻

If a brief conclusion may be allowed to open a new subject, it is worth pointing out that the subscribers themselves, real or potential, have often been forgotten in this branch of research. They were long-suffering, since they often had to wait interminably for multi-volume works to be completed well behind schedule. If they were *really* interested in the subject matter, this could be intolerable. Sometimes, of course, they died or lost patience, with the consequence that incomplete sets – of the *Monde primitif*, for example – are found in libraries or on the market.[57] Keeping track of one's own subscriptions, especially after 1814 when part publication flourished, could be a laborious business fraught with problems. I have tried to illustrate the experience of Marshal Davout and his family in this respect in a paper entombed in the first K. V. Sinclair Festschrift.[58] The Davouts at least were in France and, after the Marshal's return from provincial banishment, back in Paris. Across frontiers it could be more difficult again, witness the letter – published in facsimile by its owner the Grolier Club – sent by Thomas Jefferson to his favourite Paris bookseller on 26 May 1795. Jefferson did not know that Froullé had gone to the guillotine more than a year before, but his remarks speak eloquently about the frustrations of all distant subscribers. Thus he complains of a box of books having taken more than a year – from December 1792 to February 1794 – to reach him badly affected by water. Consequently he recommends better packing and calls for replacement of four volumes of plates from the *Encyclopédie méthodique*. These were 'so entirely rotten that the leaves, on attempting to open them, fell into powder'. A heartfelt plea is made: without substitutes 'my edition of the work will be incomplete & and of little value. I hope that an original subscriber who has taken the work from the beginning & means to do it to the end will be indulged in this.' Detailed instructions follow on the requirements of a punctilious customer who was not to live to see the conclusion of the most ambitious subscription enterprise of all.[59]

Effective subscribers are one thing; those who decline are another. A letter received by Montfaucon in March 1727 demonstrates some of the obstacles in the way of his second subscription and presents an elegant model for polite refusal:

Mon Reverend pere:

si la facilité d'avoir de L'argent repondoit à L'inclination que j'ai de faire honneur aux Sçavans de notre Congregation, en avançant la moitié du prix des ouvrages dont ils – proposent la souscription, je serois des premiers à leur donner cette marque de mon estime et de L'approbation si justement dûë à leurs travaux. Les vôtres, mon – Reverend pere, qui sont immenses meritent surtout cette consideration. si avant que le tems de souscrire soit expiré, L'occasion de ménager 40 ou 60ll se presente, je la saisirai et j'aurai soin d'envoyer cette somme à votre Rece. J'ai l'honneur d'être avec bien du respect

Mon Reverend pere
Il y a peu de gens à Meaux
assez dans le goût des livres pour
souscrire
   a St Faron le 8e mars 1727

Votre tres humble et
très obéissant serviteur
et Confr. fr. Bonaventure
Aubert OSB[60]

This simple text is in fact rich in suggestions for the historian of books. It may help to explain why this researcher is prepared to investigate subscription publishing across more than one frontier and hemisphere.

REFERENCES

1. For a retrospect after twenty years see Wallace Kirsop, 'Literary History and Book Trade History: the Lessons of *L'Apparition du livre*', *Australian Journal of French Studies*, 16 (1979), 488–535.

2. See, for example, remarks made in Robert Darnton, *The Business of Enlightenment. A Publishing History of the* Encyclopédie *1775–1800* (Cambridge, Mass., and London: The Belknap Press of Harvard University Press, 1979, esp. pp. 1–3) and the countering argument in G. Thomas Tanselle, *The History of Books as a Field of Study* (Chapel Hill: The Hanes Foundation for the Study of the Origin and Development of the Book, The University of North Carolina at Chapel Hill, 1981).

3. See Martyn Lyons, 'Texts, Books, and Readers: Which Kind of Cultural History?', *Australian Cultural History*, 11 (1992), 1–15.

4. See Jonathan Rose, 'Rereading the English Common Reader: A Preface to a History of Audiences', *Journal of the History of Ideas*, 53 (1992), 47–70.

5. The emphasis on scribal culture is inspired by a number of important recent publications, e.g. Harold Love, *Scribal Publication in Seventeenth-Century England* (Oxford: Clarendon Press, 1993), *De bonne main. La communication manuscrite au XVIIIe siècle*, ed. by François Moureau (Paris and Oxford: Universitas and Voltaire Foundation, 1993) and the July–September special number of *XVIIe siècle* in 1996.

6. Historians of books could profitably look at studies such as Jackson Lears, *Fables of Abundance. A Cultural History of Advertising in America* (New York: Basic Books, 1994) and Richard Ohmann, *Selling Culture. Magazines, Markets and Class at the Turn of the Century* (London and New York: Verso, 1996) as well as at the growing literature on the history of shopping and consumption.

7. See P. J. Wallis, 'Book Subscription Lists', *The Library*, 5th s. 29 (1974), 255–86, and F. J. G. Robinson and P. J. Wallis, *Book Subscription Lists. A Revised Guide* (Newcastle upon Tyne: Harold Hill & Son Ltd for The Book Subscriptions List Project, 1975).

8. See W. Kirsop, 'Pour une histoire bibliographique de la souscription en France au XVIIIe siècle' in *Trasmissione dei testi a stampa nel periodo moderno*, II: *II Seminario internazionale Roma-Viterbo 27–29 giugno 1985*, ed. by Giovanni Crapulli (Rome: Edizioni dell'Ateneo, 1987), pp. 255–82; W. Kirsop, 'Keeping Réaumur's *Mémoires pour servir à l'histoire des insectes* in print', *Bibliographical Society of Australia and New Zealand Bulletin*, 17 (1993), 127–33; W. Kirsop, 'Un projet de dictionnaire alchimique en 1784' in *Alchimie: art, histoire et mythes. Actes du 1er colloque international de la Société d'Etude de l'Histoire de l'Alchimie (Paris, Collège de France, 14–15–16 mars 1991)*, ed. by Didier Kahn and Sylvain Matton (Paris and Milan: S.E.H.A. and Archè, 1995), pp. 749–56; Patricia Gray, 'Subscribing to Plutarch in the Eighteenth Century', *Australian Journal of French Studies*, 29 (1992), 30–40.

9. See the copy of the prospectus in Paris, Bibliothèque Nationale, Collection Clairambault 490, fols 108–111.

10. For example editions of St John Chrysostom and St Basil, Dom Michel Félibien's *Histoire de la ville de Paris* and the *Veterum Scriptorum et Monumentorum ecclesiasticorum et dogmaticorum Collectio* of Martène and Durand.

11. *Encyclopédie, ou dictionnaire raisonné des sciences, des arts et des métiers [. . .]* (Paris edition), XV (1765), 416–17 and *Dictionnaire universel françois et latin, vulgairement appelé Dictionnaire de Trévoux* (new edition, Paris, 1771), VII, 810.

12. See Sarah L. C. Clapp, 'The Beginnings of Subscription Publication in the Seventeenth Century', *Modern Philology*, 29 (1931), 199–224, and G. Pollard and A. Ehrman, *The Distribution of Books by Catalogue from the Invention of Printing to A.D. 1800 based on material in the Broxbourne Library* (Cambridge: privately printed for members of the Roxburghe Club, 1965), pp. 178–97.

13. See Peter T. van Rooden & Jan Wim Wesselius, 'Two early cases of publication by subscription in Holland and Germany: Jacob Abendana's *Mikhlal Yophi* (1661) and David Cohen de Lara's *Keter Kehunna* (1668)', *Quærendo*, 16 (1986), 110–30. I have not seen Otto S. Lankhorst, '"De snode uitwerkzels van een listige eigenbaat". Inventarisatie van uitgaven bij intekening in de Republiek tot 1750', *De zeventiende eeuw*, 6 (1990), 129–36.

14. See Saugrain, *Code de la librairie et imprimerie de Paris* (Paris, 1744), pp. 126–30.

15. See the fragmentary list (1725–1759) in 'Registre des Permissions accordées par Monseigneur Le Garde des Sceaux pour les Souscriptions de Liures', Paris, Bibliothèque Nationale, fonds français, 21844, fols 89–92.

16. *Lutetia Parisiorum erudita sui temporis [. . .]* (Nuremberg, 1722), pp. 67–80, and *Neuester Gelehrter Staat von Paris [. . .]* (Jena: J. F. Bielcken, 1724), pp. 99–115.

17. *Les Monumens de la monarchie françoise*, of which five folio volumes appeared between 1729 and 1733, remained unfinished. See H.-J. Martin, 'Les Bénédictins, leurs libraires et le pouvoir. Notes sur le financement de la recherche au temps de Mabillon et de Montfaucon' in *Mémorial du XIVᵉ centenaire de l'abbaye de Saint-Germain-des-Prés. Recueil de travaux sur le monastère et la Congrégation de Saint-Maur* (Paris: Vrin, 1959), pp. 273–87 and Dom Yves Ricaud's remarkably documented article on Montfaucon in *Dictionnaire des Lettres françaises: Le XVIIIᵉ siècle*, ed. by Cardinal Georges Grente, rev. by François Moureau (Paris: Fayard, 1995), pp. 923–35.

18. See W. Kirsop, 'Following the Money Trails: Selling Books before, during and after the Revolution', *Australian Journal of French Studies*, 29 (1992), 266–87.

19. *Catalogue hebdomadaire ou liste des livres, estampes, cartes, ordonnances [. . .]*, 19 vols (Paris: 1763–1781), then *Journal de la Librairie ou Catalogue hebdomadaire [. . .]*, 8 vols (Paris: 1782–1789).

20. *Œuvres pastorales de M. Merthghen, traduites de l'allemand par M. le baron de Nausell [. . .]*, 2 vols (Paris: Belin, 1783). Printing of these 18mo volumes was apparently completed in 1782. The prospectus bound into volume I of my set was approved in December 1782.

21. See Cissie Fairchilds, 'The production and marketing of populuxe goods in eighteenth-century Paris' in *Consumption and the World of Goods*, ed. by John Brewer and Roy Porter (London and New York: Routledge, 1993), pp. 228–48.

22. (Berkeley, Los Angeles, Oxford: University of California Press, 1991).

23. The text of the *arrêts* of 1777 can now be conveniently consulted in Antoine Perrin, *Almanach de la librairie*, ed. by Jeroom Vercruysse from the 1781 version (Aubel: P. M. Gason, 1984), pp. 163–89.

24. See *Idée générale de l'histoire de la ville de Bordeaux [. . .]*, 1761 prospectus bound with Dom Devienne, *Histoire de la ville de Bordeaux [. . .]* (Bordeaux: 1771), Bibliothèque Nationale, Rés. 4° Lk⁷.1120.

25. See Reinhard Wittmann, 'Subskribenten- und Pränumerantenverzeichnisse als lesersoziolo-gische Quellen' in *Buch und Leser. Vorträge des ersten Jahrestreffens des Wolfenbütteler Arbeitskreises für Geschichte des Buchwesens 13. und 14. Mai 1976*, ed. by Herbert G. Göpfert (Hamburg: Hauswedell, 1977), pp. 125–59.

26. Bibliothèque Nationale, Collection du Vexin 46, fols 73 sqq.

27. See the article 'Un projet de dictionnaire alchimique en 1784' cited in note 8 above.

28. See the article 'Keeping Réaumur's *Mémoires pour servir à l'histoire des insectes* in print' cited in note 8 above.

29. R. A. Leigh, *Unsolved Problems in the Bibliography of J.-J. Rousseau*, ed. by J. T. A. Leigh (Cambridge: Cambridge University Press, 1990). See also R. A. Leigh, 'Rousseau, his pub-lishers and the *Contrat social*', *Bulletin of the John Rylands University Library of Manchester*, 66.2 (Spring 1984), 204–27.

30. See W. Kirsop, 'Paper-Quality Marks in Eighteenth-Century France' in *An Index of Civilisation. Studies of Printing and Publishing History in honour of Keith Maslen*, ed. by R. Harvey, W. Kirsop and B. J. McMullin (Clayton: Centre for Bibliographical and Textual Studies, Monash University, 1993), pp. 55–66 (esp. pp. 59–60). Mérande's *Fables de La Fontaine, quatre volumes grand in-folio. Proposé par souscription, au nombre de trois cents exemplaires* (8°, 8pp.) was approved in March 1774 (copy in personal collection). The Desaint registers that have recently come to light in the trade reveal that Mérande sold a set of the *Fables* to his Paris confrère on 13 July 1768 for 180 *livres*. I am extremely grateful to André Jammes for allowing me to work briefly on this sensational find in November–December 1996.

31. See the article cited in note 25 above, esp. p. 148.

32. See *L'Art du livre à l'Imprimerie nationale* (Paris: Imprimerie nationale, 1973).

33. The relevant documents are to be found in Archives Nationales, O^{1}610 and 611, as well as in O^{1}609: Bibliothèque du Roi, n° 28.

34. See Hélène Richard, *Une grande expédition scientifique au temps de la Révolution française: le voyage de d'Entrecasteaux à la recherche de La Pérouse* (Paris: Comité des travaux historiques et scientifiques, 1986), pp. 229–30, 343–4.

35. See W. Kirsop, 'Cultural Networks in Pre-Revolutionary France: some Reflexions on the Case of Antoine Court de Gébelin', *Australian Journal of French Studies*, 18 (1981), 231–47.

36. A comprehensive bibliography of this work cannot be given here. Many of Giles Barber's valuable contributions were brought together in *Studies in the Booktrade of the European Enlightenment* (London: The Pindar Press, 1994). Robert Darnton's *The Forbidden Best-Sellers of Pre-Revolutionary France* (New York and London: W. W. Norton & Company, 1995) and *The Corpus of Clandestine Literature in France 1769–1789* (New York and London: W. W. Norton & Company, 1995) sum up much of his writing over the last two decades.

37. (Oxford: Clarendon Press, 1992).

38. (New Haven & London: Yale University Press, 1995).

39. W. Kirsop, 'Les mécanismes éditoriaux' in *Histoire de l'édition française*, tome II: *Le livre triom-phant 1660–1830*, ed. by Henri-Jean Martin and Roger Chartier (Paris: Promodis, 1984), pp. 21–33, esp. p. 32.

40. Dena Goodman, *The Republic of Letters. A Cultural History of the French Enlightenment* (Ithaca and London: Cornell University Press, 1994), p. 176.

41. See note 8 above.

42. Goodman, p. 177.

43. See the letter Court de Gébelin sent to the President and Fellows of Harvard College via John Adams on 2 March 1780 accompanying the first six volumes of the *Monde primitif* (Harvard University Archives, UAI.5.120, Corporation Papers). Part of the text is reproduced in *Adams*

Family Correspondence, ed. by L. H. Butterfield and Marc Friedlaender (Cambridge, Mass.: The Belknap Press of Harvard University Press, 1963–), IV (1973), 5–6. I discussed this episode *inter alia* in a work-in-progress talk (at the Houghton Library on 25 September 1995) on 'Subscription Publishing in Eighteenth-Century France'. A full account is being prepared for the *Harvard Library Bulletin*.

44. Paris, Bibliothèque Nationale, fonds français 17701–17713.

45. Paris, Bibliothèque Nationale, fonds français 19641.

46. See the article cited in note 35 above. The Court correspondence in the Bibliothèque publique et universitaire in Geneva is a mine of information on these topics.

47. Copies of La Mottraye's *Relation* are bound with two sets of the *Voyages* in the Bibliothèque Nationale (J. 920$^{(2)}$ and Rés. J. 591). On Johnson see B. J. McMullin, 'T. Johnson, Bookseller in The Hague' in *An Index of Civilisation*, pp. 99–112.

48. Paris, Bibliothèque Nationale, Joly de Fleury 2491, fol. 98$^{r–v}$.

49. Two illuminating papers on the North American phenomenon were given at the Fourth Annual Conference of SHARP in Worcester, Massachusetts in July 1996: Nancy Cook, 'Intertextuality and Corporate Practice: The Example of Hartford Subscription Publishers, 1867–1880' and Sheryl A. Englund, '"An Excellent Likeness of the Author": Mapping a Subscription Sales Encounter, *c.* 1889'.

50. See Geraldine Sheridan, 'Voltaire's *Henriade*: a history of the "subscriber" edition, 1728–1741', *Studies on Voltaire and the Eighteenth Century*, 215 (1982), 77–89.

51. Goodman, p. 176.

52. Subscribers to the Kehl edition of Voltaire clearly did not expect to be listed. However, the illustrator Moreau le Jeune later approached them to take the engravings he was doing for the enterprise. See the letter Jacques Olivier-Desmont sent from Bordeaux on 18 January 1783 to Court de Gébelin to solicit his help in the process: 'J'ai souscrit pour la belle édition des œuvres de Volt^{re} avec Les Caractères de Baskerville, entre les mains de M. Beaumarchais Mr Moreau Jeune, dessinateur & graveur du Cabinet du Roi propose une souscription d'une Suite d'Estampes, destinée à décorer cette belle édition. Il m'a ecrit pour celà. Je ne puis éviter de souscrire.' (Paris, Bibliothèque de la Société de l'Histoire du Protestantisme français, MS L 1237, n° 11).

53. In the prospectus to *L'Antiquité expliquée*, BN, Coll. Clairambault 490, fol. 111^r, and at the end of the first subscriber list in Abbé Expilly's *Dictionnaire géographique, historique et politique des Gaules et de la France*, 1762, I, sig. c2^v.

54. (M.A. thesis, Monash University, 1985).

55. See the letter cited in note 43 above.

56. *Les Voyages de Pythagore [. . .] Par S** M*** Bibliothécaire. Ouvrage proposé par soumission* (Paris: David Monier, An V).

57. See the seven volumes originally subscribed for by 'M. LAMAIGNERE, Greffier du Sénéchal de Guyenne, à Bordeaux' that found their way to the library of the Real Academia Española in Madrid.

58. W. Kirsop, 'From the First Empire to Romanticism: the Subscriptions of the Davout Family' in *Essays in Honour of Keith Val Sinclair: an Australian collection of modern language studies*, ed. by B. Merry (Townsville: Dept of Modern Languages, James Cook University of North Queensland, 1991), pp. 76–82.

59. See *'Books which mr Froullé is desired to send me'. A letter from Thomas Jefferson to a Paris bookseller, Monticello in Virginia May 26, 1795* (New York: Grolier Club, 1971).

60. BN, f. fr. 17702, fols 60^r–61^v.

COMMODIFICATION AND VALUE: INTERACTIONS IN BOOK TRAFFIC TO NORTH AMERICA, *c*.1750–1820

JAMES RAVEN

THE DIFFERENT CONNOTATIONS of literary commerce were strikingly evident in the course of transatlantic book traffic. Alongside written correspondence, the exchange of printed texts was conducted through the business and barter transactions common to all commodities. Textual despatch and consumption, also included the free disposal of literature, benevolent donations, authorised propaganda, and the determination to pursue connections and exchange despite economic disadvantage and more cost-effective alternatives. Cultural agendas underpinned literary (and thereby ideological) commercial transactions; strictly economic criteria were tempered by social and political considerations.

The following explores both the supportive and qualifying cultural dimensions of book acquisition and library building in eighteenth- and early nineteenth-century North America. Its starting point are the processes associated with the literary 'commodification' of the period. We are unlikely to be surprised that the importation of books from mother countries was the mainstay of bookselling in the early, sparsely-populated years of colonial settlement, but by the mid-eighteenth century, greater domestic production might have been expected to have reduced the need for overseas orders. The increasing rather than declining volume of book imports to North America during the eighteenth century and then (in relative terms at least) the beginnings of decline from the 1790s raises many questions about the economics of the transatlantic trade, the relative qualities of domestic and foreign productions, the predictability of the market, and the ordering, transportation and financial mechanisms that sustained or limited the trade. Even more telling, however, is a further feature of the changing profile of literary imports: the social and geographical bifurcation of the booktrade. As American domestic publication advanced at the end of the eighteenth century, the continuing importation was sustained by luxury and institutional demand and the supply-line service to isolated communities. In explaining this, quantification by number and volume is not the only measure of achievement.

The broad history of this book traffic is simply described. Until at least the mid-eighteenth century – one hundred years after printing began in New England – more than 90% of all books in North America were imported. North American presses provided no serious challenge to the increasing volume of European books imported to the ports of the eastern seaboard. Print had first arrived in the lands north of Mexico by overland routes,[1] but by the mid-seventeenth century the volume of books entering the scattered Spanish settlements beyond the Rio Grande was eclipsed by developments further north. From the late seventeenth century, British and continental book merchants and agents began to respond seriously to colonial book demand from New England down to Virginia. From 1700 to 1780 45% of English book exports by volume departed for the British colonies, including the West Indies.[2] Between the mid-seventeenth and the early nineteenth centuries, most books in British America were published in and purchased and shipped from London. Late seventeenth-century colonial booksellers' invoices and inventories reflect a transition from what has been called the 'dribbles and drabbles' of English importation to its later near monopoly of supply.[3] In the eighteenth century the supplies from London (later supplemented by some other British ports) increased tenfold despite some obvious counter-pressures. In placing an order, formidable obstacles had to be overcome. The achievement of the dominant market and legal advantages of London early in the century was that they continued to override even the complexities of transatlantic transit and financial transactions, the time, costs and inconvenience. Only by accounting for the surmounting of some of these difficulties and for the persistence and intensification of others, can we begin to understand the nature of the import boom in the eighteenth century – and the reasons for its eventual decline.

Increased shipment of books from Britain was an obvious consequence of the limited and unbalanced growth of colonial printing. From the early decades of commercial importation, legal monopolies to publication remained in place, with patents reserved for printing rights to bibles, prayer books, psalters, almanacs, and certain law books and other specialist works. Further political and legal impediments endured within the colonies. In some, restrictive local licensing remained in force until 1730, founded on British colonial commerce in the second half of the seventeenth century. The Navigation Acts of 1651 and 1660, together with new enforcement measures in 1696, limited colonial commerce to English and colonial vessels. The closed system was designed to benefit all citizens of the empire and to encourage both colonial and metropolitan initiatives. Beyond this, basic economic considerations of paper, printing equipment, and labour costs also figured largely. For most of the century few provincial and colonial booksellers were able to challenge the oligopolistic dominance of London with its economies of scale, trade organisation and the use of established distributive agents. In the eighteenth century book traffic between Britain and North America boomed. Its persistence was a consequence of metropolitan commercial hegemony, social pressures to sustain particular imports, and the refinement of mechanisms to overcome the various financial and transit difficulties caused by distance. All added to the retardation of American domestic supplies and services, which, in the early years at least, was reinforced by the closed colonial trading system and British and colonial legal sanctions. The perilous Atlantic crossings and the frequent interruptions of war were constant obstacles, but advances were made in the provision of information about books published in Britain, in the means to order and purchase them – both financial and in simple terms of communication by letter or agent – and in the means to have the goods shipped back. Also reduced were the transaction and distribution costs of inventorying, insurance, commission and handling charges, shipping, freight.

Elsewhere, based on customs and invoice records, I have suggested an average annual total for all book and pamphlet imports from English ports to the British mainland American colonies in the early 1770s of some 120,000 items, or something like 4% of total British annual output (or nearly 5% of total English annual output).[4] Although such estimates remain highly artificial, they are at least suggestive of the immense volume of book imports in this period. Between 1660 and 1780 the overall annual growth rate of the mainland colonial population was somewhere between 2.4% (the estimate for New England) and 4.3% (the estimate for the lower South), and by 1780 the total population reached some 2.5 million, or the equivalent of some 27% of the total population of England, Scotland and Wales of just under 9 million.[5] This colonial population, therefore, comprising just over a fifth of all the peoples of British mainland America and Britain (excluding Ireland) combined, was supplied with something between one-twentieth and one-thirtieth of total annual British literary production. After the War of Independence the situation became more complicated, with some evidence of a decline in demand for certain imported books and a gradual decline relative to American book production, but evidence also of greater regional variation and of a healthy recovery in the overall upward trend of imports.

At first sight, this impressive eighteenth-century expansion of book imports to North America from Britain and Europe can be explained in simple terms of consumer demand and commodification. Despite calculations of lower per capita consumption between about 1720 and 1750, in absolute terms (and with corresponding changes in the social profile of consumption) the colonies imported three times as many goods in 1750 than in 1700. From the late 1740s a major increase in per capita consumption also began. The practice of purchases supported by current financing was increasingly replaced by use of credit advanced by British merchants.[6] The thirteen colonies were in many respects 'cultural provinces' of the mother country, attempting to adopt cosmopolitan standards of taste. Books were notable luxury goods – totems of respectability and conveyers of metropolitan thought.[7] Fashion of a secular kind – rather than evangelism or scholarship – played a prominent part in growing demand. London booksellers were to supply a market society straddling the Atlantic. 'In the last ships' became the familiar boast of booksellers' newspaper advertisements listing imported titles. This appetite for literary commodities has even been seen as revolutionizing political discourse and creating 'an indispensable foundation for the later political mobilization of the American people'.[8] If there was a strong link between newly imported material culture and new nationalism, however, Independence brought no less and in certain areas even more clamour for things European. In the Federalist period, in the words of one of its historians, 'peace brought a riot of luxury', and a New England 'codfish aristocracy' were both envied and mocked for pursuit of a new cosmopolitanism.[9]

The consumer revolution in print was enabled, in part, by an information revolution. At the beginning of the eighteenth century, the immediate obstacle to purchasing books from Europe was the far from simple question of acquiring precise information about publication and availability; the next task was to set about securing a resident agent to manage the affair on the other side of the Atlantic. Both problems were generally faced by all the commercial customer groups: wealthy or well-connected individuals; institutional customers including colleges, churches, libraries, and gentlemen's societies; and colonial booksellers and general merchants. The provision of information was transformed during this period, ultimately perhaps at the cost of lifting expectations to unattainable levels. By the mid-eighteenth century almost all the leading London booksellers printed catalogues of new or in-stock titles. Colonial traders further advertised imports in newspapers. More important still, London newspapers and periodicals from the mid eighteenth century provided individual and institutional customers with ever greater opportunities to read of new publications. The critical reviews, in particular, with their attempt at comprehensive notices together with extracts and criticisms, were not only popular imports in their own right but led to exacting orders sent either to the colonial bookseller or directly to the London wholesaler or agent.

By the 1790s the surge in North American demand for print also underpinned the emergent domestic printing and publishing industry – and especially the reprinting of standard editions. During the 1790s the development of native supplies, although uneven, did begin to lower domestic book production costs and create real alternatives to importation. Although new services and expertise were all advanced during the century, information, transport and associated transaction costs always threatened to make transatlantic trade unviable – and certainly did so once the handicapped domestic printing industry reached an effective stage of development. Distance ensured lapses of time that aggravated the trials of credit, money transfers and interest, and long-term planning was made difficult by all the transatlantic obstacles. For at least the smaller London booksellers and their colonial bookselling partners, the pricing constraints of the London trade told in the end. The evidence from the surviving correspondence and business records of John Murray I is that his colonial trade was hardly worth it. He always retained hopes that the trade would build up. Overseas orders did accumulate, but very slowly, and what appears to have been a normal credit agreement for payment within six months of the invoice despatch, was honoured by some but not every customer.[10] As Stephen Botein concluded, 'the conventional pricing arrangements of the London booktrade presented only minimal incentive for expansion of transatlantic business.'[11]

Nevertheless, transatlantic book traffic continued. For the colonial customer, the need to be attached to European culture was a powerful compensation to otherwise marginal or even negative economic equations. Indeed, in absolute terms, the total volume of book exports from Britain to North America probably remained stable and possibly even expanded in the first decades of the nineteenth century. Certainly, the particular and changing nature of colonial demand promoted commercial initiatives on both sides of the Atlantic. These brought alterations both in the kinds of literature exported and in the types of exporter. An early change was to the state of books ordered, where the increase in the number and quality of American binders reduced the demand for luxury bound British and European publications.[12] Domestic book printing developed more slowly, but was first advanced by the production of almanacs and other small practical books until by the end of the century imported books were more likely to be of particular types. Throughout the century, for example, the relatively cheap price of many imported English editions of popular novels could not be matched by home reprints.[13] Again, periodical publications were first the leading edge and then among the most problematic of British imports.

The ranks of London exporters were also changing by the end of the century. Major general merchants increasingly served as professional collectors in London, and firms such as Lackington and Allen of Finsbury Square and then Pall Mall and Piccadilly developed export and clearing-house expertise. Such firms claimed to undercut the more old-fashioned types of wholesalers who were described as disenchanted and no longer efficient in the transatlantic trade. As one of these merchants firms took care to explain to their American customers: 'we beg leave to remark that by the mode of a direct supply from the Bookseller the Book costs much more than if the order had passed thro our hands, Our Commissions as Merchants would have been far short of the

The catalogue of the booksellers Daniel Boinard and Alexander Gaillard was published in Philadelphia in 1784, listing 1600 French titles, and six years later Claudius Raguet of the same city issued his own list of French titles.[28] The revival of British imports after the War of Independence was also paralleled by the re-establishment of trade in German books centred upon Philadelphia. In the 1790s German booksellers such as Johann Christian Krieger of Giessen attempted to build up an American business by publishing annual priced catalogues. In Lancaster, Pennsylvania, Christian Jacob Hütter offered from 1798 new catalogues promising 'the most complete collection of the newest and best German books ever imported. Every month, depending on the regularity of shipping, I will receive new issues of periodicals, continuations and all the best and most interesting new publications in the field.'[29] This second phase of German-American book trading was relatively shortlived however. The French Revolutionary and Napoleonic Wars brought havoc to delivery lines. A decline in new German immigration and a growing indifference to the language in Philadelphia also undermined demand and blocked recovery of the German trade in the early nineteenth century.[30]

The continuing strength of European luxury book imports to the south was supplemented by more general commerce to remote outposts. A broad spectrum of European imports reached French planters in South Carolina, Dutch and German communities, and even, in the Spanish territories, isolated settlements of Italians and 'Mediterraneans'.[31] New British trade at the end of the century included ventures to new south-eastern settlements and missionary activity. The Panton and Leslie and later Forbes firms, founded in 1783 and 1804 respectively, were probably the major conveyers to points south of the Carolinas.[32] Missionaries like Rev. John Forbes, sent by the SPG to St Augustine in 1765, arrived with a folio bible and two folio prayerbooks for each church in the 3,000-strong community.[33] Books from Robert Wells of Charleston were also despatched with the troops sent to St Augustine from the mid-1760s.[34]

In Louisiana printing arrived only in 1764, two years after the colony had been ceded to Spain by France. An import trade had been long established, however, led by general merchants. A 1730 Louisiana estate inventory lists nearly 100 books, and another for the Provost estate in 1769 details 300 books, almost all printed in, and imported from, France.[35] Under Spanish governance, Alejandro O'Reilly planned in 1771 a school library in New Orleans, also open to 'clergy and honest persons'. The surviving inventory of the carefully packed books sent from Cadiz records 122 classical Latin texts, but others clearly intended to promote Spanish culture over French including 2,883 volumes in six boxes 'to be sold to the pupils in the schools'.[36] The inventory of the effects of Don Manuel Gayoso de Lemos, Governor of Spanish Louisiana in 1799, included some 411 volumes, of extraordinary range, and many forbidden by the *Indice ultimo*.[37] Of the 173 separate works, only three appear to have been Mexican imprints, and only two were printed in the United States. By contrast 40 had been printed in Madrid, 30 in London, twenty in Paris, three in Amsterdam and two in Edinburgh. French imports further revived in Louisiana, after Spanish withdrawal in 1800, although this was curtailed by the Purchase in 1803.[38] The scale, though, was extremely modest. In 1803, when the population of New Orleans stood at about 8,000, its newspaper, the *Moniteur*, listed 288 printed books and 200 account books imported into the city during the previous twelve months,[39] but such activity, together with the imports through Canada, is the only way of explaining the numbers of French – usually Parisian – books listed in the many surviving library inventories of early settlers to St Louis and the northern Mississippi Valley.[40] It is also notable that general importers to New Orleans were able to switch to advertising imported London titles only a couple of seasons after American acquisition.[41] Further east, Florida remained Spanish until 1821, the new regime marked by poverty and unrest. In the early years at least, however, it was a time of Hispanic high hopes, and Governor Vicente Manuel de Zéspedes set out to continue relations with the English mercantile firm of Panton and Leslie.

The result was a spattering of far-flung shipments of books, mirrored by the support given to small French, German, Italian and other European settler communities. In 1777 John Fitzpatrick, writing from his swampy settlement on the banks of the Mississippi at Manchac, British West Florida (now Louisiana), hoped that John Waugh, English merchant, still had for sale 'Rollins Antient History & them tuo Vols. that are on Physick' because he had a lodger, one Dr West, who wanted them sent on to him by boat.[42] Waugh was then in New Orleans, owned ships on the Mississippi, and made frequent voyages between London and Pensacola, West Florida. Fitzpatrick also somehow managed to assemble a book collection, albeit engagingly gap-ridden. His 1791 inventory listed a total of 80 volumes, including the eight volumes of Rollin's history, three of the four volumes of Catherine Macaulay's history, odd volumes by Pope, Milton, Smollett, and 'the works of Jonathan Swift in fourteen volumes, lacking volumes one, two, seven, eight, ten and thirteen.'[43]

Elsewhere, details of direct trade are sketchy, with only enigmatic glimpses of the frontier book world. In California annual overland and shipped consignments of books from Mexico (with many books originating from Spain) supplied the 21 missions established between 1769 and 1823 in the region between San Diego and Sonoma.[44] In other remote places special needs for importation continued well into the new century. The Sulpician missionary Gabriel Richard, for example, was not only a founder of one of Detroit's earliest presses (as well as of the University of Michigan), but from 1798 until his death in 1832 he ordered large shipments of religious, educational and literary works from his native France.[45] Most exotic of all, perhaps. was the establishment by Nicholas Rezanof in about 1807 of the Kodiak library at Sitka in the Russian territory of what is now Alaska. Some 1,200 books were imported on the ship Neva from St Petersburg, the majority Russian, but a quarter French.[46]

In the more affluent eastern seaboard importation declined at least relatively to the success of local American supply, but the course of demand was partly tied to the high expectations of colonial customers. In the absence of local publications and reprints there had been no alternative to imported books, yet even when the American presses were more active, the social valuation of imported literature remained strong. The fashionable customer was also the customer who most expected to be able to order new things from London. This social dimension to the import trade contributed to the evaluation of the costs and attractiveness of the domestic product. Demand for British and European books was never uniform, but now it was increasingly driven by particular groups and interests. As with the book boom in England, increased demand had derived proportionately more from those already active in the market and from institutions such as the new proprietary and circulating libraries, than from the increase in the total numbers buying books. In North America, this was paralleled in the profile of the decline of imports, where certain outstanding features remained as the more general demand for overseas print melted away. At the turn of the nineteenth century demand in the book import trade appeared narrower, both socially and geographically.

At the social level, it was largely a luxury market that survived. For those American booksellers and merchants whose trade was based on the sale of small imported books, the development of the American publishing and reprint market was felt first. Given the risk of importing expensive stock that might be difficult to move, the business of most commercial American importers of the second half of the eighteenth century was grounded on the type of low-value print that was, for similar production and demand reasons, to be the leading edge of expanding American publication.[47] The lasting export from England of high-value, luxury books, and the virtual collapse of both the bible and the cheap book and almanac trade, fed into the commercial restructuring of the transatlantic book business, with its revised strategies, new operators and specialisms.

The great proprietary libraries, some more public than others, were especially important. The Library Company of Philadelphia was founded in 1731, the Library Company of Darby, Pennsylvania, in 1743, the Redwood Library, Newport, Rhode Island, in 1747, and the Charles Town Library Society in 1748. This last foundation opened five years before the British Museum and ten years before the first major proprietary subscription library in Britain.

Here, the demand for new and expensive literature was sustained by the ostentatious wealth of the Charleston elite. All were eager for their flourishing port to be accepted as a great city of the Empire. The Library Society aspired to imitate the shelves of European learned societies, and in pursuit of these ideals it achieved a swift accumulation of both members and volumes. The 1770 Catalogue listed 184 folios, 115 quartos, 555 octavos and smaller volumes, and an additional 135 classical titles. By 1819 the Library commanded 280 members, 13,000 volumes, a capital in funded debt of $10,000 and a yearly income of $3,000.[48] A visitor in 1810 described the interior:

The library contains Boydell's elegant edition of Shakespeare, and the large prints are framed and hung up round the room. The portraits of the king and queen, belonging to that edition, are placed on either side the door-way leading to the inner room . . . There is a large painting, executed by a Mr White, of Charleston, exhibited in the library . . . The subject is the murder of Prince Arthur . . . some new casts from the Apollo, Belvidere, Venus de Medicis, Venus rising from the sea, &c. were deposited in the Library to be exhibited for a short time . . . The library also contains a few natural curiosities, such as fossils, minerals, mammoth bones, snakes, armadilloes, poisonous insects in spirits, &c. and two remarkable deer's horns which were found locked together.[49]

For wealthy individual customers and institutions like the Charleston Library Society, direct correspondence with London agents and booksellers continued well into the nineteenth century. At mid-century, the New York Society Library engaged John Ward as its London agent bookseller,[50] but in 1771, faced by silence from his successors, the Society resolved 'to find out and settle a Correspondence with some Bookseller in London who will supply the Library with such books as may be ordered from Time to Time upon the best Terms'. The New York Society Library gave prudent leave to its bookseller, 'when ever he observes any Sett of Books want to be completed, to take particular care to supply the Additional Vol.'[51] The Library Company of Philadelphia ordered its London and European books first from Peter Collinson, a Quaker merchant, and then, after various other agents including Franklin when in London, the general Quaker merchant firm of Woods and Dillwyn until at least the mid-nineteenth century.[52]

Yet little was easy about such trade, however rich and famous you were, and however expansive overseas literary commerce appeared to be. Appointments as bookseller to the Charleston Library Society, for example, included some of the most distinguished and successful London traders of the age, but they rarely served long. Failure to understand a commission or to prevent a slow sea-passage usually brought a termination of business – and quite possibly some relief in London.[53] The Library Company of Philadelphia and bibliophiles like James Logan of the same city, declared that they employed book agents to avoid enslavement to a bookseller's ignorance or deceit.[54] The

Charleston Library's Secretary was always ready to convey the belief of members that their bookseller was lazy, exercising bad judgment or unloading unsaleable books. After brief reliance on the exiled Charleston bookseller (and former Library Society committee member) Robert Wells, in 1787, the Society turned to and then away from the pro-American John Stockdale for the year 1791–92.[55] His dismissal for incompetence – against which Stockdale sent an aggrieved protest – was followed by a new policy of employing the firm of general merchants, Bird, Savage and Bird, to collect orders from the supplier booksellers. For ten years the firm served the Society well, until, in the early months of 1801, it encountered business difficulties and declined trade.[56]

The London book trade now included businesses capable of dealing more efficiently with the book-search demands of overseas literary societies and libraries. The firm of Lackington and Allen certainly presented itself as such a business, and the breadth of its stock, together with the thoroughness of its cataloguing, impressed the Charleston Library Society who elected the company its Bookseller in September 1801. Lackington and Allen was successor to the extraordinary enterprise of James Lackington, who had first set up shop in London in 1774.[57] The empire was built from remaindered books sold at discount, from large and rapid turnover, and originally from the controversial refusal of credit. The firm gained increasing respect, not least because of its width of stock. Moreover, booksellers elected by the library societies had always been required to collect books from other wholesalers, and very often from antiquarian dealers to complete orders. This, as Bird, Savage and Bird explained, had become very difficult and time-consuming for a single bookseller like Stockdale. Lackington and Allen's Emporium was a different matter.

The redirection of the Library Society's London orders was also accompanied by changes in the type of literature requested. As the Society's President admitted to Bird, Savage and Bird in 1793, 'the bulk of the Catalogue [the Society's requirements] inumerates Books of much lighter reading than our last, but in a Society such as ours, we are obliged to consult all tastes and to have many books of mere amusement as well as books of instruction and science'.[58] But if the founding ambition of Charleston's 'Et Artes trans Mare Currunt' was forgotten, the amnesia was widespread. In 1801, the Secretary of the New York Society Library declared that 'the Taste of several of the Members of the Library is so much turned to the reading of novels that it will be absolutely necessary to have a supply of this kind of Books'.[59] The change suited Lackington and Allen's shelves and connections very well.

This traffic had to survive major crises. Some four years after Lackington and Allen's appointment, in June 1805, the ship carrying the Library Society's large winter consignment was captured within a few miles of Charleston by a privateer sailing under French letters of marque during the second year of renewed war between Britain and France. It was a catastrophe. The *Charleston Courier* of 7 June estimated that the full cargo was worth between £80,000 and £100,000. The literary loss was especially severe. It included thirteen trunks of books from Lackington and Allen, containing the Library Society's books (worth a little over £170), but also a special order to supply a library and some scientific instruments to the South Carolina College in Columbia, South Carolina. The College order was valued at over £970. In addition, were 2,000 letters in the ship's bags 'all of which were detained by the Frenchman'.[60]

Although the ship was eventually recaptured by a British brigantine, taken to Jamaica (where the goods were resold), and the ship and the books for the Library Society and the College returned to Charleston under British naval convoy in mid-October, the episode reaffirmed the importance of insurance.[61] During the eighteenth century the effective charge on transatlantic insurance was lowered by between ten and twenty per cent, with coverage increasing to within one or two per cent of the loss. Nevertheless, insurance rates remained unpredictable and the outbreak of hostilities brought sudden hikes in charges – which often led, as in the Charleston example, to certain items and costs remaining uninsured. More aggravating than the uninsured portion, however, was the time that it took to settle with the underwriters. In June 1806, six months after the Library Society's instructions reached London, Lackington and Allen reported that the underwriters had not yet paid out. The settlement was not finally made until August 1807, but by 14 November, when a new order was sent, the Library Society remained ignorant of its details.[62] In Charleston incompetence and obstinacy now seemed to accompany interminable delays for the latest publications from London. Library Society frustration turned to real anger, however, when not only its books and journals but also acknowledgements of payments and orders failed to arrive. Between August 1807 and March 1809 the Librarian heard nothing from Lackington and Allen, and therefore had no advance notice of whether any of the Society's books were carried by the vessels that did arrive at Charleston – or by those that were reported as lost or captured.

It might be argued that the Library Society was once again assuming that it could ignore worldly realities. Britain and France were still at war, and American vessels were especially disrupted by the Berlin Decree, the retaliatory Orders-in-Council of 1806, and then the deeply unpopular Embargo Act of December 1807, suspending all commerce with the rest of the world. The replacement Nonintercourse Act of March 1809 still prohibited trade with Britain and France. In May of that year, the Library Society turned to a domestic supplier, William W. Woodward of Philadelphia, who was importing books from London as well as dealing in American imprints.[63] Until then, the Society had appeared resolute in depending directly on London booksellers, even though New York, Boston, and Philadelphia wholesalers were now the main and often cheaper suppliers of London-imported books to American customers, and increasingly of American publications and reprints.

Nevertheless, the experiment with Philadelphia ordering is instructive. When Woodward commended his new shipment of books from London – testimony to the poor enforcement of the Nonintercourse Act – he offered to search through this for any books that he was unable to supply to date, but warning that 'if any should have been imported they will be extravagantly dear'. The Librarian was horrified by the new charges, replying that 'as the Books from London come so high you will please to stop sending any more of that description'.[64] As a result, perhaps, the Charleston Library Society replaced Lackington and Allen for another London supplier, reverting to a general mercantile firm. Other major American libraries, notably the Library Company of Philadelphia, also persisted with direct London suppliers, but its committee, like that of the New York Society Library, conducted its affairs through long-established agents. The Charleston Society also continued to seek a direct London bookseller supplier and in June 1809 John Hopton, merchant in London and friend of the Society, wrote to its President to 'recommend to your attention Messrs F. C. & J. Rivington, who as well as their Father & Grandfather, were Booksellers on the same site, St Pauls Church Yard, for about a Century, & are undoubtedly as respectable as any in that trade'. He added that the Rivingtons' prices were slightly higher than those of some booksellers, but that they supplied quality goods.[65]

From the mid-eighteenth century, transatlantic book traffic was very much part of a broad consumer boom, and against the prestigious London product local manufacturers were relatively constrained, other than in newspaper, almanac and cheap book production. For the London wholesaler the costs of production together with those of distribution, had to be less than the revenues that could be received from selling the books elsewhere, and this meant maintaining pricing rigidities in the face of ever-increasing under-cutting opportunities by direct bookseller-client operations. In many ways the London monopoly was upheld by the powerful mix of initial economic advantage and increased social consumerism. The boom in book imports ultimately declined partly because of the interruptions of war and the eventual advance of the domestic printing industry, but much more because of the inherent fragility of the transatlantic trading structure. This fragility was exposed by the very success of new trading endeavours and new types of rapidly produced and fashionable publications which heightened customer expectations. Imports did not slacken because of any lessening interest on the part of many colonial booksellers or new specialist London merchants. Some London booksellers did abandon the American business because of increased burdens caused by new colonial demands, but in a competitive industry, others were ready to take up the challenge. Although the transaction costs of the transatlantic trade were lowered by the end of the century, changing demand, increasingly led by serial publication and *belles lettres* proved impossible to satisfy given the distance and time delays of the Atlantic. It many ways it is remarkable how long economic and social dependency on the colonial metropolis had been sustained in this literary commerce. Rising demand was one inevitable spur to cheaper alternatives, but changing demand and the appetite for the latest books ultimately created a bifurcated market, one satisfying the need for bibles, newsprint and new American literature, and the other dealing in more expensive European products. Institutional, special-case and peripheral imports were the survivals of the overseas trade.

REFERENCES

1. James Raven, 'The Importation of Books to Colonial North America', *Publishing History* 42 (1997): 21–49; and James Raven, 'Sent to the Wilderness: Mission Literature in Colonial America', in James Raven, ed., *Free Print and Non-Commercial Publishing since 1700* (London and Vermont: Ashgate Press, 2000).

2. Giles Barber, 'Books from the Old World and for the New: the British International Trade in Books in the Eighteenth Century', *Studies on Voltaire and the Eighteenth Century* 151 (1976) 219–24; and Giles Barber, 'Book Imports and Exports in the Eighteenth Century', in Robin Myers and Michael Harris, eds., *Sale and Distribution of Books from 1700* (Oxford: Oxford Polytechnic Press, 1982); p. 94. For the West Indies, excluded from this discussion, see Roderick Cave, *Printing and the Booktrade in the West Indies* (London: Pindar Press, 1987).

3. Stephen Botein, 'The Anglo-American Book Trade before 1776: Personnel and Strategies', in W. L. Joyce, et al., eds., *Printing and Society in Early America* (Worcester: American Antiquarian Society, 1983), pp. 48–82; and Stephen Foster, 'The Godly in Transit', in *Seventeenth-Century New England* (Boston: Colonial Society of Massachusetts, 1984), pp. 185–238; both discussed and revised in Hugh Amory, 'Under the Exchange: The Unprofitable Business of Michael Perry, a Seventeenth-Century Boston Bookseller', *Proceedings of the American Antiquarian Society* 103 (1993), 33–35, 45–50.

4. Details are given in Raven, 'Importation of Books'; and James Raven, 'I viaggi dei libri: realtà e raffigurazioni', in Maria Gioia Tavoni and Françoise Waquet, eds., *Gli spazi del libro nell'Europa del XVIII secolo* (Bologna: Pàtron Editore, 1997), 177–200.

5. John J. McCusker and Russell R. Menard, *The Economy of British America 1607–1789* (Chapel Hill and London: University of North Carolina Press, 1985), pp. 217, 218, fig. 10.1; R. D. Lee and R. S. Schofield, 'British Population in the Eighteenth Century', in Roderick Floud and Donald McCloskey, eds., *The Economic History of Britain since 1700* 2d edn, 3 vols. (Cambridge: Cambridge University Press, 1994), 1: pp. 17, 21.

6. James A. Henretta, *The Evolution of American Society, 1700–1815: An Interdisciplinary Analysis* (Lexington, MA: D.C. Heath and Co., 1973), pp. 41–42.

7. John Clive and Bernard Bailyn, 'England's Cultural Provinces: Scotland and America', *William and Mary Quarterly*, 3d ser. 11 (1954): 200–213; Ralph Davis, *The Rise of the Atlantic Economies* (London: Weidenfeld and Nicolson, 1973), esp. pp. 304–08; and Carole Shammas, 'Consumer Behavior in Colonial America', *Social Science History* 6 (1982): 67–86.

8. T. H. Breen, '"Baubles of Britain": The American and Consumer Revolutions of the Eighteenth Centuries', *Past and Present* 119 (1988), 87.

9. Samuel Eliot Morison, *The Maritime History of Massachusetts 1783–1860* new edn (Cambridge MA: Riverside Press, 1961), p. 35, and cf pp. 25, 125–33. In fact, these observations have a long pedigree; see Thomas J. Wertenbaker, *The Golden Age of Colonial Culture* (New York: University Press, 1949).

10. Of various examples, John Murray Archives, Albermarle St., London, John Murray I Day Book, fol. 409 (27 Nov. 1773); Account Ledge, fol. 170 (6 June 1774, 7 July 1774, 16 Feb. 1775).

11. Botein, 'Anglo-American Book Trade', pp. 20, 27.

12. Hannah D. French, 'Early American Bookbinding by Hand 1636–1820', in Hellmut Lehmann-Haupt, ed., *Bookbinding in America: Three Essays* (Portland, Maine: Southwold-Anthoensen, 1941), pp. 3–127; and William Spawn, 'The Evolution of American Binding Styles in the Eighteenth Century', in John Dooley and James Tanis, eds., *Bookbinding in America 1680–1910* (Bryn Mawr, PA: Bryn Mawr College Library, 1983), pp. 29–36.

13. The only exceptions, towards the end of the century, were short novels; see Robert B. Winans, 'Bibliography and the Cultural Historian: Notes on the Eighteenth-Century Novel,' in Joyce, et al., eds., *Printing and Society*, pp. 178–81.

14. James Raven, *London Booksellers and American Customers: Transatlantic Literary Community and the Charleston Library Society, 1758–1812* [hereafter *LBAC*] (Columbia, SC: University of South Carolina Press, 2000), letter 52, Bird, Savage and Bird to Gov. Chas. Cotesworth Pinckney, 22 Sept., 1792.

15. Henry Lemoine, *Present State of Printing and Bookselling in America [1796]*, Douglas C. McMurtie, ed., (Chicago: private edn, 1929), p. 19.

16. Raven, *LBAC*, chs. 2, 7.

17. JMA Letter Book 3, Murray to Robert Miller of Williamsburg, 17 Aug., 1772.

18. JMA Letter Book 4, Murray to Miller, 5 Dec., 1773.

19. Further discussed in Raven, 'Sent to the Wilderness'.

20. See C. A. Weslager, 'The Swedes' Letter to William Penn,' *PMHB* 83 (1959), 91; Edwin Wolf II, *The Book Culture of a Colonial American City: Philadelphia Books, Bookmen, and Booksellers* (Oxford: Clarendon Press, 1988), pp. 8–9, 17–18.

21. Otto Lohr, 'Die deutsche Sprache in Nordamerika im 17. Jahrhundert', *Mitteilungen der Deutschen Akademie* 1 (1933): 90–103. See also Henry A. Pochmann, *German Culture in America: Philosophical and Literary Influences, 1600–1900* (Madison: University of Wisconsin Press, 1957), pp. 26–7, 30.

22. Adolph Benson, ed., *The America of 1750: Peter Kalm's Travels in North America* (New York, 1937) 2: 685.

23. Robert E. Cazden, 'The Provision of German Books in America during the Eighteenth Century', *Libri* 23 (1973): 81–108.

24. Hendrik Edelman, *The Dutch Language Press in America* (Nieuwkoop: De Graaf, 1986), p. 5.

25. Leonard W. Labaree, et al., eds., *The Papers of Benjamin Franklin* 30 vols. (New Haven CT, and London: Yale University Press, 1959–), 4: 484, Franklin to Peter Collinson 9 May, 1753.

26. John, Lord Sheffield, *Observations on the Commerce of the American States* 6th edn (London: J. Debrett, 1784), p. 234.

27. This trade is detailed in Robert E. Cazden, *A Social History of the German Book Trade in America to the Civil War* (Columbia, SC: Camden House, 1984), pp. 3–31. See also Robert B. Winans, *A Descriptive Checklist of Book Catalogues Separately Printed in America 1693–1800* (Worcester, MA: American Antiquarian Society: 1981), nos. 39, 63, 70, 84, 86, 89.

28. Winans, *Descriptive Checklist of Book Catalogues*, nos. 103. 143.

29. Cited in Cazden, 'Provision of German Books', p. 15.

30. ibid., pp. 16–17.

31. Bruno Roselli, *The Italians in Colonial Florida* (Florida: The Drew Press, 1940).

32. Papers of Panton, Leslie, and Co., Florida Hist. Soc., Univ. South Florida Library, Tampa; William S. Coker, *Historical Sketches of Panton, Leslie and Company* (Pensacola: University of West Florida, 1976).

33. Wilbur Henry Siebert, *Loyalists in East Florida 1774 to 1785* 2 vols. (Deland, FA: Florida State Historical Society, 1929), 1: 5.

34. Calhoun Winton, 'English Books and American Readers in Early Florida', in Samuel Proctor, ed., *Eighteenth-Century Florida and the Revolutionary South* (Gainesville, FL, 1978: University Presses of Florida, 1978): 110–21 (pp. 114–15).

35. Roger Philip McCutcheon, 'Books and Booksellers in New Orleans, 1730–1830', *The Louisiana Historical Quarterly* 20 (1937): 606–18.

36. David Bjork, ed., 'Documents Relating to the Establishment of Schools in Louisiana, 1771', *Mississippi Valley Historical Review* 11 (1924–5): 561–9 (p. 565).

37. Archivo General de Indias, Seville, México, Papeles de Cuba, leg. 169, no. 101, 239ff; Irving A. Leonard, 'A Frontier Library, 1799', *The Hispanic American Historical Review* 23 (1943): 21–51. Identification of many titles given in the 'Causa Mortuoria' can be approximate only.

38. Roger Philip McCutcheon, 'Books and Booksellers in New Orleans, 1730–1830', *The Louisiana Historical Quarterly* 20 (1937): 606–18.

39. John M. Goudeau, 'Booksellers and Printers in New Orleans, 1764–1885', *The Journal of Library History* 5 (1970): 5–19 (p. 7). The Moniteur he cites seems to provide evidence of 288 rather than the 488 printed books he suggests.

40. Listed in John Francis McDermott, *Private Libraries in Creole Saint Louis* (Baltimore MD: Johns Hopkins Press, 1938), 'Early Libraries', pp. 23–74.

41. McCutcheon, 'Books and Booksellers', p. 610, citing various newspaper advertisements.

42. Fitzpatrick to Waugh, Apr. 22, 1777, cited in Margaret Fisher Dalrymple, ed., *The Merchant of Manchac: The Letterbooks of John Fitzpatrick 1768–1790* (Baton Rouge and London: Louisiana State University Press, 1978), p. 243.

43. ibid., 23, 431–2, App. 1.

44. Maynard J. Geiger, 'The Story of California's First Libraries', *Southern California Quarterly* 46 (1964): 109–24.

45. Leonard A. Coombs and Francis X. Blouin Jr, eds., *Intellectual Life on the Michigan Frontier: The Libraries of Gabriel Richard & John Monteith* (Ann Arbor, MI: University of Michigan, 1985), pp. 1–9.

46. Clarence L. Andrews, 'The Historical Russian Library of Alaska', *Pacific Northwest Quarterly* 29 (1938): 201–04.

47. See for example, Hannah D. French, 'The Amazing Career of Andrew Barclay', *Studies in Bibliography* 14 (1961): 145–62.

48. J.L.E.W. Shecut, *Shecut's Medical and Philosophical Essays: Containing: 1st Topographical, Historical and Other Sketches of the City of Charleston* (Charleston, 1819), p. 41.

49. John Lambert, *Travels Through Lower Canada, and the United States of North America, in the Years 1806, 1807, and 1808* 3 vols. (London, 1810), 2: 363–4.

50. NYSL Archives, NYSL First Minute Book 1754–72, fol. 29, Mar. 27, 1758.

51. NYSL First Minute Book, fol. 32–3, Mar. 27, 1758.

52. Library Company of Philadelphia, Minute books, 2 (1768–85), 3 (1785–94), 4 (1794–1816), 5 (1816–32) copies of correspondence with Joseph Woods and William Dillwyn, 1783–1812 (and with Samuel Woods from 1812 to at least 1824).

53. The early history is discussed in Raven, *London Booksellers and American Customers*.

54. Edwin Wolf 2nd, *The Library of James Logan of Philadelphia 1674–1751* (Philadelphia: Library Company of Philadelphia, 1974); and in particular, Logan to John Whiston, 27 July 1748, copy, Hist. Soc. Pennsylvania, Logan Papers, Letterbook 1748–50, f. 5.

55. Stockdale's American contacts are discussed in Eric Stockdale, 'John Stockdale of Piccadilly:

Publisher to John Adams and Thomas Jefferson', in Robin Myers and Michael Harris, eds., *Author/Publisher Relations during the Eighteenth and Nineteenth Centuries* (Oxford: Oxford Polytechnic Press, 1983), pp. 63–87.

56. See George C. Rogers Jr, *Evolution of a Federalist: William Loughton Smith of Charleston (1758–1812)* (Columbia SC: University of South Carolina Press, 1962), pp. 99, 203, 273–5, 355.

57. Charles Knight, *Shadows of the Old Booksellers* (London: Bell and Daldry, 1865), pp. 282–99; George Paston [pseud.], *Little Memoirs of the Eighteenth Century* (London and New York: Grant Richards and E. P. Dutton, 1901), pp. 205–34; Richard G. Landon, 'Small Profits do Great Things: James Lackington and Eighteenth-Century Bookselling', *Studies in Eighteenth-Century Culture*, 5 (1976): 387–99; and others listed in James Raven, 'Selling One's Life: James Lackington, Eighteenth-Century Booksellers and the Design of Autobiography', *Writers, Books and Trade: An Eighteenth-Century English Miscellany for William B. Todd*, edited by O. M. Brack, Jr (New York: AMS Press, 1994): 1–23 (notes 33–35). In 1827 the firm moved to 4 Pall Mall East; it variously changed partners and was finally Harding, Triphook and Lepard.

58. *LBAC* letter 57, C. C. Pinckney to Bird, Savage and Bird, 17 Apr. 1793.

59. NYSL archives, Keep papers, J[ohn] Forbes, draft of a letter for the Purchasing Committee, to Revd John M. Mason, Glasgow, 1 Oct. 1801. I am indebted to Sharon Brown, NYSL, for her assistance in locating this.

60. *Charleston Courier*, 7 June 1805.

61. *Charleston Gazette*, 30 July and 14 Oct. 1805.

62. *LBAC* letters 107, 108, LA to Davidson, 5 Aug. 1807, and Davidson to LA, 14 Nov. 1807.

63. William Wallace Woodward, printer, bookseller and stationer of Chestnut St. (1796–1801) and South Second St. (1802–20), Philadelphia. See H. Glenn Brown and Maude D. Brown, *A Directory of the Book-Arts and Book Trade in Philadelphia to 1820 Including Printers and Engravers* (New York: New York Public Library, 1950).

64. CLS archives MS 29, CLS Letterbook 1758–1811, Woodward to Davidson, 24 May 1809, and Davidson to Woodward, 20 June 1809.

65. *LBAC*, letter 114, Hopton to DeSaussure and Roper, 24 June 1809.

BEYOND BOUNDARIES: BOOKS IN THE CANADIAN NORTHWEST[1]

FIONA A. BLACK

IN 1789 JEDIDIAH Morse's *American Geography* informed readers that Canada was bounded in the 'West by unknown lands.'[2] Morse might have been intrigued to hear of a surveyor in those same 'unknown lands' a few years later, settling down to read the 1792 London edition of his work.[3] What is more intriguing perhaps is the manner in which the surveyor acquired it. This paper discusses book selection and acquisition by those readers who were scattered across the lands claimed by 'The Governor and Company of Adventurers of England Tradeing into Hudson's Bay.' Studies of books crossing boundaries, borders or frontiers tend to focus on nations, their neighbours and colonies.[4] In doing so such studies discuss, amongst other factors, transportation, communication, financial transactions and general business practices which were all affected by the presence of various physical and metaphoric boundaries. However, there were other regions, exemplified here by the Canadian Northwest, which were neither nations in their own right nor colonies, and which therefore had distinctive geographic, administrative and trade boundaries which informed and shaped the nature of their links with more developed areas.

The Hudson's Bay Company received its charter from King Charles II in 1670 and the Company's officers and men were not a part of any military plan or colonial scheme, with the attendant development of settled communities and the establishment of retail business networks. Giles Barber's wisely cautious comment that the geographic region of Hudson's Bay 'apparently never received any books at all' from Europe in the eighteenth century is a reflection of the distinctiveness of the various boundaries surrounding the Bay.[5] Although considerable physical boundaries were involved, the lack of trade boundaries and regulations, in this instance, affected the business practices regarding exported goods and, in turn, affect our ability to recover information about the movement of books. No shipping owned by general merchant houses from Britain ever sailed into Hudson's Bay bearing books, as it did into the harbours of Halifax or Quebec. The steady though comparatively small movement of books to Hudson's Bay is therefore not researchable via some of the more familiar channels of book history enquiry.

Using the resources of the Hudson's Bay Company Archives in Winnipeg, Manitoba, it is possible to illustrate how these readers used the corporate communication and transportation systems to gain long-distance access to the book stocks of English, and sometimes Scottish, booksellers. This small study, of a relatively small group of literate men,[6] aims to help shed a comparative light on contemporary book availability in more settled regions of Canada.[7]

There was no print culture among the indigenous peoples of North America before the coming of the explorers and fur traders. However, there certainly was a highly organised culture of communication, involving a variety of sign systems for transmitting or recording information.[8] The men of the Hudson's Bay Company benefited directly from the geographical and environmental knowledge of the tribes with whom they came in contact, for example by use of the maps drawn by native guides.[9] In addition to this sharing of information, the native-trader contact included family ties. Traders married native women and had children by them. They also forged ties with other traders who shared their interests, a seasonal 'correspondence by letter' being kept up between the forts and posts, aided by native carriers.[10] This then was the intellectual and social climate of the traders who brought with them their characteristic modes of acquiring information and entertainment from the world of printed materials. The boundary of distance (from the sources of supply of books and serials) was not, to judge from the evidence, a deterrent to these readers. This paper summarises book availability and ownership from the 1780s to the early twentieth century; a period which embraces changes not only in the types and amounts of material available but changes in the corporate policies affecting the provision of books in the Northwest. While the social and cultural life of the fur trade has been a subject of research, a systematic survey of book availability and the mechanisms of acquisition has not hitherto been undertaken.[11]

The Hudson's Bay Company Archives holds over 7,000 linear feet of textual records and several hundred volumes of books. These books are the remnants of the nineteenth-century fur trading post libraries which were moved to the Archives in the 1930s, some of them bearing the unmistakeable traces of birds having roosted on them and monstrous northern mosquitoes having been swotted with them. However, these same volumes of monographs and bound periodicals had not always been so neglected. By the light of whale oil lamps, catalogues listing them had been pored over and discussed by officers (and latterly by servants also) as they sat around the sturdy pine tables in forts hundreds and sometimes over a thousand miles distant from each other. Selections were made and 'commissions' were filled out in the various post record books – always in duplicate, one set to remain at the fort or post and one set to be sent with the returning supply ships to the little wharf at

Gravesend on the Thames and thence to Company headquarters in Fenchurch Street in London.

These private and group commissions provide the base data for this study which aims to chart what the explorers and traders gained access to within the Northwest itself, rather than what they may have read or purchased when they were on leave in Britain.[12] In addition, books purchased in Britain and shipped to the Northwest when the employee was hired do not form a part of this study. Perhaps the most frequently cited example of this category of book collection is the personal library of 1,400 volumes which Joseph Colen arranged to have shipped back to England at the end of his term in 1798.[13] Only the volumes which were ordered by Colen whilst he was in the Northwest are included in this survey.[14] Indeed, even if there had been no book orders to be found in the Company ledgers, other commissions attest the existence of readers and book owners. For example, whether or not he had read William Buchan's injunction about reading by candlelight,[15] Joseph Howse requested '1 pair of neat spectacles with green glasses – to save the eyes when reading by candlelight – not to magnify at all.'[16] In addition, Thomas Stayner's request in 1797 for 'Additional mahogany for a bookcase' certainly indicates the presence of books in his life.[17]

Contemporary accounts indicate that some travellers, such as the military scientist John Henry Lefroy, were very surprised not only by the range of books found in relatively isolated spots, but by the wide knowledge of the officers in the fur trade.[18] From the preliminary work described here, it would seem that there may have been defining characteristics of a book culture in the Northwest which set it apart from that of other parts of the continent. For example, by the 1830s readers in Upper and Lower Canada (Ontario and Quebec) could purchase cheap (usually pirated) American editions of British titles and by 1870 the *Canada Bookseller* made the broad statement that Canadians, at least for fiction, largely read material published in the United States.[19] Throughout this period readers in the Northwest however, were paying the standard British retail price for what one of them called 'sterling English editions' of the same works.[20] The Northwest offers an interesting example of a geographic area which was, due to exploration and scientific activity, increasingly embraced as an important part of the fledgling Canada[21] while at the same time having links exclusively to Great Britain, rather than to continental sources, concerning access to printed materials.

The reasons for this reliance on British sources of supply for books and periodicals are embedded in the history of the Northwest itself. The land the fur traders explored and inhabited was either Company land or Company-controlled land; the fur traders' links with the outside world were massively constrained by their terms of employment. Prior to the Company merger of 1821, they were to regard the rival companies trading out of Montreal as enemies, even unto death, and all of their own communications and purchases and supplies had to travel via the Company shipping route of London to Hudson's Bay. The only way books could move was on the three annual supply vessels which sailed from Gravesend each May. Even when Lord Selkirk bought land from the Company for his famous and troubled settlement on the Red River, the colonists received all of their supplies, including books for their library, via York Fort on Hudson's Bay, not up from the Great Lakes and the St Lawrence River.

Thus, business history and human geography inevitably mingle in this study which describes book availability, via sale or loan, within the 'frail but coherent culture of fur trade and exploration.'[22] Was this Northwest print culture a generalisable entity or was it characterised by isolated examples of a more or less vibrant intellectual life? The evidence uncovered so far seems to suggest that beginning with starkly isolated individual efforts at book ownership from the late seventeenth century, the book culture of the Northwest evolved along parallel lines with rural Britain, until, in the mid- to late-nineteenth century, there was a pattern of local book availability in libraries which included all but the smallest of fur trading outposts. Prior to the establishment and maintenance of libraries however, those traders who wished to read could supply themselves with both standard works of reference, critical reviews and current works in many fields, notably, as might be expected, the pure and applied sciences, and technology. Who were the readers who acquired or borrowed such materials? The fur trade involved several occupations which required literacy, beyond the obvious administrative needs of the chief traders and chief factors. The officer class also included the Bayside sloop masters, surveyors and surgeons, as well as apprentice clerks and writers. At each post there would be varying numbers of officers, one or two clerks, a postmaster and a number of skilled tradesmen, artisans, labourers and canoe men. These latter two groups were asked to perform a wide variety of tasks most of which did not require the ability to read. From a preliminary analysis of signing ability on the Company contracts signed at Stromness in Orkney in the 1780s, over 50% of the men signed with their full name, rather than just initials or a mark. Due to the fact that the Parish Schools in Orkney taught reading before writing, as was the general practice at that time, the percentage of servants who could read may have been higher than these figures suggest.

Was there much time within the fur trade culture for recreation and reading? Work at the posts was highly seasonal, with the most intense activity taking place in early summer when the vessel arrived from London, via Orkney, and then again in late summer loading the furs gathered from the inland posts or brought directly to the Bay by the native hunters. Even during these busy times, the Company Governors made it clear that Sundays were not for work. Michael Payne's meticulous research of everyday life at York Fort indicates that leisure time, at that major post at least, was filled with a variety of sports and games as well as with reading.[23]

The paternalistic provision of books for those in navies (to which the fur trade has been likened) was not unknown.[24] There are certainly parallels, logistically, between sailors and fur traders; they shared a total reliance on sea communication routes and provision of goods in ports. Therefore it would seem pertinent to ask what reading matter, if any, was provided by the Governors. Since the seventeenth century the Governors in London had provided Bibles[25] and 'good books . . . in order to promote Virtue and discourage Vice.'[26] In addition, by the 1790s, they were also beginning to realise that the children born in the Northwest might form a useful new pool of recruits to alleviate a labour shortage for the Company caused by the revolutionary wars. Because literacy was important for several fur trade occupations, in 1794 the Governors began supplying spelling books and primers for small schools which they felt would be easily run and with little preparation, by the Post Surgeons, whom the London Committee felt must have considerable free time. These schools petered out after 1811 when increasingly intense competition forced some fiscal restraint.[27] It was not to be until well into the nineteenth century that the Governors shipped a relatively wide array of titles to the Northwest for use in Company libraries. Even then, the impetus for such subscription and circulating libraries came from interested officers and men who paid for the materials.[28]

From the earliest days, the Company provided each post with one sheet almanac, which was duly listed on the shipping invoices each May. Overall though the Company did little in the way of providing reading materials.[29] However, efficient transportation was crucial to the Company's economic success and as an offshoot it facilitated trade interactions of a less formal nature, including the movement of printed materials. This background forms the context for the individual commissions sent annually to the Secretary in London. There was a lively variety of individual orders, from yards of the best plaid to magic lanterns, particular types of fireworks, silver teaspoons, broadswords and a gravestone for a baby.[30] The orders for books are interspersed in the ledgers with all of these other items.

The remainder of this paper is arranged in two sections, the first of which discusses this individual effort to acquire pertinent reading materials for professional and recreational purposes, and the second of which describes the access the officers and men gradually came to enjoy through the Post libraries. The paper concludes with a preliminary comparison of book availability in the Northwest and that in the colonial regions.

INDIVIDUAL BOOK CULTURES

As with any literate people, readers in the fur trade had personal preferences which were reflected in the books they owned. These preferences were, of course, informed by the individual's level of education, social background and disposable income.[31] Servants of the company (as opposed to officers) ordered very few books in the early period, to judge from the surviving evidence, and when they did order it was often a family Bible or a technical manual related to their position in the Company. One might suppose that the most well-educated and most highly-paid amongst the Officers would own the broadest-ranging personal book collections. This was not always the case however. When the relatively well-paid physician Thomas C. Rowland of Moose Factory died from an overdose of his own sedatives, his estate inventory listed only seven medical books, two magazines, three prayer and hymn books, one Bible and one guide to Scotland.[32] By contrast Peter Fidler, who has been termed 'Canada's forgotten surveyor'[33] built, primarily whilst he was in the Northwest, a collection of hundreds of books, 500 of which he bequeathed on his death in 1822 to the Red River library.[34] Dr Rowland died at the end of the nineteenth century and may have had ample access to books at the Moose Factory library, whereas Fidler was active in the Northwest a century earlier and, if he were to have access to the materials he clearly both needed and wanted, he had no alternative but to purchase them. Once books were in the Northwest they did not necessarily remain in the ownership of the person who first acquired them. Judith Beattie has demonstrated clearly that the provenance evidence in the remaining volumes attests to a steady resale, exchange or gift system being in operation.[35] Fidler acquired a small proportion of his books in this way.

The discovery of what books were newly published was made by some of the officers when they were at home on leave, but for others such as Fidler, who stayed for most of his life in the Northwest, publication information as well as books themselves travelled the same route. Sometimes, as was typical then as now, other works published by the same publisher were listed at the front or back of the volumes shipped.[36] In addition to these non-ephemeral publication notices, it might be reasonable to assume that at least a small number of publishers' broadsides and catalogues made their way to the Northwest. However, not surprisingly, there is no proof of this in the official Company records such as bills of lading, invoices for goods, or staff accounts. The proof rests with Fidler who used these items as endpapers in the volumes he bound in deerskin.[37] He used catalogues from a variety of London book-sellers, including J. White, W. Baynes, H. D Symonds, Francis Wingrave, W. Strahan and T. Cadell and Lackington, Allen and Co. Indeed Fidler did not only receive ephemera relating to the book trade, he also used broadsides for the ubiquitous Solomon's Balm of Gilead and for De Velnos' Vegetable

Pills for the Scurvy when he bound his copies of the *Monthly* and *Critical Reviews*.

The presence of these literary magazines is a telling factor in determining the fur traders' knowledge of recent publications. From the evidence, it seems clear that the Northwest was in some regards an extension of contemporary provincial Britain – the reviewing journals which were available to the men were exclusively British, understandably therefore focussing on British publications. No copies of *The Canadian Magazine and Literary Repository*, published in Montreal, apparently made their way to the fur trading posts – again a stark reminder of the crucial influence of the Company transportation and communication routes. This is not to imply that Canadian periodicals would have been wholly unknown to the men, it is simply a useful reminder that their intellectual world was more British-centric than North American, the political and corporate boundaries in this case superseding the physical boundaries. The post-1820 surviving volumes in the Company Archives offer overwhelming support for this, in that 75% of the books were published in London and a further 12% in other British towns, notably Edinburgh, although the single surviving work in Gaelic was published in Glasgow.[38] The United States is represented by four works from New York and one from Chicago, while Canada has a single remaining representative of its growing publishing industry, the work by Henry Youle Hind bearing the McKenzie River Library bookplate: *Essay on the Insects and Diseases Injurious to Wheat Crops*, published by Lovell and Gibson of Toronto in 1857.[39]

One of Fidler's orders provides a possible example of his uses of magazines as sources of information. By the supply ship returning from York Fort to London in 1799, Fidler placed an order for Charles Hutton's *Mathematical and Philosophical Dictionary*, which had been published in London in 1796.[40] A few weeks previously, when the ship had arrived in the Bay, he had received his previous year's requests and these included the *Monthly Review* for 1798. In the February and March issues of that periodical,[41] there was a lengthy review and abstract of Hutton's work; it seems reasonable to conclude that this may be how Fidler knew of it or at least may be what spurred his decision to place an order.

Sometimes the men wanted to order a work on a certain topic but did not have an exact title in mind. This did not deter them from ordering, as when Mr Topping requested simply 'The latest book on domestic medicine' in 1809.[42] The title sent is unknown, but it cost Topping 13s 3d. Although Fidler usually knew precisely what he wanted, he too sometimes placed such subject requests and relied on the Company Secretary to find the needed item. For example, in 1803 Fidler requested 'The latest & most complete Astronomical Tables for calculating the places of the Sun, Moon, Planets & Jupiters Satellites.' The Secretary wrote 'Vince's System of Astronomy' above his request and the price, which was £3 8s.[43] Occasionally there is evidence in the commissions of a specific edition being ordered, such as Cooke's pocket editions or French works from Dilly and from Wingrave.[44] One regular feature is a specification as to size – octavo or duodecimo being frequently requested. However, considerations of portability certainly did not restrict some of the fur traders in their selections; in 1798 Thomas Stayner received the eighteen-volume *Encyclopedia Britannica*.[45]

How the Company Secretary filled the orders prior to 1801 is difficult to deduce.[46] Surviving imprint evidence is not reliable as so many imprints were of course sold by a wide variety of London booksellers. By 1801, the Officers' and Servants' Accounts offer clear evidence of which booksellers were being used; and, as might be expected from Peter Fidler's endpaper evidence, the firm of Lackington and Allen was indeed used. That bookselling emporium was in Finsbury Square, about 3/4 mile from Company headquarters, Hudson's Bay House on Fenchurch Street. Table 1 details some of the bills listed in the Officer's and Servants' Accounts in the early nineteenth century. Unfortunately these bills have no title information attached to them.

Table 1
Examples of Individuals' Book Bills, 1805–1814[47]

Year	Bookseller	Amount	Name	Post
1805	Johnson	£8 18s 8d	William Auld	Prince of Wales
1806	Johnson	£4 2s 6d	Peter Fidler	York Factory
		£2 8s [magazines]	Jacob Fesinmeyer	Moose Factory
1808	Lackington & Allen	£2 15s 11d	Joseph Howse	York Factory
		£20 13s 5d	Peter Fidler	
1811	Lackington & Allen	£1 5s	James Kirkness	York Factory
		£3 13s 6d	J.P. Whitford	York Factory
1812	Lackington & Allen	£2 8s 11d	Joseph Howse	
1813	Bernard Hennington	£3 19s	Thomas Vincent	Albany
		£0 12s	William Harper	Albany
		£2 17s	Peter Fidler	York Factory
		£4 7s	George Atkinson	Eastmain
		£3 8s	James Clouston	Eastmain
1814	Bernard Hennington	£4 13s	Thomas Vincent	Albany
		£3 14s 6d	L.R. Stewart	Albany
		£6 18s 10d	Peter Fidler	Moose Factory

The 1811 orders for magazines, filled by Hennington on the 1812 supply ship, came to a total of £46 19s 7d,[48] which was, perhaps understandably, significantly less that the bills for groceries, but it was more than was paid to several other merchants, for sundry items.

Hennington's bills for fur trade orders varied each year. In 1813 his bill came to only £15 3s, 3.1% of the total tradesmen's bills for that year which were £475 0s 5d. His percentage of the total was higher, at 4.9%, the following year, with his own bill being similar, at £15 6s 4d, but the total being only £309 2s 3d.[49] This snapshot of one particular bookseller's bills may simply indicate the obvious – that book orders fluctuated as did the orders for other items. However, there is one small but notable aspect of the book orders which differs from orders for, say, crystal decanters and luxury groceries. These latter commissions sometimes had notes appended to them explaining that nothing further would be supplied to the employee until their arrears were settled. No examples have been found of book orders being turned down for non-payment of previous bills, though one may only speculate about the possible reasons for this.

Using both surviving volumes and the business records of the Company, it is possible to trace what the officers and men ordered and owned in the period up to 1814. Overall, a wide array of subjects is in evidence, but it is by no means comprehensive or wholly representative of what was available. John Feather offers a preliminary analysis of British books by subject for the eighteenth century.[50] In addition, Simon Eliot offers figures extracted from the *Nineteenth Century Short Title Catalogue* for the period up to 1815.[51] Feather's work indicates that British presses produced significantly more titles in religion and the social sciences (including politics), than in any other subject, though literature, history and geography are also well represented.[52] Science and technology lag far behind in the number of titles published. The data in Figure 1 can only be offered as a preliminary outline of the differences between production and fur trade acquisition not least because the date ranges of the datasets involved are not identical.[53] Nevertheless, it would seem that the fur trading readers had a pattern of acquisition notably different from the general pattern of production. For example, taken together, the fur traders' books in all branches of science and technology form over 30% of the total and far outweigh those in any of the humanities, which is in direct contrast to the evidence from Feather's survey of production. The large percentage of titles produced in both religion and the social sciences (the latter including thousands of political items) is another contrast with the items which the fur traders requested. Sermons and political tracts and pamphlets seem to have been uncommon in the Northwest in the early period, though the bundles of newspapers which were apparently sent out with the supply ships would have contained some of the current political controversies and opinions. In addition, the fur traders appear to have had an unusual interest in dictionaries and grammars in both English and other languages. This interest may reflect a self-improvement mentality amongst some of the officers and men, and a willingness of some of the more literate to instruct their less educated messmates. William Howse appears to have been teaching himself Spanish and Italian, to judge from his book orders,[54] and a North West Company officer, Daniel Harmon, referred in his journal to teaching another man to be 'fond of books.'[55]

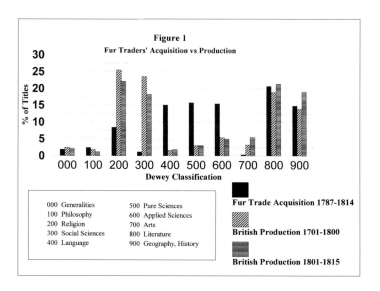

Figure 1
Fur Traders' Acquisition vs Production

The reasons for the preponderance of scientific and technical titles are multi-faceted, but the fur trade society had distinctive occupational traits, including surveying and scientific observation, which are reflected in the figures. The majority of almanac titles ordered, for example, were nautical, providing necessary information for the surveying activities. The practical handbooks ordered included astronomical tables as well as such items as shipwrights' and builders' assistants. Although not classified under science, the travel accounts hold special interest because they were sometimes the published versions of the very travel journals the readers and their colleagues were creating. Although there is evidence, in journals kept by Peter Fidler and other surveyors, that a few manuscript copies of the exploration and travel narratives circulated in the Northwest, they were apparently rare.[56] An interesting omission is that of chapbooks (although one or two of the titles within 'Religion' are possibly in this category, from the evidence of their low prices). Chapbooks would have been the staple of many of the servant class, if they read at all when at home in Orkney. It is possible that they owned them from purchases made in Britain, but did not join in the book ordering from the

Northwest for cultural and social reasons.[57] It is certainly apparent that arti-sans' and labourers' orders were rare. Indeed the apparent lack of pamphlets and chapbook literature, if it is confirmed by further research, may be one of the defining characteristics of the early Northwest print culture compared with other parts of Canada. By later in the nineteenth century, missionaries were supplying religious chapbooks to the Northwest for the use of Company servants as well as for evangelical work with native peoples. However, from the 1760s onwards, there is evidence that chapbooks, both religious and non-religious, were being exported from London and the Clyde ports for sale in a variety of stores in the settled areas of the Maritimes and the Canadas (Quebec and Ontario).[58] So, while the highly literate officers might not have fared so ill compared to some of their compatriots in Halifax or Quebec, the servants did not seem to have had the same access to print that they would have had elsewhere on the Continent.

In addition to a subject analysis, one might speculate whether the subjects varied amongst the differing occupational groups within the fur trade. However, of the 65 men who ordered books and/or serials prior to 1820, only 35% have been identified to date by occupation. Even with such scant data, it seems apparent that there is no clear demarcation of certain subjects being the exclusive domain of single occupational groups (medical works were ordered by many more officers than the surgeons for example) with the exception of astronomical works for the explorer-surveyors. The surveyors would regularly order nautical almanacs up to four years in advance, forcing the secretary in London to write 'not published' beside many of these requests.

Serials were ordered regularly, in addition to books, and Table 2 lists the titles as given in the commissions, and the number of staff who requested each one.

Table 2
Serials Ordered, 1787–1814[59]

Subject	Title	No. of Staff
General	*European Magazine*	2
	Monthly Magazine	15
	Oeconomist's Magazine	8
	Reflector	1
Science/Technology	*Journal of Natural Philosophy, Chemistry and the Arts*	1
	Repository of Arts and Manufactories	2
Medicine	*Medical and Chirurgical Review*	2
Literature	*Monthly Review*	2
	Novelist's Magazine	1
Women	*Lady's Magazine*	1

Women are singled out as a subject in this table because, during the period covered, there were no white women in the Northwest. The orders may perhaps be viewed as an indication of the evolution of the broader fur trade culture. For example, by the late 1790s, not only was one staff member ordering magazines for women, a variety of novels were being ordered which may have been destined for female readers. In 1798, James Bent at Albany River ordered *Duties of Woman* along with works of history, travel and fiction.[60] These orders may have been a spur towards (or, conversely, a reflection of) a greater acceptance by the Governors and Committee of the presence of women in the lives of their staff in the Northwest (it was during this period that the London Committee sent a General Letter to their staff insisting that the native wives and children of fur traders should be provided for by the men when they left the Northwest and/or when they died).

The serial orders also hint that for at least some of the officers the great distances involved did not appear to lessen their expectations of good service. In 1798 Thomas Thomas informed the Company secretary that 'There was a mistake made in the Medical and Chirurgical Review sent this Year, for it is only part of the . . . 3rd vol. wereas I intended to have had the whole completed. The Numbers sent are from Jany 1796 to Dec 1796 inclusive.'[61] Returning unwanted items for credit was also not unkown. In 1799 William Auld returned four numbers of 'Natural Philosophy' for a credit of ten shillings.[62] The fact that Auld returned them to London, rather than selling them to a colleague, is perhaps revealing about the highly individual nature of some book orders.

Some men ordered critical reviews repeatedly for a number of years and apparently never ordered books at all through the Company Secretary. An element of the serial orders which seems to differ from the book orders is that repeatedly several men at the same post would order the same magazines – *The Monthly Magazine* and the *Oeconomist* being those most often ordered. If the various officers and servants had pooled their resources, they could have had a greater variety of magazines to share. Part of the explanation why this did not occur may lie in the strict rank/strata within fur trade communities, as in other communities of the time.[63]

Personal orders for serials and monographs did not stop when there were circulating collections in the Northwest. For example, in 1864 James Yates, bookseller in London's Goswell Street, filled orders for at least eleven individuals at various posts, as well as for the York Factory Library and the Moose Factory Book Club.[64] Serials form a particular link between the earlier personal collections and some of the later library catalogues. Dr Tolmie, referring to the Fort Vancouver collection in 1836, stated that 'a circulating library of papers, magazines, and *some* books' was operating 'full blast.'[65]

FUR TRADE POST LIBRARIES[66]

During the nineteenth century, there were eight forts which had libraries, some of which were subscription libraries, akin to those in the colonial regions, which would circulate books to more distant readers, in this case those at other posts in the same district.[67] Some of the remaining volumes in the Company Archives bear flyleaf notations concerning which outpost the books were held at. In 1852, James Anderson sent a circular letter from Fort Simpson to the Company officers in charge of posts in the Mackenzie River District. Anderson states, in part:

> The men and officers here have agreed to subscribe 5/- per annum towards establishing a District Library . . . the books will be periodically exchanged, and after they have gone through the District, will be deposited at Headquarters. Lists of the books there deposited will be forwarded to all the Posts, so that any person may get the book or books he may want thence, exclusive of the annual supply . . . [68]

Prior to the establishment of such circulating libraries, small collections were used by officers. A small collection at Fort George, for which there is an 1821 inventory, provides a glimpse of this type of specialised library for officers. The 50 titles (in 59 volumes) are analysed by subject in Table 3.

Table 3
Extract from 'Inventory taken at Fort George, fall 1821'[69]

Subject	Titles	% of Titles
Science and Technology	21	42
Medicine	17	34
Language and Literature	7	14
Travel	4	8
Philosophy	1	2

Although taken from only one surviving sample, this subject breakdown looks in some ways similar to that of the personal book collections already referred to. In fact it is likely that these books had been privately acquired and then left at the post for others to use, as regularly seems to have occurred. These were definitely for broader access by the men at the post but the collection had not been deliberately planned under institutional or committee control. Such control was exercised by the later libraries which had sets of rules and regulations, fees for subscribers and committees of officers who would select books on an annual basis to be purchased on their post account. These books, as with the personal orders, all came from Britain. In 1846 for example, Forbes Barclay, the designated librarian at Fort Vancouver on the Columbia

River, requested that the Secretary in London procure books to be charged to the library's account and to be shipped at the 'first opportunity,' via Cape Horn (see Figure 2). He added to his letter, 'and please to continue sending the Periodicals as opportunities occur.'[70] This indicates that by this date the single annual supply run to Hudson's Bay was no longer a limiting factor for book acquisition, as it had clearly been for Peter Fidler and the others placing individual orders.

Figure 2

Fort Vancouver Library, 1846

'List of Books requested to be sent'[71]

Continuation of Foreign Quarterly Review
Laing's Travels in Sweden, or through the Continent of Europe, but not in
    Norway, as we have already that work in the Library
2 Copies of the Annual Register, from the year 1841, up to the latest date
    published
The Last of the Plantagenets
One Copy of 'Punch' from its commencement up to [the] latest date, bound in
    quarterly or half yea[rly] setts
Chambers' Edinburgh Journal from 1st January 1843 up to the latest date,
    bound in half yearly or yearly setts
The 'Mirror' for the years 1844 and 1845, bound in yearly or half yearly setts
Continuation of United Service Journal
Life of Lord Eldon in 3 vols. 8vo 24/-
Frederic the Great, his Court & Times by J. Campbell 21/-
Twelve Years Military Adventures 2 vols. 24/-
Curiosities for the Ingenious 2/6
Clarke's Hundred Wonders of the World 10/6
Murray's Colonial & Home Library, from its commencement up to latest date,
    half bound, 2/6 per number

The books listed in Figure 2 range in first publication date from the 1820s onward, but The Life of Lord Eldon is probably referring to *The Public and Private Life of Lord Chancellor Eldon* which was published in London in 1844;[72] so in this case fairly recent publication information was available seven and a half thousand miles away. Periodical orders are again evident and this is the earliest order so far noted which requests a set of Murray's Library.

Although London booksellers were overwhelmingly the usual suppliers of the fur traders' books, the national background of the majority of the Hudson's Bay Company officers and servants was Scottish or Orcadian[73] and occasionally there were familial links between fur traders and booksellers in Scotland which led to deliberate arrangements being made for books to be supplied from there. An example of such an arrangement occurred in 1852. A library was being proposed, in the 1850s, for the men in the Mackenzie River District – a library separate from the one already established for the officers there. A relative of the Glasgow bookseller, Thomas Murray, worked in the Northwest. Through this kinship an arrangement was proposed to the Governors in London for their approval. Murray agreed to fulfil the order for books 'at as cheap a rate as any wholesale house in London.'[74] He was to send the shipment to Orkney for pickup in June; Murray would be paid by the London office and the men at Mackenzie River would pay the London office through the usual Book Debt arrangements at the posts. The books ordered on this occasion were overwhelmingly the miscellanies in the currently popular sets such as 'Knight's Shilling Volumes', 'Chambers's People's Editions' and 'Routledge's Railway and Popular Library.'[75] These works are a far cry from the specialised scientific, technical and medical collection held at Fort George thirty years before. The MacKenzie River list emphasises personal improvement with its works of history and manners. Fiction is represented almost exclusively by Dickens, and generic magazines are included such as *The Family Herald*, *The London Journal*, and *The Family Economist*. This is clearly a non-elite library, deliberately aimed at a wide readership and would have been akin to similar libraries in the colonies or in Britain. Library inventories from various locations in the Northwest offer snapshots reflecting similar ranges of materials, such as the newly formed James Bay Library with 73 volumes, which was created at Moose Factory in 1873. The subscription fee in this case was 10s for residents of Moose Factory and 8s for those who lived at outlying posts in the District. The latter were allowed loans of one year duration, but within the factory the loan period was one month.[76] The James Bay Library, which was added to each year, can be characterised by its huge preponderance of fiction: Trollope, Lytton, Kingsley and Miss Braddon all being well represented.

The libraries which existed later in the nineteenth and into the twentieth century can also be researched in some detail, and they indicate a similar focus on fiction for the leisure time of the men. An example is the library at York Factory which was a circulating collection for the Nelson River District, for which there is a typescript catalogue from 1918 in classified arrangement (Table 4).

Looking at numbers of titles by no means tells the whole story. More instructive, for the purposes of availability of certain classes of literature to widely dispersed readers, is the number of volumes in each category (Table 5).

Although fiction is still clearly far ahead, Table 5 illustrates the great importance of periodicals in libraries in the Northwest. Lefroy's and other comments about the knowledgable fur traders may owe more to the presence of

Table 4
Nelson River Library 1918, by Number of Titles[77]

Subject	Titles	% Titles
Fiction	873	65.9
Religion	109	8.2
History	100	7.5
Science, Technology and Medicine	51	3.9
Travel	46	3.5
Biography	39	2.9
Poetry and Drama	38	2.9
Dictionaries and Encyclopaedia	32	2.4
Magazines	30	2.3
Essays	7	0.5
Total	1,325	100

Table 5
Nelson River Library 1918, by Number of Volumes[78]

Subject	Volumes	% of Volumes
Fiction	1,014	50.8
Magazines	394	19.7
History	177	8.9
Religion	112	5.6
Poetry and Drama	66	3.3
Biography	65	3.3
Science, Technology and Medicine	60	3.0
Travel	51	2.6
Dictionaries and Encyclopaedia	44	2.2
Essays	11	0.6
Total	1,996	100

general magazines, with their excerpts from new publications on a wide array of topics, than has hitherto been acknowledged.

Although much further work is needed in order to offer comparative details of the fur traders' libraries with those in contemporary Britain, the subject content of those surveyed to date can be compared with book production. For the nineteenth century in general, there are several sources available for the study of subject content of books published and Simon Eliot has used these to offer a preliminary overview.[79] Some of Eliot's figures indicate that fiction formed over 25% of titles by late in the century, a proportion apparently reflected in the fur trade library stocks. The electronic file of the *Nineteenth Century Short Title Catalogue* (NSTC) can now be searched for the period 1801–1870. Figure 3 offers percentage figures of titles for that period, and Geography, History and Biography (900s) are the only subject grouping which indicate greater production than literature (which of course incudes poetry, drama, essays as well as fiction). Although any such large overviews require caveats regarding sources, data collection and recording methods, the general picture of production gleaned from NSTC may approximate the true situation, and in this case seems to indicate that few science and technology materials were requested for the fur trade libraries compared with the rate of production. These libraries seem to have had a clear emphasis on recreational rather than utilitarian uses of print.

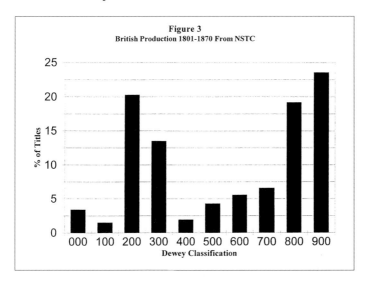

Figure 3
British Production 1801-1870 From NSTC

Whilst in operation the library collections described briefly here appear from contemporary evidence to have functioned efficiently in circulating books. However, they were not the only library institutions engaged in this activity in the Northwest. For several years in the 1860s, Mudie's well-known commercial library sent books regularly to individuals in the far West. The run of ledgers headed simply 'Invoices for Canada' include the forwarding and receiving of 154 titles from Mudie's, moving on Company ships from 21 January 1861 to 25 February 1864.[80] These include much fiction, travel and history, but especially the reviewing magazines the *Quarterly* and the *Edinburgh*. The length of loan period must certainly have been a year or longer, but whether interlending within the Northwest was officially permitted is not mentioned in the extant Company records.

There were other means of moving books to the fur trading posts other than the two focussed on here of private and collective purchase through company channels. The officers and men could request that books be sent to them by friends in Britain. Unfortunately, recovering details from this method is hindered by the fact that the contents of private boxes which were shipped to Hudson's Bay were not listed on the bills of lading. In addition to personal ordering through friends, sometimes missionary interest was aimed at the servants of the Company (rather than at the native population), such as occurred in 1846 when the Reverend Alexander Millar of South Ronaldsay in the Orkney Islands wrote to Archibald Barclay, the Company Secretary, asking permission to have a small library collection from the Religious Tract Society shipped free to York Factory from Stromness. While Revd. Millar expressed his interest in the books' use by the numerous Orkneymen who went to the Northwest, he did add that they were 'for *all* at the Factory who may choose to avail themselves of it.'[81] Whether or not these little chapbooks were read as avidly as some of the other materials at the Factory, is not recorded, but such heavily illustrated items would perhaps appeal to the Orkneymen who could barely sign their names on the Company contracts.

COMPARISON AND ANALYSIS OF BOOK ACQUISITION IN THE NORTHWEST AND OTHER PARTS OF CANADA

Although this research is not at a stage where firm conclusions may be drawn, it is possible to see that there were overlapping stages in the book culture of the fur trade, just as there were in contemporary Britain – the early collections were all private though some were definitely shared, then there were a few small collections for officers and finally circulating libraries open to all for a fee. The nature of the geographic boundaries, and the lack of some legal and business-related boundaries between the fur trading readers and their sources of supply, meant that the aspects of book acquisition which most constrained readers in the colonial regions were not necessarily present in the Northwest. While Hudson's Bay only had direct contact with Britain once a year the communication system between the readers and their 'book agent' (the Company secretary in London) was clearly organized, highly efficient, virtually error-free and would have been the envy of colonial booksellers and their British suppliers who had to send multiple copies of business letters, book orders and invoices in the hope that one at least would arrive safely.[82] In addition, the payment system was straightforward and did not involve the supplying bookseller in a credit arrangement with long-distance customers.[83] The Company Secretary paid for the books and the officers and men in turn paid the Company through a structured system of book debts recorded at each post. James Anderson wrote in 1852, 'Anything tending to the improvement of their servants, will I think meet with the approbation of the Governor & Committee, and to encourage it, they would probably allow the Books to be imported freight free, and at prime cost.'[84] When this type of arrangment was made, the readers in the Northwest paid the standard London price for their books unlike the colonial prices which usually included commercial freight and insurance rates.[85] On the other hand, the British booksellers were always, in their dealings with the fur traders, reacting to specific orders; no books were ever sent on speculation to the Northwest. Therefore new plays, novels and poetry were proportionately far rarer in the Northwest than in the colonial regions.

It is possible from the evidence gathered here to make some further, though tentative, suggestions concerning similarities and differences with the book culture of other parts of Canada, especially regarding three elements: place and date of publication and subject matter. Unless the surviving evidence is overwhelmingly misleading, it seems that the fur traders' knowledge of Canadian, and indeed North American, publications was scant compared to that of readers in Montreal and Quebec for example. However, it is not just by geographic origin of publication that there is a possible distinctive bias in the Northwest book culture – the dates of publication of items surviving from nineteenth-century libraries both in the Northwest and in the colonial towns differ widely. To use selected Maritime towns as an example, more than 2,200 titles are listed in *Pre-1701 Imprints in Nova Scotia Collections*,[86] and these offer evidence of the presence of early modern European books in various towns in the nineteenth century – books which were often bought deliberately for the fledgling academic institutions. Early printed books were also bought for personal libraries in colonial towns, although evidence uncovered for a parallel project would indicate that the rare book market was largely under-developed in early Canadian towns compared with towns in provincial Britain.[87] Older works were not wholly unknown in the Northwest; York Fort's Library held a work by Jean Baptiste DuHamel, published in Rouen in 1675, as well as a seventeenth-century edition of Pliny. These were very unlikely to have been deliberate library purchases however; they were probably donated by Joshua Halcro, an officer of the Company, whose name appears on the title pages.[88] It was certainly not common, if it ever happened, that the libraries or individual orders would include requests for early publications. The orders were almost entirely for works in current editions. Private libraries, which were shipped into the Northwest and then out again after the owners' terms of service, remained almost entirely unrecorded; they may well have included older rarer items.

The emphasis on fiction and periodical literature in the library collections of the Northwest can possibly be matched by collections in Montreal and Halifax, though a direct comparison awaits further research. However some differences can be noted; there were no specialised circulating collections such as those which were built for the Mechanics' Institutes in towns and cities to the East. The research reported on here does show that individuals ordered such technological items as were common in the Mechanics' Institute libraries, but the libraries in the Northwest were notably lacking in such items. Also interesting is the general lack of published exploration literature regarding the Northwest in the library collections. A corporate library was held at Beaver House in London, which apparently held all available accounts from the Northwest in published format.[89] However, the travel accounts favoured in both the individual and collective book cultures of the Northwest seemed to emphasise an interest in tales of the South Seas, Scandinavia, Africa, etc. – in other words, perhaps understandably, anywhere *other* than where the men actually were.

In conclusion, the records of the expatriate Scots and English who formed the staff of the Hudson's Bay Company offer an insight into book availability across various types of boundary in Canada. The evidence found so far would seem to indicate that the book culture of the Northwest differed in some respects from that of other parts of Canada. The research reported on here could be enhanced in the future: the orders placed by servants could be added to the growing body of evidence about working-class readers and their book selections;[90] and the book acquisition mechanisms described here might be compared with such mechanisms for the officers and men of other eighteenth century 'companies of adventurers' such as the East India Company. In addition, there are avenues of fur trade print culture which have not been mentioned here, such as the fur traders as authors[91] and the effect which the book availability described here may have had on their writing. There is certainly scope for research to extract the references to books in the manuscript and published fur trade journals.[92] The present study has focused almost exclusively on the men who were staff of the Hudson's Bay Company. The notable rival, the North West Company, while leaving fewer records, offers other avenues for research, particularly into the reading habits of individuals such as Roderick MacKenzie who apparently left a bound volume of manuscript notes including 219 pages of notes on his reading.[93] The men of the North West Company offer a potentially useful comparison with those of the Hudson's Bay Company as the former had their headquarters in Montreal and accessed the Northwest from the St Lawrence River system. Their channels of communication and access to books therefore differed. In spite of these avenues which await further research, it is hoped that this preliminary investigation of the ways in which books crossed various types of boundary in order to be read in the vast Northwest, will add detail to the general picture of print culture in Canada in the eighteenth and nineteenth centuries.

REFERENCES

1. Portions of this research were first presented at two conferences: 'Beyond the Periphery: Books by Express Canoe in the Canadian Northwest,' Annual Conference of the Society for the History of Authorship, Reading and Publishing (SHARP), Edinburgh, July 15–17, 1995; and, 'By Brig, Sloop and Canoe: Book Availability in the Canadian Northwest,' Founding Conference for a History of the Book in Canada, Ottawa, May 23–25, 1997. An abbreviated version of the SHARP paper has been published as 'Books by Express Canoe in the Canadian Northwest, 1750–1820,' *The Bibliotheck* 21 (1996): 12–33.

2. Jedidiah Morse, *The American Geography* 2nd ed. (London: John Stockdale, 1792) 474.

3. Peter Fidler's copy is held in the Hudson's Bay Company Archives, Public Archives of Manitoba (HBCA, PAM). Rare Book Collection. RB FTL PF 16. Morse was using 'Canada' to refer to modern Quebec and parts of Ontario. For the sake of simplicity and clarity, the term is used throughout this paper to refer to the modern country of Canada.

4. For macro studies see, for example, Giles Barber, 'Books from the Old World and for the New: The British International Trade in Books in the Eighteenth Century,' *Studies in Voltaire and the Eighteenth Century* 151 (1976): 185–224 and James Raven, 'The Export of Books to Colonial North America,' *Publishing History* 42 (1997): 21–49. For micro studies see, for example, Françoise Parent-Lardeur, 'Les envois de livres de Paris au Bas-Canada de 1824 à 1827,' *Livre et lecture au Québec, 1800–1850.* dir. Claude Galarneau et Maurice Lemire (Québec: Institut québécois de recherche sur la culture, 1988) 29–42.

5. Giles Barber, 'Book Imports and Exports in the Eighteenth Century,' *The Sale and Distribution of Books from 1700*, ed. Robin Myers and Michael Harris (Oxford: Oxford Polythechnic Press, 1982) 96.

6. Overall numbers at each post varied year by year. For example, at York Factory, a key post on the Bay, there were 63 servants and 10 officers in 1824–25, but in 1829–30 these numbers dropped to 37 and 5 respectively; Michael Payne, *The Most Respectable Place in the Territory: Everyday Life in Hudson's Bay Company Service, York Factory, 1788 to 1870* ([Ottawa]: National Historic Parks and Sites, Canadian Parks Service, Environment Canada, 1989) 44.

7. The author's dissertation (Loughborough University, 1999) focusses on book availability in the Canadian colonies compared with that in contemporary provincial Scotland.

8. An early attempt at printing in an indigenous language is explained in Jan Shipley, 'The Cree Syllabics,' *The James Evans Story* (Toronto: Ryerson Press, [1966]) 75–80.

9. Richard I. Ruggles, *A Country so Interesting: The Hudson's Bay Company and Two Centuries of Mapping, 1670–1870* (Montreal: McGill-Queen's University Press, 1991) Plates 19– 20, 22–23 and 26; and R. Cole Harris, ed., and Geoffrey J. Matthews, cartographer, *Historical Atlas of Canada Volume 1 From the Beginning to 1800* (Toronto: University of Toronto Press, 1987) Plate 59.

10. HBCA, PAM, E.2/12, Andrew Graham, 'Observations on Hudson's Bay, 1792' p. 427.

11. Two very useful studies which contribute to the intellectual history of the fur trade from a book history perspective are Michael Payne and Gregory Thomas, 'Literacy, Literature and Libraries in the Fur Trade,' *The Beaver* 313.4 (1983): 44–53; and Judith Hudson Beattie, '"My Best Friend": Evidence of the Fur Trade Libraries Located in the Hudson's Bay Company Archives,' *Épilogue* 8.1–2 (1993): 1–32.

12. If some of the readers had relied solely on acquiring books for themselves when on leave, they would have had few opportunities: Andrew Graham was in the Northwest for 20 years before his first visit home to Scotland; HBCA, PAM, E.2/12, Graham, 'Observations' p. 339.

13. HBCA, PAM, A.5/4 p. 76–77, Letter from Governing Committee to John Ballenden cited in Alice M. Johnson, ed., *Saskatchewan Journals and Correspondence: Edmonton House,*

1795– 1800, Chesterfield House, 1800–1802 (London: Hudson's Bay Record Society, 1967) xcviii-xcix, note 9.

14. For examples of Colen's orders from the Northwest, see HBCA, PAM, A.16/111 fol. 7d for his 1788 order, and fol. 23 for his 1794 order.

15. William Buchan, *Domestic Medicine* (London: A. Strahan and T. Cadell; Edinburgh: J. Balfour and W. Creech, 1792) 57.

16. HBCA, PAM, A.16/112 fol. 70. The glasses were shipped to Howse and he was billed £1 11s 6d for them. Howse might have read Buchan in the Northwest, as copies had been ordered by John Ballenden in 1795 and by Nicol Spence in 1799; A.16/111 fol. 25d and fol. 53.

17. HBCA, PAM, A.16/111 fol. 40d, Officers' and Servants' Commissions, 1797. Stayner was billed £2 7s for his wood. In the previous year David Thompson received a 'Book Stand' for £3 3s; HBCA, PAM, A.16/111 fol. 35.

18. Payne and Thomas 52 and Beattie 5–6; Lefroy's comment, cited in both of these papers, was made in a letter dated at Fort Simpson, March 29, 1844.

19. Allan Smith, 'American publications in nineteenth-century English Canada,' *Papers of the Bibliographical Society of Canada* 9 (1970): 15.

20. Payne and Thomas 48.

21. Suzanne Zeller, *Inventing Canada: Early Victorian Science and the Idea of a Transcontinental Nation* (Toronto: University of Toronto Press, 1987).

22. Germaine Warkentin, ed. *Canadian Exploration Literature: An Anthology* (Toronto: Oxford University Press, 1993) xi.

23. Payne, *The Most Respectable Place* 65–92.

24. Harry R. Skallerup, *Books Afloat and Ashore: A History of Books, Libraries and Reading Among Seamen During the Age of Sail* (Hamden, CT: Archon Books, 1974) 1–16, 109–133 passim.

25. HBCA, PAM, A.24/13 fol. 13. Twelve Common Prayer Books were listed on the Invoice of Goods for Prince of Wales Fort, 1777. In the following year, a similar invoice for Albany lists twenty-four Common Prayer Books, a quarto Bible, and a large Common Prayer Book with Psalms; A.24/13 fol. 43.

26. HBCA, PAM, A.6/7 fol. 110, London General Letters Outward, 1741.

27. Payne, *The Most Respectable Place* 108–111.

28. William Campbell, a Clerk from 1885–1910, referred to a library at York Factory in which 'the books were collected by the Officers of the Company at their own expense.' HBCA, PAM, A.12/FT 340/1/5 fol. 10–11, London Subject Files on the Fur Trade, Staff File on William Campbell, cited in Beattie 9–10.

29. Other paternalistic institutions eventually provided books in the Northwest, notably the Church Missionary Society which set up a press at Moose Factory, 1853–1859. This press was primarily for the purposes however of 'spreading the Word' to the aboriginal peoples rather than to provide reading matter for the fur trading staff; see Joyce M. Banks, 'The Church Missionary Society Press at Moose Factory: 1853–1859,' *Journal of the Canadian Church Historical Society* 26.2 (1984): 69–80.

30. The commissions are in HBCA, PAM, A.16/111 and A.16/112. The request for the gravestone (complete with inscription) is found in A.16/112 fol. 5. The run is unbroken from 1787 to 1814, with the exception of 1789–1791, for which years there is no data in the ledgers of commissions.

31. Wages varied widely between officers and servants. See Glyndwr Williams, ed., *Andrew Graham's Observations on Hudson's Bay 1769–91* (London: Hudson's Bay Record Society, 1969) transcribed in Warkentin, *Canadian Exploration Literature* 104–105. See Payne, *The Most Respectable Place* 108 for comments on rising wages in the early nineteenth century.

32. HBCA, PAM, A.12/FT 340/4/10, Inventory of the property of the late Mr T.C. Rowland,

Medical Officer to the Hudson's Bay Co.

33. James G. MacGregor, *Peter Fidler: Canada's Forgotten Surveyor, 1769–1822* (Toronto: McClelland and Stewart, 1966).

34. HBCA, PAM, Search File, Peter Fidler. Typescript dated 2.2.1933 of Fidler's Will, 'Original at Somerset House, Records of the Prerogative Court of Canterbury.' The Red River Library had been founded in 1816.

35. I am very grateful to both Judith Hudson Beattie of HBCA and to Leslie Castling of the Legislative Library of Manitoba for granting access to the volumes owned by Fidler and for the provision of copies of cataloguing records and title pages.

36. An example, offering twelve titles and price information, is included in HBCA, PAM, RB FTL McKR 51. P. Brydone. *A Tour Through Sicily and Malta*. Vol 1. London: Printed for W. Strahan and T. Cadell, 1776. This list covers several subjects including travel, law, history, politics and medicine.

37. As more of Peter Fidler's books survive than those of any other individual in the fur trade, his collection has been the focus of several enquiries. See for example Debra Lindsay, 'Peter Fidler's Library: Philosophy and Science in Rupert's Land,' Peter F. McNally, ed., *Readings in Canadian Library History* (Ottawa: Canadian Library Association, 1986) 209–229.

38. HBCA, PAM, Rare Book Collection. The Gaelic work is RB FTL McKR 219A. *Eachdraidh na H-Alba* (Glasgow: A. Sinclair, 1867). An edition with this date does not appear in Mary Ferguson and Ann Matheson, *Scottish Gaelic Union Catalogue* (Edinburgh: National Library of Scotland, 1984) [SGUC]. The SGUC refers to an edition by the same publisher in 1863; SGUC #1652.

39. HBCA, PAM, RB FTL McKR 65.

40. Fidler paid £3 8s for the 2 volumes and they are now in the Rare Book Collection in the Legislative Library of Manitoba; F1–1, F1–2.

41. HBCA, PAM, RB FTL PF 34.

42. HBCA, PAM, A.16/112 fol. 79d.

43. HBCA, PAM, A.16/112 fol. 6.

44. HBCA, PAM, A.16/112 fol. 36d. This includes Joseph Howse's order of 1805, for three French titles.

45. HBCA, PAM, A.16/111 fol. 51. The encyclopedia cost Stayner £22.

46. However, in 1801 and 1802 the name Lindsell appears beside several individual commissions.

47. HBCA, PAM, A.16/111 and A.16/112, Officers' and Servants' Commissions, 1787–1814.

48. HBCA, PAM, A.16/113 p. 15.

49. HBCA, PAM, A.16/113 p. 42–43.

50. John Feather, 'British Publishing in the Eighteenth Century: A Preliminary Subject Analysis,' *The Library* 8.1 (1986): 32–46.

51. Simon Eliot, *Some Patterns and Trends in British Publishing, 1800–1919* (London: The Bibliographical Society, 1994) 130, Appendix C, Table C8.

52. Feather 35–37.

53. The figure also excludes approximately 3% of the fur trade titles which have been classified as 'miscellaneous.'

54. HBCA, PAM, A.16/111 fol. 57. William Howse's book order, 1799. This includes, amongst others, requests for 'Palermo's Amusing Practice of the Italian Language' and 'A Spanish Dictionary.'

55. W. Kaye Lamb, ed., *Sixteen Years in the Indian Country: The Journal of Daniel Williams Harmon 1800–1816* (Toronto: Macmillan, 1957), entry for July 12, 1805 cited in Warkentin, *Canadian Exploration Literature* 251.

56. HBCA, PAM. E.3/5 fol. 1d. Peter Fidler's Journal of Exploration and Survey, 1807–1808. Letter from Peter Fidler, York Factory, to the governing committee in London, August 22,

1808. In this instance, Fidler refers to topographic information from the journals of William Linklater and Malcolm Ross.

57. See Michael Payne's work on the social life of the fur trade, for example his dissertation 'Daily Life on Western Hudson Bay, 1714 to 1870: A Social History of York Factory and Churchill.' Ph.D. dissertation. Ottawa: Carleton University, 1989.

58. See for example the 'Small histories' advertised by the merchants Campbell and Stewart in Saint John; *Royal Gazette and New Brunswick Advertiser* (October 17, 1786): [3].

59. HBCA, PAM, A.16/111 and A.15/112, Officers' and Servants' Commissions.

60. HBCA, PAM, A.16/111 fol. 51.

61. HBCA, PAM. A.16/111 fol. 48d.

62. HBCA, PAM. A.16/111 fol. 55d.

63. Payne, *The Most Respectable Place* 28, 31–33.

64. HBCA, PAM, A.67/28 fol. 298–305, Bills and Receipts, 1840–1900.

65. Quoted in Payne and Thomas 47, emphasis mine.

66. For a list of the extant book inventories and catalogues, see Beattie 11–15, Appendix A. I am indebted to Judith Hudson Beattie for sharing further unpublished research materials on the various post libraries.

67. Payne and Thomas 46.

68. HBCA, PAM, B.200/b/26 p. 41, Anderson to Officers, March 9, 1852.

69. HBCA, PAM, B.76/d/2 fol. 30d-31, Inventory dated November 12, 1821, listed by John Lee Lewes and A. MacDonald.

70. HBCA, PAM, A10/21 fol. 219, London Inward Correspondence General, 1846.

71. HBCA, PAM, A10/21 fol. 220.

72. *Nineteenth Century Short Title Catalogue* [CD-ROM] (Newcastle-upon-Tyne: Avero, 1996) #2S8676 and #2T21364.

73. Jennifer S.H. Brown, "A Parcel of Upstart Scotchmen', *The Beaver* (February/March 1988): 4–7; and for details of place of origin of one post's staff, see Payne, *The Most Respectable Place* 34–37, 47, Tables 1–3 and Table 5.

74. HBCA, PAM, A.10/31 fol 245, Letter from James Anderson, Fort Simpson, to Eden Colvile, 16th March, 1852.

75. HBCA, PAM, A.10/33, List of Books for McKenzies [sic] River Library, to be purchased from Mr. Thomas Murray, 8 Argyle Street, Glasgow.

76. HBCA, PAM, B.3/2/4 Box 1, dated Moose Factory, September 6, 1876.

77. HBCA, PAM, RG3/4A/4, Catalogue of Nelson River Library, York Factory, Man., May 1918.

78. HBCA, PAM, RG3/4A/4, Catalogue of Nelson River Library.

79. Eliot 43–58, Section C and 127–133, Appendix C.

80. HBCA, PAM, A.24/45, Invoice Book of Shipments to Hudson's Bay, General.

81. HBCA, PAM, A.10/21, London Inward Correspondence, General. Alexander Millar to Archibald Barclay, May 20, 1846.

82. The correspondence of David Hall, bookseller in Philadelphia, offers many examples of the system of sending multiple copies of documents by different ships; American Philosophical Society, Hall Papers, Letter Books, 1750–1771; for example Hall to Alexander Kincaid, Edinburgh, December 5, 1767.

83. For details of credit arrangements, see James Raven, 'Establishing and Maintaining Credit Lines Overseas: The Case of the Export Book Trade from London in the Eighteenth Century, Mechanisms and Personnel,' *Des personnes aux institutions réseaux et culture du crédit du XVIe au XXe siècle en Europe.* dir. Laurence Fontaine et Paul Servais (Mons, Belgium: Fucam, 1997) 144–162.

84. HBCA, PAM, A.10/31, Anderson to Colvile, March 16, 1852.

85. Not all colonial booksellers built insurance and freight charges into their retail book prices,

however. See for example, Robert Fletcher's advertisement in Halifax in which he offers 138 titles at the 'London Price' *Nova Scotia Gazette and Weekly Chronicle* (May 7, 1771): [3].

86. Mark C. Bartlett, comp. *Pre-1701 Imprints in Nova Scotia Collections* (Halifax: [s.n.], 1994).

87. See Note 7.

88. HBCA, PAM, RB FTL YF 25, Jean Baptiste DuHamel, *De Consensii Veteris et Novae Philosophiae Libri Quatuor* (Rouen: Jacobum Lucas, 1675); RB FTL YF 17, Pliny the Younger, C. *Plinii Caecilii Secundi: Vita Epistolarum Panegyricus.* [title page missing].

89. HBCA, PAM, A.46/7, 'The following is a List of the Company's Books in the Book Case in the Board Room [1802–1819].' 63 titles are listed in 121 volumes (the latter includes 20 volumes of Statutes). Exploration and travel literature for the Northwest, and other parts of the continent form the largest subject group.

90. For lists of servants' book orders see, for example, Jan Fergus, 'Provincial Servants' Reading in the Late Eighteenth Century,' *The Practice and Representation of Reading in England*, ed. James Raven, Helen Small and Naomi Tadmor (Cambridge: Cambridge University Press, 1996) 202–225.

91. For explorers and fur traders as authors see, for example, Ian Maclaren, 'Exploration/Travel Literature and the Evolution of the Author,' *International Journal of Canadian Studies/Revue internationale d'études canadiennes* 5 (1992): 39–68.

92. For example, Andrew Graham refers by specific page numbers to Guthrie's 'Dissertation on the Climate of Russia' published in the *Transactions of the Royal Society of Edinburgh*. HBCA, PAM, E.2/12 Graham, 'Observations' p. 602. However, much care must be taken with such apparent evidence of book availability in the Northwest; Graham wrote much of this particular journal in Scotland after his retirement and therefore his references might have been added then.

93. Saskatchewan Archives Board (Saskatoon). Morton Papers. II A 32 A 5 xiii. Morton refers to the Masson Collection in the Dominion Archives (now the National Archives of Canada). Roderick McKenzie's volume of notes is M420 in the collection.

CRUSOE'S BOOKS:
THE SCOTTISH EMIGRANT READER IN THE NINETEENTH CENTURY[1]

BILL BELL

AFTER I HAD been there about ten or twelve days, it came into my thoughts that I should lose my reckoning of time for want of books and pen and ink, and should even forget the sabbath days from the working days; but to prevent this I cut with my knife upon a large post, in capital letters, and making it into a great cross I set it upon the shore where I first landed, viz. 'I came on shore here on 30th Sept. 1659' . . . among the many things which I brought out of the ship in the several voyages . . . in particular, pens, ink, and paper, several parcels in the captain's, mate's, gunner's, and carpenter's keeping, three or four compasses, some mathematical instruments, dials, perspectives, charts, and books of navigation, all of which I huddled together, whether I might want them or no; also I found three very good Bibles which came to me in my cargo from England, and which I had pack'd up among my things; some Portugueze books also, and among them two or three popish prayer-books, and several other books, all of which I carefully secur'd.

THUS DEFOE PROVIDES a carefully chosen catalogue of items essential for Crusoe's survival in a strange land. Perhaps predictably, among the principal items to be secured in his forays out to the wrecked vessel are the paraphernalia of science – charts, mathematical instruments, compasses; yet, as experience has taught him, just as important to personal definition and orientation in an unfamiliar landscape are the precious commodities of books, ink, and paper. Cultural memory is in exile contingent on – even reinforced by – the continued practices of reading and writing.[2]

The pages that follow will attempt to explore the relationship between the text and the experience of the exile. How exactly does the act of reading reinforce or challenge the cultural assumptions of the reader far from home? What, in more general terms, is the connection between the circulation of texts and the preservation of cultural identity under strange skies? Although most of the following examples will relate to the Scottish diaspora in the nineteenth century, it is hoped that some of the larger questions addressed in this essay will suggest something of the contribution that the sociology of the text can begin to make towards what might be called a geography of communications.

PORTABLE CULTURE

One important aspect of Scotland's complex fate over the past 300 years has been the scale of its mass migrations. From the first Highland Clearances in the eighteenth century to the assisted passages taken to Australia, Canada, and New Zealand in the twentieth, Scots have been on the move. By the early nineteenth century the Scottish emigrant experience was one that was surrounded by print, from before departure, throughout the journey, and if anything even more intensely so after arrival.[3]

The great wave of nineteenth-century Scottish emigration was to occur at a time of conspicuously growing literacy and so it was perhaps no coincidence that the causes of reading and emigration were to be constantly associated in the rhetoric of the period. 'After the daily labour of cultivating their new fields,' opined one Glasgow newspaper on the establishment of a settlers library in Upper Canada in 1820, immigrants would now be able 'to retire and cultivate the best of fields, the human mind'.[4] One Presbyterian minister advised his Australian-bound audience in 1851 that they might profitably employ their time on the long voyage 'in reading what will improve your mind and your heart also. . . in order to keep up with what is contemptuously styled the 'march of intellect'.[5] With the latter in mind, John Mathison of Aberdeen published in 1834 his *Counsel for Emigrants* to North America in which it was enthusiastically claimed that 'a very great number of works relating to Canada may be perused with advantage', several of which could be purchased 'for less than a shilling, afford both information and amusement for the Emigrant, and are wonderful instances of the perfection to which cheap literature is brought'.[6] Reverend David McKenzie even went so far as to prescribe a healthy supply of cheap literature as an antidote to shipboard mischief:

Shipboard is your place of study. Consider every hour valuable, and diligently employ it in reading or meditation. It is want of employment that has been the most frequent occasion of quarrels among passengers on a long voyage. . . . In ancient times, those who went down to the sea in ships might no doubt have seen great wonders in the deep, for everything was then new, and before the art of printing . . . the information of mankind was very limited; but *tempora mutuantur,* – for neither the 'Penny Encyclopædia' nor 'Chambers' Information for the People' was then known.[7]

So continued a series of concerted campaigns on the part of improvers, church organisations, and government agencies to promote overseas settlement, as tracts, pamphlets, newspaper articles, and posters poured from the presses in Glasgow, Edinburgh, and London. Although not unique to the nineteenth century, the circulation of advertisements publicising the emigration cause was by mid-century at an all-time high. In 1851 John Hill Burton remarked that in the most destitute parts of Britain 'one may read, stuck to the walls as decorations, the announcements of the Emigration Board'.[8] From the 1860s on, the production of promotional maps and guides was made a public priority, with agencies regularly providing reference rooms where prospective emigrants could read the literature freely, consult maps, and inspect registers of available property. Such advertising would become increasingly pervasive as the century progressed. Requesting in 1878 a subsidy for the publication of a newspaper for the promotion of emigration, Henry Simpson wrote to the Minister of Agriculture in terms explicitly connecting the causes of emigration and literacy: Canada, claimed Simpson, was 'almost a sealed book to the ordinary British farmer and small capitalist'. He need not have feared. Within a decade, a government directive had gone out requiring a map of Canada to be displayed in every British school and a copy of the *Hand Book for Settlers* was presented to every pupil.

Perhaps the most successful means of publicising emigration was in the 'letter home', a format which appeared regularly in the popular press. These were usually anonymous accounts of life in the New World, written apparently for the benefit of the settler's family, and usually concluding with an exhortation to family and friends. So successful was the format to become that government officials, recognising its effectiveness as propaganda, had by mid-century begun to solicit favourable accounts from the colonies. Malcolm Cameron, Minister of Agriculture, adopted the practice in his promotion of Canada in the 1850s, one of the most prolific suppliers being Alexander Somerville of Hamilton who for seventeen years (1860–77) wrote for publication in the British press for a regular monthly fee of twenty dollars.[9]

Experience in the New World was, to say the least, heavily mediated in such documents. Predictably, many of those who read with delight glowing accounts of life in Utopia would fail to recognise the place when they landed. Throughout the century commentators were to remark on the disparity between emigrant experience and official representations of colonial life. One of the most critical opponents of emigration propaganda was John McDonald, who wrote in 1821 that 'it is by no means the ideal paradise which it is represented to be . . . all the truth which has both been written and printed respecting Upper Canada, would not cover one-half of the lies which have been told'.[10] By mid-century the situation had not improved, causing one commentator to remark in 1851 on 'how large – how formidably large – are the elements of deception in the means of information which the emigrant has usually at hand'.[11] Such a sobering view of official print culture was often confirmed by nineteenth-century emigrants themselves, who frequently wrote home bitterly about how they had been misled by published information. 'It is absurd to think that all the *Otago Journal* is true', wrote one disappointed emigré to his family in 1849. 'The gammon that the first comers wrote home', commented another wryly, 'and which is come back here in the New Zealand journals, is dreadfully absurd exaggeration, nonsense, foolishness'.[12]

Such propaganda was to generate widespread mistrust of the printed word among working class communities, causing the Scots-Canadian poet Alexander McLachlan to write bitterly:

> And pious folks with their tracts,
> When our dens they enter in,
> They point to our shirtless backs,
> As the fruit of beer and gin . . .
> And they quote us texts to prove,
> That our hearts are hard as stone.[13]

As one witness to the Select Committee on Postage reported in 1839, as a result of their increased scepticism about the reliability of officially produced documents the poor had learned to privilege the private letter over the printed text as a source of information. In his study of nineteenth-century immigrant communities in Australia, Richard Broome observes how compensation was found by 'many colonists [who] travelled "home" in their thoughts. Thousands of wax-sealed letters crossed the sea . . . precious lifelines between the old and new worlds'.[14] In settler society, the letter from home could function as a community event as well as a private mode of communication, these precious documents often being passed from hand to hand, and routinely read aloud. In a world of dubious print, the correspondence between communities of friends and relatives was one of the most important means of maintaining a sense of authentic collective identity for the nineteenth-century settler.

Another way in which the individual could participate in familiar cultural networks after arrival was through the casual flow of unofficial print that was regularly sent out and back from the colonies, between family members and friends. Perhaps the best source of information about actual reading conditions on the nineteenth-century frontier is to be found not in the printed record but in the accounts left by settlers themselves in diaries and letters, many of which contain requests for reading matter from home. Local newspapers seem to have been particularly desirable, not simply because they were relatively cheap to procure – although this was clearly a factor – but also because the newspaper represented a more immediate and tangible link with the home community. As Ross Harvey observes in his study of the New Zealand press in this period, the newspaper from home carried intense symbolic significance for the immigrant, not least in its power to evoke nostalgia for the culturally familiar.[15] Thus we find the Toronto farmer James Reid writing to an Ayrshire friend in 1849, 'I employ a great deal of my time reading. I have the whole of Thomas Dicks works, Dr Chalmers, and Stackhouses History of the Bible and . . . a number of inferior works. Please send me a newspaper or two in the Spring with an account of the ploughing matches and you will oblige an old friend.'[16]

Despite the optimism of the experts, with a severely limited cargo allowance (a mere 20 cubic feet per passenger bound for Australia in the 1850s) with houses to build and furnish, children to feed and clothe, and crops to plant, it is unlikely that many books beyond Bibles and catechisms – perhaps the odd volume of *Pilgrim's Progress* – would have found their way on the voyage. Those that did would most likely have been locked up tight in the hold throughout the journey. As one official source advised Montreal passengers in 1842 'the baggage of emigrants should consist only of their wearing apparel, with such bedding and utensils for cooking as may be required on the voyage . . . any articles not to be used at sea, ought to be packed in water-tight cases, or trunks, not exceeding 80 or 90 pounds in weight'.[17] A further prohibition was the high duty payable on the importation of printed matter, a luxury which it was often assumed the steerage passenger could well do without. As the British Vice-Consul and Agent of the Canada Land Company warned would-be emigrants in 1833, they would 'have to pay duties on little which they commonly have – say . . . linen . . . tools . . . books'.

In response to such privation, several philanthropic organisations were to offer financial assistance for the subsidy of reading on board emigrant vessels, even in some cases offering to offset the high cost of importation. In 1821, the Committee on Emigration from the West of Scotland to the Settlements in Upper Canada resolved at their Glasgow meeting:

that the luggage of the Emigrants be restricted to their body and bed-clothes, pots and pans, a small assortment of crockery ware, and a few articles necessary for their own immediate use; and that no furniture be carried out, such as chests of drawers, clock-cases, bed steads, chairs, tables, or washing-tubs, unless the emigrants are in sufficient circumstances to pay for the transport of the same from Quebec to the place of settlement; but the books which they may have, as their private library, may be allowed; and the whole must be closely packed in small and sufficient chests, boxes, or bagging.[18]

With private libraries (such as they were) packed away, steerage passengers would sometimes be invited to entertain themselves with devotional and improving reading matter issued on board by emigrant societies and church organisations. By the first half of the nineteenth century such arrangements appear to have been common on emigrant vessels. John Frazer of Glasgow records in his Canada-bound diary for 1837, 'Mr John M Hamilton and myself, by request of the Captn. distributed religious tracts among the Passengers, many of whom could not read, those who could accepted them with avidity.'[19] In some instances the distribution of shipboard reading matter was more carefully orchestrated in the form of lending libraries. Upon his arrival in Sydney in February 1850, schoolmaster Richard Murphy was pleased to report that 'the box of books granted by the Committee of the Emigrant School Fund was found very serviceable, was well read by the emigrants, and distributed to them on leaving'.[20] In 1848 the Otago Association similarly acknowledged a liberal bequest of books donated by various civic organisations for the founding of the Dunedin community, among them a copy of the *Encyclopædia Britannica* contributed by the publisher and Lord Provost of Edinburgh, Adam Black. The library, reported the Association with unrestrained pride, was 'despatched with parties of emigrants in three ships, to whom doubtless they have been a profitable source of amusement and instruction at sea'.[21] Despite these official attempts to alleviate the situation, the relative scarcity of shipboard reading matter continued to be a problem, even on vessels where some provision had been made (for all of the optimistic committee reports, we know that only one book per week among six adults was in actuality provided on board the three Otago vessels).[22] The most compelling evidence of attempts to compensate for the paucity of shipboard entertainment are perhaps to be found in the many letters and journal entries left by emigrés themselves. As one traveller noted in his shipboard diary 'tho' the forgoing pages of this journal may not be particularly important or interesting to any, yet they may help to while away the tedium of the hour, while nothing better can be had.'[23]

TRANSPLANTED NETWORKS

According to Benedict Anderson, the imagination of cultural synchronicity across vast distances was to a great extent made possible in the nineteenth century through the mediation of what Anderson calls 'print-capitalism':

> It became conceivable to dwell on the Peruvian altiplano, on the pampas of Argentina, or the harbours of 'New' England, and yet feel connected to certain regions or communities, thousands of miles away, in England or the Iberian peninsula. One could be fully aware of a shared language and a religious faith (to varying degrees), customs and traditions, without any great expectation of meeting one's partners.[24]

Thus Anderson situates commercial textuality at the centre of the colonial project, mediating and defining a common imperial identity for geographically disparate groups. Without print, so the argument goes, the colonial project would not to the same extent have been possible. In her recent survey of *Colonial and Postcolonial Literature*, Elke Boehmer argues similarly for the importance of what she calls the 'textuality of empire':

> At its height the British Empire was a vast communications network . . . [and] at least in part, a textual exercise. . . . The Empire in its heyday was conceived and maintained in an array of writings – political treatises, diaries, acts, and edicts, administrative records and gazetteers, missionaries' reports, notebooks, memoirs, popular verse, government briefs, letters "home" and letters back to settlers.

Through such communications networks, argues Boehmer, 'colonization seeded across widely separate and vastly different territories cultural symbols which exhibited a remarkable synonymity'.[25]

Helpful as they are in defining the mechanics of imperial ideology, such totalising perspectives do little in the end to account for the actuality of settlement life. To pay due attention to the *specificity* of emigrant experience is to be sceptical of the very 'synonymity' which is bound up with the homogenising rhetoric of Empire. Furthermore, analyses that unproblematically deploy the opposition of coloniser/colonised avoid at their peril questions of race, religion, gender, and class difference *between* and *within* settler communities, close examinations of which militate against the very idea of a homogenous 'British' colonial practice. Immense diversity can alone be seen in the multiple versions of Scottishness that were transplanted in a myriad of different complexions and intensities across the world, as variations of class, language, and religion to be found at home were time and again replicated overseas, often in exaggerated forms. Whenever we think of the Scottish immigrant community, therefore, it must always be with the awareness that we are not speaking of a single cultural unit, but a whole range of regional, religious, economic groups with their own distinct (though sometimes related) cultural networks.

In his study of the Irish in America, Charles Tilly has coined the phrase 'transplanted networks' as one way of explaining the heterogeneity of immigrant experience. Variant identities in a colonial context, argues Tilly, are not the result of monolithic imperial ideologies, nor are they spontaneous social constructs, but historic consequences of simultaneously existing information networks which replicate and modify themselves in new geo-political contexts. Offering an alternative to conventional models of immigration history in what he calls 'network structure', Tilly argues that 'instead of a series of individual transformations in the direction of a dominant . . . culture, migration involves negotiation of new relationships both within and across networks. Instead of individual status-striving, collective efforts to cope. Instead of wholesale transplantation, selective re-creation of social ties.'[26]

One way in which social ties were selectively recreated within settler communities was through the extension of familiar textual networks. 'For many networks,' argues Tilly, 'North America simply represented one more extension of circuits that had long served the same purpose within Europe'.[27] It was in the area of religion in particular that a devotion to cultural difference was most conspicuously in evidence, as throughout the nineteenth century vigorous campaigns were launched by missionary organisations to build infrastructures that would allow Scots wherever they were to resist assimilation through the practice of religion on their own familiar terms.[28] Unsurprisingly, it was in this area that Scottish settlers appear to have had the most clearly defined textual requirements.[29]

In the battles for the hearts and minds of displaced congregations, the printed word was often seen as an important point of stasis and authority in an otherwise unpredictable and unfamiliar environment. Some of the best efforts to ecumenise frontier religion were to be met, at best, with indifference; at worst, with outright antagonism. Reverend James Nisbet, who travelled on behalf of the Canada Sabbath School Union in 1848 met resistance from Anglicans and Methodists who, reported Nisbet, 'objected to our books as not going far enough in stating the truth respecting the Sacraments'.[30] Presbyterians could be just as intractable, if not more so. In an effort to maintain religious and cultural separatism the Biblical verse 'ye are a peculiar people' was regularly invoked by Scottish clergy in missionary sermons and tracts. One of the most zealous of these was John Dunmore Lang (famous for his use of the phrase 'there's nae folk like our ain folk') who was responsible for the resettlement of 4,000 Highlanders in Australia in the 1830s. Lang's scheme proceeded on the assumption that their religious beliefs, combined with their reliance on Gaelic, would make his charges impervious to the corrupting influence of convicts and Catholics, providing an antidote to the moral plague that Lang believed transportation had spread in the New World. Their language itself would place them, in his words, 'beyond the reach of contamination'.[31]

One of the most dramatic examples of this kind of socio-religious separatism at work is to be found in the New Zealand settlement of Waipu, involving the double migration of the followers of the Reverend Norman McLoud, who had settled around St Anne's, Nova Scotia, in the first half of the nineteenth century and who were to move *en masse* with their leader to north-west New Zealand on six ships between 1855–59. At a time when the colonial government was implementing its policy of so-called 'contiguity and concentration' its geographical isolation appears to have been what most commended Waipu to McLoud and his 900 followers. In her ethnographic study of the double migration, Maureen Molloy stresses the importance of the connection between isolation and kinship. 'The repeated emphasis on isolation from strangers', observes Molloy, suggests that the desire of the Nova Scotian settlers 'to maintain a geographical boundary between themselves and others was strong'. Before arrival the Normanites had arranged for the purchase of adjoining tracts of land in order to ensure that no contiguous blocks would be inhabited by non-Nova Scotians, in their words 'to prevent any strangers from being placed among them'.[32] It is this very isolation that today makes Waipu most intriguing from the point of view of the historian, providing as it does an interesting laboratory in which to try a range of cultural questions, not least those relating to reading habits and the circulation of texts in exile.

Among the farm implements, kitchen utensils, photographs, and letters, today's visitor to the Waipu settlers museum can find a relatively small but significant library of over a hundred volumes, which taken together offer a fascinating window on the book owning and reading habits of a small community over the better part of a century. Most revealing are the precious twice-travelled books that a number of emigrants were to bring with them from Scotland to Nova Scotia and thence on to New Zealand in the 1850s. The fly-leaf of one Gaelic Psalter intimates that it was 'used by Rev Norman McLeod, in his churches in Scotland, Nova Scotia, and Waipu, and by the pioneers in their homes for Family Worship'. Prior to his departure for Nova Scotia in 1845 Colin McDonald, a 35 year old native of Gourock, purchased a Gaelic New Testament printed in Edinburgh two year earlier. The same book accompanied him to New Zealand when he re-emigrated over a decade later.

Other members of the community were to acquire books during their sojourn in North America. In June 1846 Neil Campbell purchased a 16th edition of Crosby's *Key to Walkinghame's Tutor's Assistant* (1843), printed by Wilson & Co in York, Upper Canada, and was later to take it with him on board the Spray bound for Waipu in 1856. Daniel Robertson brought with him a family Bible printed in New Brunswick that he had acquired while he was living in Churchville, Nova Scotia. Norman McLennan had in 1847 purchased a brand new copy of Joseph Worcester's *Dictionary* (printed in Boston that same year) while he was living in Wareham, Massachussetts. This too came to Northland in 1855.

Books seem to have served important social as well as purely religious functions at Waipu and Scottish texts in general appear to have had high cultural significance. In 1884, an Edinburgh edition of *The Poetic Works of Robert Burns* was presented to the third-generation settler Christine McMillan by her prospective husband. Burns has always held strong symbolic importance for the emigrant Scot, and we can see in such gestures just how intimately bound up with the reading experience are expressions of kinship and ethnicity.[33] At a time when many New World Scots were happily participating in hybrid literary cultures, what is perhaps most remarkable is the length to which the Waipu settlers and their descendants went to acquire Scottish imprints well into the twentieth century, at a time when North American and Australian versions were far easier to obtain.[34] Of the Scottish imprints found at Waipu, almost half appear to have been purchased after settlement. If anything there appears to have been an increased bias towards texts of Scottish origin as time passed. At a meeting of the Waipu Library Committee in November 1890 'after some discussion, in regard of getting new Books . . . it was proposed that we send to Edin. for books to the value of £6'. In the following May 'correspondence & receipts in regard to Books received from Home was read . . . it was proposed that we pay half the expenses of getting the Books out from Home'. In spite of two migrations – one might even say because of two migrations – tangible links with a home many had never seen became increasingly important, and reading was one of the symbolic acts that made this possible.

In her study of reading practices in the American republic, Cathy Davidson – following Rolf Engelsing's account of the transition from an 'intensive' to an 'extensive' relationship with print – has argued that by the end of the eighteenth century 'the quality and the nature of reading was changing'. Instead of a highly concentrated and meditative relationship with the text, principally through the Bible, sermons, and tracts, secularisation and the widening availability of books had transformed the way that print was consumed. Davidson's account of the move from 'intensive' to 'extensive' reading patterns is one based on a belief in the more general transformation of political subjects into an active republican citizenry, and so the argument goes from 'elementary to advanced literateness'. 'The whole mentality of reading was changing,' argues Davidson, 'and, clearly, the Bible and the Psalter no longer occupied the singular place they once had in the life of the community or of the individual reader.'[35]

Such wholesale transitions do not necessarily apply to the many isolated settlements across nineteenth-century North America where the Bible and Catechism still held a privileged place in the daily life of the reading community, and where the preservation of religious values was often itself regarded as a deliberate act of opposition to the larger world beyond. In his account of the Normanite settlement in 1840s Nova Scotia, Neil Robinson remarks that 'in this conservative community . . . reading occupied a different role from that it enjoys today. The Bible provided an inexhaustible well of drama, poetry, and spiritual inspiration. . . . Even when the reader had memorised whole sections of them, he would return, in his rare intervals of leisure, to the comfort of the written word'. As society was becoming more generally secularised, so an active resistance to the dominant culture was exercised by a number of ethno-religious groups in the New World, influenced by and in turn necessitating an intense relationship with the authoritative text.

By the late nineteenth century, however, Scottish communities in industrial conurbations like Montreal, Sydney, and New York were becoming by degrees secularised and culturally integrated. Over time, the majority of settlers and their descendants – particularly urban dwellers – would take their place in increasingly hybrid print cultures, retaining only nominal links with home through letters, newspapers, and books. Yet myths of national origin have a tendency to gain potency in proportion to the extent that a community feels its ethnicity threatened, and it is at the very moment when Scots are becoming increasingly assimilated – religiously, racially, socially – that signifying practices emerge which serve to renew a sense of cultural difference. As Carl Klink observes in the context of Canadian literary culture, it was at the point of assimilation that a new form of Scottish writing was to emerge which was 'a reflection, in part, of a consciousness of race – racial origins, potentialitites, and disasters – a feeling which became increasingly intense towards the end of the century'.[36] It is perhaps no coincidence that the great wave of global

Caledonian activity occurs at exactly this moment. Witness the number of colonial editions of Burns that were produced from the 1870s on, as well as the volume of Scots vernacular poetry being written and read by second and subsequent generation immigrants who had never in their lives spoken the language. Yet the establishment of Highland games, clan gatherings, Scottish Rite temples, St Andrews and Burns societies, from Waipu to Hamilton, Melbourne to Johannesburg, often taken as evidence of a cultural confidence, might rather be the most obvious consequence of a crisis of identity, not so much a celebration as a reaction to the threat posed by emergent nationalism.

It is nevertheless those who can readily assimilate both culturally and economically that make the greatest success stories in the birth of a nation. Wherever there is money to be made, Robert Louis Stevenson once commented, there you will find Scots, and this was perhaps never truer than in Canada. As early as 1806 Judge Robert Thorpe could complain about an already established 'chain' of 'Scotch pedlars . . . linked from Halifax to Quebec, Montreal, Kingston, York, Niagara, & so on into Detroit' so powerful that it was proving detrimental to competitive trade.[37] The tendency of Scots to consolidation in business dealings was as true in the book trade as in other areas of commerce. 'Down to 1900', as one historian has observed, 'the Canadian village outside Quebec typically had its leading Kirk and minister, its Scottish schoolmaster and its Scottish-derived editor and printer'.[38] Though there was nothing unusually Scottish about his stock, in establishing his Quebec City business in 1795 with apprentices from Glasgow, John Neilson was not the last to set up shop with labour and equipment imported from home. Many of the dominant figures in the Canadian book trade before and after Confederation would continue to be part of a powerful network of booksellers, printers and publishers who had learned their professions in Aberdeen, Glasgow and Edinburgh and who kept themselves supplied by drawing on their trade connections at home and abroad: Armour & Ramsay of Montreal, Adam Stevenson & Company of Toronto, James Dawson of Pictou, and of course William Lyon McKenzie, to name but a few.

The role that the production, circulation, and reception of texts has had to play in the formation and preservation of cultural networks should be self-evident. Until recently, however, the study of emigration history has developed in relative isolation from a history of communications. And although historians have done much to analyse patterns of production and consumption, even where terms such as 'trade', 'distribution', and 'circulation' have been used, the tendency has been to regard the market from the perspective of *either* manufacturer *or* consumer, rarely in terms of the larger geographical neworks in which such transactions take place.

Over three decades ago, Wilfred Egglestone challenged the literary historian 'to trace the importance of . . . books in pioneer North America', arguing that no credible account of early Canadian culture would be possible until adequate attention had been paid to 'the reading public, the educational apparatus, the libraries, the printing presses, the publishers, the bookshops' that had made it all possible.[39] Thanks to the recent efforts of a number of scholars, this task has begun.[40] Much work remains. This article has offered no more than a brief *resumé* – by no means complete – of a number of areas that will reward further, more careful enquiry. To recognise the importance of textual communication to the emergence of societies is to begin to realise some of the ways in which the history of the book is now beginning to inform the history of culture.

REFERENCES

1. A version of this paper originally appeared in the *Papers of the Bibliographical Society of Canada,* 36:2, Fall 1998, 87–106, to which I am grateful for permission to reproduce it here.

2. Apart from the Bible and *Pilgrim's Progress, Robinson Crusoe* was throughout the nineteenth century among the most frequently recommended reading matter for the prospective emigrant, the protagonist himself representing the embodiment of Protestant self-reliance. 'To teach the mechanic the use of inventive resources in an emigration field,' wrote one Scottish writer in the 1850s, 'there could be no better book than *Robinson Crusoe'*. [John Hill Burton, *The Emigrant's Manual* (Edinburgh: Chambers, 1850), p. 23.] A decade earlier, James Brown had even referred unironically to Scottish settlers in British North America as 'Canadian Crusoes'.

3. For a more detailed account of reading practices on emigrant ships, see B. Bell, 'Bound for Australia', *Journeys through the Market*, eds. R. Myers and M. Harris (Oak Knoll, 1999, 119–140).

4. Robert Lamond, *A Narrative of the Rise and Progress of Emigration from the Counties of Lanark and Renfrew to the New Settlements in Upper Canada* (Glasgow: Chalmers & Collins, 1821), p. 14.

5. David MacKenzie, *Ten Years in Australia* (London: William Orr, 1851), pp. 152–3.

6. John Mathison, *Counsel for Emigrants and Interesting Information* (Aberdeen: Mathison, 1834), p. x.

7. MacKenzie, *Ten Years in Australia,* pp. 152–3.

8. Burton, *Emigrant's Manual,* pp. 13–14.

9. Eventually, professional letter writers were dispatched for the express purpose of providing sympathetic accounts for the home reader. One of these, Peter O'Leary, was sent to Canada in 1884 for 'the purpose of writing letters to the English papers' about favourable conditions in the North-West. For a detailed discussion of emigration propaganda in a Canadian context, see chapter three, 'Wooing the Emigrant', in Norman MacDonald, *Canada: Immigration and Colonization 1841–1903* (Toronto, Macmillan), pp. 30–48.

10. John McDonald, *Voyage to Quebec and Journey from thence to New Lanark in Upper Canada* (Edinburgh: Andrew Jack, 1821), p. 12.

11. Burton, *Emigrant's Manual,* pp. 11–12

12. *Emigrants' Letters: Being a Collection of Recent Communications from Settlers in the British Colonies* (London: Trelawney Saunders, 1850), p. 92

13. Alexander McLachlan, *The Emigrant and Other Poems* (Toronto: Rollo & Adam, 1861), p. 202.

14. Richard Broome, *The Victorians Arriving* (McMahons Point, NSW, 1984), pp. 36–37. See

also Jane E. Harrison, *Until Next Year: Letter Writing and the Mails in the Canadas, 1640–1830* (Wilfred Laurier University Press, 1997).

15. See Ross Harvey, 'The Power of the Press in Colonial New Zealand,' *Papers of the Bibliographical Societies of Australia and New Zealand*, 20:2, 1996, 133.

16. James Reid to Thomas Gibson (January 1849), Archives of Ontario: MU 2382. It is possible that Reid purchased the books he mentions in Canada. Local Scottish newspapers would of course have been more difficult to acquire.

17. Cattermole, *Advantages of Emigration* [quoted in Mathison, 107]. Luggage allowance could vary widely: on the Shaw, Saville, & Albion Line to New Zealand in the 1860s, 'Every passenger in the first and second class was allowed half a ton measurement of luggage free of charge and in the steerage, a quarter of a ton [560lb]. Anything in excess of this had to be paid for at a fairly steep price.' [See Frank Bowen, *The Flag of the Southern Cross* (n.d.), p. 23]

18. Minutes of the Committee on Emigration from the West of Scotland to His Majesty's Settlements in Upper Canada, March 1821, quoted in Lamond, *A Narrative*, p. 40.

19. Journal of a voyage from Glasgow to New York. National Archives of Canada: MG 24 I 197:

20. *Emigrants' Letters: Being a Collection of Recent Communications from Settlers in the British Colonies* (London, 1850), p. 123.

21. *Otago Journal*, May 1848, pp. 30–31

22. One passenger reported to relatives that 'the congregational library was opened once a week, when books were returned and new ones issued' (*Otago Journal*, p. 42). In his shipboard journal the expedition's leader, Reverend Thomas Burns, dutifully records on February 1 1848: 'Issued from box No. 7 one volume of the Congl. Library to each mess'. [Rev Thomas Burns, Shipboard Diary, MS Otago Settlers Museum]. From a diary kept by another passenger we learn that a mess on board the Philip Laing constituted at least one male adult and four or five others. Thus was there provided one book per week between six passengers.

23. National Archives of Canada: MG 24 I 197. Another solution to the scarcity of print on board ship was the occasional publication of a shipboard newspaper. Detailed research on Australian shipboard newspapers, of which several examples survive, is currently being undertaken by Des Cowley and Shona Dewar at the La Trobe Library, Melbourne. Passengers on board the *Philip Laing* we know had access to two manuscript newspapers, one published weekly 'by a cabin passenger . . . another by a steerage passenger as often'. (*Otago Journal*, p. 42).

24. Benedict Anderson, *Imagined Communities: Reflections on the Origin and Spread of Nationalism* (London: Verso: 1991), p. 72.

25. Elleke Boehmer, *Colonial and Postcolonial Literature,* (Oxford University Press, 1995), pp. 13, 52.

26. Charles Tilly, 'Transplanted Networks', *Immigration Reconsidered,* ed. Virginia Yans-McLaughlin (Oxford University Press, 1990), p. 87.

27. Tilly, 'Transplanted Networks', p. 89.

28. The amount of archival material for the study of missionary publishing and printing for Canada alone is vast. Thanks to Leslie Howsam's work on the British and Foreign Bible Society, John Wiseman's work on the distribution of nineteenth-century missionary literature in Ontario, and John Moir's edition of the papers of the Glasgow Colonial Society, we are beginning to understand how these print networks were actually created and functioned on a daily basis.

29. George Parker has drawn attention to the case of Walter Johnstone, who reported to the Scottish Missionary Society that he found at the Charlottetown Despository no Psalms bound in with the Bibles, 'a sorry state of affairs for Scottish Christians'. [*The Beginnings of the Book Trade in Canada* (Toronto: University of Toronto Press, 1985), p. 19.] A helpful account of the book exporting activities of one of the most active religious organisation is provided in John S. Moir, 'Through Missionary Eyes: The Glasgow Colonial Society and

the Immigrant Experience in British North America,' *The Immigrant Experience,* ed. C. Kerrigan, (Guelph, 1989), pp. 95–109.

30. Diary of Rev James Nisbet, 1848. National Archives of Canada: MG24 J2S.

31. Quoted in Don Watson, *Caledonia Australis: Scottish Highlanders on the Frontier of Australia* (Sydney: Collins, 1984), p. 66.

32. Maureen Molloy, *Those who Speak to the Heart: The Nova Scotian Scots at Waipu 1854–1920* (Palmerston North: Dunmore, 1982), p. 126.

33. See Carol McGuirk, 'Burns and Nostalgia', *Burns Now*, ed. Kenneth Simpson (Edinburgh: Canongate Academic, 1994), pp. 31–69.

34. An analysis of imprints where place of origin can be determined demonstrates that a clear majority of the Waipu books were produced in Scotland (60), compared to 32 produced in England (though a number of these are in Gaelic. Although the community's principle spoken language was for many years Gaelic, most of its reading appears to have been, by necessity, in English. A high proportion of the Normanites devotional, and therefore most prized, books were in the native language). Nine titles originate in North America, and only three in New Zealand.

35. Cathy Davidson, *Revolution and the World* (Oxford: Oxford University Press, 1986), p. 72.

36. Carl Klink, *Literary History of Canada*, 2nd edition, volume one (Toronto: University of Toronto Press, 1976), p. 254.

37. Quoted in *DCB*, VII, 920.

38. Olive and Sydney Checkland, *Industry and Ethos: Scotland 1832–1914* (Edinburgh University Press, 1989), p. 158.

39. Wilfred Egglestone, *The Frontier and Canadian Letters* (Toronto: McClelland and Stewart, 1957), pp. 56, 33.

40. For the first sustained treatment of book trade links between Britain and Canada, see George Parker, *The Beginnings of the Book Trade in Canada*. More recent developments include Fiona Black on Scottish books in Canada [see, for example, 'Newspapers as primary sources in Canadian-Scottish book trade history: the example of Halifax, Nova Scotia, 1752–1820', *Epilogue* 10 (1995), 43–51; 'A Scottish element in Canadian print culture: some preliminary questions on definition and evidence', *Eighteenth-Century Scotland*, 10 (1996), 11–14; and ' "Advent'rous merchants and Atlantic waves": a preliminary study of the Scottish contribution to book availability in Halifax, Nova Scotia, 1752–1810' in *Myth, Migration and the Making of Memory: Scotia and Nova Scotia, 1700–1990*, Michael Vance and Marjorie Harper, eds. (Fredericton: Acadiensis Press, forthcoming)], Bertrum MacDonald's work on the Scottish Nova Scotian bookseller James Dawson, and John Wiseman's investigation of Ontario missionaries [see 'Bible and Tract Disseminating', *Publishing History* 18: 1985, 69–83; also 'Silent Companions: the Dissemination of Books and Periodicals in Nineteenth-Century Ontario', *Publishing History* 12: 1982, 17–50]. For a more wide-ranging consideration of the connections between the history of the book and colonial cultural history, see I. R. Willison's article in this volume.

ACROSS BOUNDARIES: THE HISTORY OF THE BOOK AND NATIONAL AND INTERNATIONAL LITERATURES IN ENGLISH

I.R.WILLISON

In September 1995 the University of London Centre for English Studies launched an MA course in the History of the Book, with an emphasis (though by no means an exclusive emphasis) on the history of the book in the English-speaking world. Unlike other courses in the subject elsewhere in the country, the London course should benefit, significantly, from the concentration and from the proximity of archival and other resources in the metropolis. At the same time the Centre is planning a similar, indeed related, course in the field of what we are calling National and International Literatures in English (NILE).

These two fields have implications for the general development of literary and cultural studies across boundaries in Europe as well as the English-speaking world. I would like to attempt a *tour d'horizon*, bringing together various elements of literary and cultural studies which, separately, are I am sure familiar enough to specialists.

I

We are involved here in issues which are both large and speculative; and I need to begin by considering their wider administrative context. Hitherto in Britain, initiatives in these two fields have been due mainly to individuals working within existing university teaching departments. Thus both the history of the book, and what was then called Commonwealth Literature, were first given a university base in the 1960s by Professor A.Norman Jeffares, head of the School of English at the University of Leeds (and one of the leading entre-preneurs in English studies at that time of substantial change within the academy). More recently, the leading post-graduate seminar in Britain in the history of the book has been established within the School of English at Oxford by our *chef d'orchestre*, D.F.McKenzie. More recently still, the first undergraduate course in the history of the book has been set up at Cambridge, in the history faculty; and in Scotland we have the courses at

Stirling and Edinburgh. Our situation in the University of London is different and, whether we in London like it or not, more high-profile – and exposed.

Because of its large complex of formal institutes for advanced research in the humanities – for example, the Warburg Institute (for the history of the classical tradition), the Institute of Historical Research, the Institute of Commonwealth Studies – the University of London has had to think of itself as the leading research university for the British Isles. However, in recent years, whatever the distinction of its individual institutes, the University of London has not exercised its leadership role effectively across the humanities as a whole – not only within Britain, but also as regards collaboration with other research centres in Europe, such as the *laboratoires* of the CNRS and the École Pratique des Hautes Études in France, or the Max Planck Institutes in Germany.

To remedy this, in August 1994 the institutes of the University of London were formally grouped into a School of Advanced Study. The aim is not only to strengthen their financial and political base *vis-à-vis* the demands of the mixed undergraduate and postgraduate teaching commitments of the Colleges within the University (which have been increasing relentlessly since the Second World War). The aim is also to train graduates for leadership in advanced research in what are perceived to be the relevant new fields of interdisciplinarity across the humanities 'where no [individual] Institute has hitherto operated'.[1] Our high profile, then, comes from the fact that the History of the Book and National and International Literatures in English are the first two fields to be thought of for promotion, in this respect, by the School of Advanced Study and its Centre for English Studies. Moreover, we need to pursue these fields in counterpoint to literary and cultural studies not only in Britain and the rest of the English-speaking world, but also in Europe, particularly in France.

II

In this connection we should remind ourselves that major changes in the rationale and structure of the humanities often follow on major, traumatic changes in the historical process itself. Thus the first systematisation of the very idea of 'research' in the universities of both France and England was, at least to some extent, a response to the violent demonstration of the political and cultural ascendancy of Germany with its victory in the Franco-Prussian War: a response embodied in the regime of Ernest Lavisse in historical, and Gustave Lanson in literary, studies in Paris; and in the regime of Lord Acton, Sir Adolphus William Ward, and their systematic, collaborative histories of politics and literature in Cambridge. In particular, Ward's *Cambridge History of English Literature*, to which George Saintsbury was by far the largest contributor (21 chapters to Ward's fourteen), involved the first systematic enlarging, and professionalising, of the study of British literary history to include an account of the history of the book (in the chapters written by H.G.Aldis, Secretary of the University Library).

Likewise, I think one can say that the promotion of the Annales school of history in France after 1945 – with its re-examining in depth of, among other things, the French *grands siècles* (and, notably, its featuring of the history of the book by Lucien Febvre, Henri-Jean Martin, and Roger Chartier) – together with the even more widely influential post-structuralism of Roland Barthes, Michel Foucault, and others, which reestablished Paris as the centre of critical intelligence in Europe, was in part a response to another *étrange défaite* at the hands of the Germans: a defeat which the *annaliste* Marc Bloch attributed, in part, to the rigidity and historical simplicities of the pre-war French educational and research establishment.[2]

Coming then to my main subject, one might say that the comparable British post-war cultural trauma was more a case of an *étrange victoire*: after victory in 1945, the dissolution of an imperial identity which had lasted for over two centuries. This identity had been constituted in no small measure by the hegemony, over much of the world, of canonical English literature (rather than music or art) – Shakespeare, Scott, Dickens, etc. – and its publishing and library infrastructure: for example, Macmillan (operating in New York and Toronto, in Bombay and Melbourne, as well as London), Nelson (textbook publisher to the Empire), Collins (Bible publisher to the Empire), and the British Museum and Bodleian libraries (archetypes for state libraries in Australia and South Africa, as well as North America).

However in post-war 'English Literature' as defined, say, by *The New Pelican Guide* (Volume 8, 'The Present'),[3] the leading position is no longer occupied by a native-born author, but by an Australian and winner of the Nobel Prize for Literature, Patrick White. A complete chapter in the *Guide* is devoted to the recipient of the first David Cohen Award for British Literature,[4] a writer from the West Indies, V.S.Naipaul (the re-issue of Volume 8 is now titled 'From Orwell to Naipaul'). Another chapter is devoted to the Nigerian writers, Chinua Achebe and Wole Soyinka, both candidates for the Nobel Prize – Soyinka being successful and now, with another West Indian (Derek Walcott), a South African (Nadine Gordimer), an Irishman (Seamus Heaney), and two Americans (Saul Bellow and Toni Morrison), the only living Nobel prizewinners writing in English. Among those mentioned in the Pelican chapter on 'India and the Novel' it is Salman Rushdie who has won the major London 'Booker of Bookers' prize[5] for his *Midnight's Children* and who 'is now widely perceived as perhaps Britain's only global writer'.[6] Many such authors write in, or include significant sections written in, a distinctive, post-colonial vernacular, or even 'creole' (showing the linguistic presence of the original, pre-colonial, inhabitants – West Indian, African, Aboriginal – as well as the classical linguistic manners of the colonists).[7] I realise that recent winners of the Goncourt, Femina and other literary prizes in France have not been by any means all native-born Frenchmen; but it is perceived that writers from the French *outremer* have been, until recently, far more effectively subjected to the hegemony of classical, metropolitan French, *négritude* or no *négritude*.[8]

Much recent thinking about our post-imperial literary and cultural experience, then, has been in terms of 'the Empire writes back' (to quote the title of a widely circulated, provocative exercise in Critical Theory),[9] across boundaries. This thinking in turn converges with the new, revisionist, interest of many general historians in the former 'peripheries' of empire interacting with the 'centre' as much through 'empires in the mind' as through trade and conquest (I refer to *The Cambridge Illustrated History of the British Empire*,[10] published in the course of 1945, and the multi-volume *Oxford History of the British Empire* now in progress and edited at Austin, Texas). Likewise new historians of the centre itself are 'determined . . . to consider Britain's changing place in the world, especially its relations with the Empire, the United States and Europe'.[11] The rationale of our project in the University of London is to attempt to bring intellectual order to what has seemed to traditional scholarship in the humanities to be mere cultural anarchy loosed upon the world (to borrow from Yeats): a search for order much assisted by concepts emerging from post-structuralist Critical Theory.

III

To make sense of the post-imperial literary and cultural experience of the English-speaking world we have to revise our concept of the autonomy, the exceptional nature, of national literatures – American, Canadian, Australian, and so on, as much as English. So far as English literature is concerned, the very idea of an English literary canon being the creation of writers born in the mother country, or assimilated from the colonies, is now beginning to be seen as an artificial construct invented for purposes of imperial cultural take-over by Adam Smith and other Scots after 1745;[12] reinforced by Macaulay in his widely influential Minute of 1835 on Indian education and the textbooks that followed in its wake;[13] then established in detail by the *Cambridge History of English Literature* in which the editors stated, airily enough, that 'the literature of the British colonies and of the United States are, in the main, the literature of the mother country, produced under other skies'.[14] (Saintsbury's contribution not only to the *Cambridge History* but also to the *British Empire Universities Modern English Dictionary*, ed. by E.D.Price and H.T.Peck (London and New York: Syndicate Publishing Co, 1914) – the only explicit 'imperial' piece by Saintsbury I have been able to identify – should perhaps be seen in this light).

On the other hand, the typically modern genre in the established English canon – the novel – can now be seen to have much of its origin and development in the experience of empire, rather than home:[15] not only the voyages etc. that provided thematic content for such as Daniel Defoe, but also the North American female captivity narratives, such as Mary Rowlandson's *The Soveraignty and Goodness of God, Together with the Faithfulness of His Promises Displayed* of 1682, which helped provide a new reading public, and therefore a new supportive structure, for the (by traditional standards) scandalous – yet compelling – enaction in narrative of endangered female virtue, famously embodied in Samuel Richardson's *Pamela*[16] and other novels (and canonised, at the European level, in Diderot's *Éloge de Richardson*). Again, the essence of the last clearly great movement in English literature – Modernism – may now be seen to have derived from writers 'writing back' in or from the former colonies, whether overseas (for example, Ezra Pound, Eliot) or the so-called 'home' colonies (for example, Wilde, Yeats and Joyce): a state of affairs continuing, it would seem, into our current 'post-modernist/post-colonial' literary phase.[17] In short a grasp of what, following Robert Crawford, we should call the 'devolved' nature of English literature enables us to see the apparent exoticism and anarchy of our post-war literary scene as merely the latest episode in the development of an essentially international literature in English.

At the same time we have to re-consider the various post-colonial literatures themselves, including the American, as parts of the same developing, international structure of literature in English. While by no means reverting to the old Cambridge doctrine of 'the literature of the mother-country, produced under other skies', such re-consideration nevertheless involves revising and enlarging our concept of 'influence' – again in terms not so much of the textual content which is specific and (so to speak) optional for a particular author, but of the governing operational strategy which is indispensable for any author: that without which he or she cannot work.

Let us take the leading case of the home-colonial Sir Walter Scott. The initial, massive influence of Scott's historical romances throughout the English-speaking world – for example, in Canada and India, as well as the United States – was not simply a matter of, say, James Fenimore Cooper ('the American Scott') choosing to 'produce' Scott's *mise en scène* 'under other skies': not simply a matter of translating the glamour of the British northern Border Country and Highlands to the new American frontier. In colonial, or newly post-colonial, cultures there was an 'absence of a distinctive authorial tradition' (as Cooper himself said, America was that country which had printers before it had authors);[18] and it was the whole 'vogue of historical romance', as a new literary genre and authorial project – a new strategy – that was 'almost immediately seized upon by critics and creative writers not only throughout America but throughout the entire Euramerican world as a model for literary nationalism, that is, for recording the history of national experience in fictive form'.[19] Even more ecumenically, the reception of Scott in India assisted the rise not only of Anglo-Indian, but also of vernacular, print-based authorship, for example the novels of the Bengali, Bankim Chandra Chatterjee (1838–1894) in which 'Scott acted as a catalyst for the feeling of nationalism that was germinating in the country'.[20]

Moreover, analysis of the common structure of literature in English and its attendant vernaculars reveals the constitutive and sustaining role, for the vogue of historical romance, of not only new but largely feminine reading publics. The work of Nina Baym on *Novels, Readers, and Reviewers – Responses to Fiction in Antebellum America*,[21] of Carole Gerson on *A Purer Taste: The Writing and Reading of Fiction in English in Nineteenth-Century Canada*,[22] and S. K.Das on the largely feminine public for Bankim's pioneering fiction[23], shows what Carole Gerson calls 'the long shadow of Sir Walter Scott' in the expansion and 'gendering' of the reading public and therefore of the literary marketplace in the English-speaking world.

Romance, then – as sustained, diversified, or (if you follow Q.D.Leavis in *Fiction and the Reading Public*) corrupted, by an ever-expanding reading public – constituted one of the major factors pervading the origins and course of literatures in English: most recently we have, for example, the demotic Onitsha Market romances in Nigeria, identified by Emmanuel Obiechina as part of the 'background to the West African novel' of Ekwensi, Achebe, Soyinka, and others.[24] However, as we see in the eventual resistance to the enduring, and even increasing, sentimentalities inherent in romance (in the case of Mark Twain in America, or Henry Lawson and the Sydney *Bulletin* school in Australia, or Frederick Philip Grove in Canada), the structural elements deriving from Scott helped bring on what, adapting Henry James's famous phrase, we might call the complex fate of post- colonial authorship. Indeed, if Northrop Frye is right in seeing Romance as one of the main conditions of literature in the Eurocentric West as a whole (the other being the Bible),[25] then it is not surprising that research into deep, pervasive, and problematic textual structures such as Romance should be indispensable for establishing and illuminating National and International Literatures in English as a field of study, one of the main characteristics of which is what post-colonial literary theorists call its 'hybridity'.[26]

However, as some other theorists go on to say, this is not to be thought of as 'an ahistorical hybridity . . . set up as a universal category . . . bracketing togther writing from very different contexts'.[27] To the historical discriminations made possible by 'extratextual research',[28] we must now turn our full attention.

IV

If the volatility of the reading public is one main structural characteristics of National and International Literatures in English from the point of view of the consumption of texts, the other characteristic, from the point of view of text production, is the deep, pervasive, and problematic influence of print: a generalisation, one might say, of Cooper's sense that in colonial and early post-colonial cultures there were printers before there were authors. Here we come to the role of the History of the Book in the London project in sharpening our whole approach to the subject.[29] All modern imperial cultures have been print-based in their origins (as has been asserted by, among others, Benedict Anderson in his influential essay, *Imagined Communities: Reflections on the Origin and Spread of Nationalism*);[30] and at least so far as the English-speaking world is concerned print culture has been, also, hybrid and volatile in its structure. In the colonial period, local printing tends to be dominated by the hyperactive, utilitarian modes suitable for the rapid construction of the local community (and then the confederation of local communities) on the frontier: the newspaper, the pamphlet. The colonial author – the Benjamin Franklin, the Joseph Howe (both printers of newspapers) – tends to emerge from within these modes. What has been called the Counterfrontier[31] – the interaction of the colonial élites, and their successors, with literary and other high-cultural traditions originating in the metropolis – depended on books, but books largely imported (or pirated) from the mother-country and archived in libraries modelled on those in the mother-country. Hence the importance of bookselling rather than publishing in the colony, with the colonial book-author, and even the transitional, early post-colonial author such as Cooper, looking to London as his main publishing base. Moreover, the eventual establishment of post-colonial literatures as seemingly independent going concerns depended on a degree of innovative collaboration between author and local book publisher that was unusual in settled literary cultures such as those in Europe. Among the classic cases are the collaboration between the first conspicuously successful home-colonial novelist, Scott, and the Edinburgh publishers Constable and Cadell, who, in their writing and publishing strategy for the *Waverley* novels, launched the three-decker as a major, characteristic format of the Victorian imperial book trade;[32] or the careful 'manufacturing' of Nathaniel Hawthorne 'into a personage' by the Boston publishers, Ticknor and Fields, which 'established "literature" as a market category' in the modern world;[33] or, in the twentieth century, the collaboration between Maxwell Perkins of Scribners in New York and Thomas Wolfe, Fitzgerald, and Hemingway, which established the creative – or at least midwifely – role of the publisher's in-house editor (as distinct from the more traditional, free-lance 'reader', such as Edward Garnett in London) in the bid for leadership in Anglophone fiction. Indeed, the conspicuousness of the impact of publishing on the structure of literary and cultural enterprise in the colonies and former colonies is one of the reasons for the pioneering contributions of North American scholars, such as William Charvat,[34] to the anglophone tradition in writing the history of the author-publisher relationship.

Such innovatory collaborations are evidence of a further and, so far, final complexity in the history of the book in the English-speaking world: that is, the shift of hegemony in publishing from London to New York, as the prelude to the current ascendancy of transnational conglomerates.[35] It is true that the earlier shift away from the traditional London book trade at the beginning of the nineteenth century, exemplified by Scott and Constable in Edinburgh, was masked by the steady expansion of Scottish enterprise down into London itself, exemplified by Murray (publisher of Byron and Darwin) and Macmillan (Hardy, James). It was this expansion and take-off in the metropolis that in fact reinforced the penetration of the emerging imperial market by publishers in Edinburgh and Glasgow: for example Blackwoods, whose *Magazine* George Orwell later pilloried as the foundation (together with Scotch whisky) of 'this godless civilisation', the British Empire;[36] or Nelsons and the influence of their school textbooks on the formation of colonial subjects;[37] or Collins, as publisher of Bibles outside Britain, and the impact of Bible reading on writers and their public in the Empire. (The project for the History of the Book in Scotland will be indispensable for illuminating this key aspect). Indeed, this earlier shift can be seen as part of the general take-over of the Empire by the home-colonial Scots from the latter part of the eighteenth century onwards that I mentioned earlier; as the shift to New York can be seen as part of the general take-over of the Empire by the Americans from 1918 onwards. In publishing this most recent shift is first shown most clearly in the willingness, and ability, of a new generation of cosmopolitan New York entrepreneurs, such as Alfred Knopf, Thomas Seltzer, Ben Huebsch and Random House to take over the task of handling the 'provincial',[38] but subversive, Modernist writers – principally Lawrence and Joyce – whose categorical demands had exceeded the moral horizon and capacity of the by then conservative London trade, and the financial capacity of the emigré, avant-garde trade in Paris and Florence.[39] The shift was reinforced by the appeal and competence of the cosmopolitan New York trade for the next generation of Modernist writers, emerging from the more remote areas of empire: for example, Random House and Faulkner from the Deep South, but most conspicuously, perhaps, the Australian Patrick White who, having found little sympathy in the London trade of the 1930s, found in Ben Huebsch 'his only lifeline in publishing' (in the words of his biographer, David Marr).[40] White's great novels, such as *The Tree of Man*, *Voss* and *Riders in the Chariot*, 'were written,' (to continue with Marr) 'in some ways, *for* Huebsch': another lead-ing case of intimate author-publisher partnership.

Looking at new elements in the story, one might think of the current phase in the interactive history of national and international literatures in English, and the history of the book, in terms of the mobilisation of new writers from the culturally remotest areas of former empire – Africa, the West Indies, the Pacific. Here the persistent vitality of oral culture has had to be harnessed to print, and to a viable reading public, by the boom in educational (rather than general or 'trade') publishing. Typical has been the story of Heinemann Educational Books, a post-war development within the traditional trade firm of William Heinemann, and of its director, Alan Hill, who developed a number of low-priced paperback series to carry these new writers into the world literary marketplace. Such were the *Caribbean Writers Series*, and above all, in collab-oration with Chinua Achebe as general editor, the *African Writers Series*;[41] the Achebe-Hill collaboration being one of the most recent of the great innovative author-publisher partnerships in our field. From the overall perspec-tive of the history of the book one might say that it was in part the financial and organisational pressures on the traditional undercapitalised 'trade' pub-lishing firm, entailed by such expansion, that exposed such firms to takeover by conglomerates riding on the post-Bretton Woods surge of the world finan-cial market.[42] As partial evidence of a process still under way, one might read the final chapters of Alan Hill's autobiography *In Pursuit of Publishing*, and its somewhat stoic account of the series of takeovers of Heinemann: by Tilling, then by BTR, by Octopus, by Reed International, and now, since the publication of the autobiography, by Elsevier.

V

To return to my opening remarks. So far as the unrivalled archival resources concentrated in London are concerned – the printed collections in the British Library, the manuscripts and papers there and in Public Record Office, and so on – I would here merely endorse Gayatri Chakravorty Spivak's general proposition: that to avoid 'succumbing to a nostalgia for lost origins', on either side of the colonial frontier, 'the critic must turn to the archives of imperial governance'.[43] The role of the critic, however, brings me, finally and very briefly, to the role of our field of study in the future development of a post-imperial, European, consortium of the humanities. This is a two-way matter.

In any new and rapidly expanding field such as ours there is a conspicuous need, as I have said, for what has become known as 'critical theory', to provide speculative concepts (such as hybridity, archive, creolisation) which enable the scholar to impose at least provisional order on the immense amount of initially strange evidence he encounters. Now in the field of post-colonial literatures in English, the leading theoreticians – for example, Edward Said and Homi Bhaba, as well as Gayatri Spivak – admit dependence on European, in particular French, speculators such as Barthes and Foucault. On the other hand, the actual practice of literature in the English-speaking world (whatever its thinness in theory) does reveal to the historian a far broader, if more complicated and problematic, base in cultural-political experience, now embodied in the imperial and post- imperial archive, than does the French dependence on exalted *maîtres penseurs* such as Hegel and Flaubert, Nietzsche and Mallarmé. The status of such *maîtres* has been conditioned, I suggest, by French, and German, reading publics of relatively stable, hier-archised, even constrained, *contrainte*,[44] structure, when compared to the Anglophone. This stability and constraint has been reflected (I further suggest) in the persistence of the essentially domestic publishing hegemony of an Hachette or an Armand Colin or a Gallimard (or in Germany, a Cotta or a Brockhaus or a Samuel Fischer), compared to the more 'imperial', yet inter-nationally seminal, base of a Longmans and a Macmillan, or a Nelson and a Collins, or an Oxford University Press and a Heinemann.

Much of all this is, clearly, not unique to the English-speaking world, and should prove applicable to, say, the history of the book and literature in the Spanish and Portuguese-speaking empires and post-empires. Be that as it may, it is researching and presenting such manifold, seminal, cultural experience, not only in London but wherever English studies are centred, that is one of the main contributions which imperial and post-imperial English Studies can make to a European cultural and scholarly community that was recently traumatised by revolution and war but is now facing permanent, post-European, global cohabitation.

REFERENCES

I am grateful to Terence Daintith, Warren Chernaik, and Warwick Gould of the University of London School of Advanced Study, and to Susheila Nasta of the NILE MA Course planning group, for looking over this paper. The opinions expressed are my own.

1. University of London, *School of Advanced Study*, (London, 1995), p.4.
2. Marc Bloch, *L'Étrange Défaite: Témoignage écrit en 1940, suivi de Écrits Clandestins 1942–1944. Avant-propos de Georges Altman* (Paris: Éditions Albin Michel, 1957), especially 'Sur la Réforme de l'Enseignement' (pp.246–262).
3. *The Present: Volume 8 of The New Pelican Guide to English Literature*, ed. by Boris Ford (Harmondsworth: Penguin Books, 1983).
4. Richard Todd, *Consuming Fictions: the Booker Prize and Fiction in Britain Today* (London: Bloomsbury, 1996), p.92.
5. ibid., p.314.
6. ibid., p.11.
7. Bill Ashcroft, Gareth Griffiths, and Helen Tiffin, 'Re-placing Language: Textual Strategies in

Post-colonial Writing', in *The Empire Writes Back: Theory and Practice in Post-colonial Literatures* (London: Routledge, 1989), pp.38–77. See also Elleke Boehmer, *Colonial and Postcolonial Literature: Migrant Metaphors* (Oxford: Oxford University Press, 1995), pp.206–22.

8. Christopher L.Miller, 'Theories of Africans: The Question of Literary Anthropology', in *"Race", Writing, and Difference*, ed. by Henry Louis Gates, Jr. (Chicago: The University of Chicago Press, 1986), p. 294: 'Ahmadou Kourouma's *Les Soleils des Indépendances* ... is to all appearances the first African novel to dare to appropriate and remold the French language to suit local conditions. Spoken African French is not identical to spoken Parisian French, but in writers like Camara Laye, one is at pains to find any difference, any Africanisms in the prose'. But see Belinda Jack, *Francophone Literatures: An Introductory Survey* (Oxford: Oxford University Press, 1996), for an extended revision of what she calls the 'extreme terms' of Miller's pioneering essay: 'It is now recognised that a plurality of literatures written in the French language or languages exists, even if the status of these literatures falls short of the autonomy of certain literatures written in English or Spanish' (p. 2), summarises her position. At the same time, whether – unlike French? – English has a 'perceived malleability' (Boehmer, p. 210), or 'merely appears more versatile because it has been used by a greater variety of people' (Ashcroft, Griffiths, and Tiffin, p. 40), would seem to be a major, complicated issue requiring further research.

9. Ashcroft, Griffiths, and Tiffin, *The Empire Writes Back*.

10. Andrew Porter, 'Empires in the Mind', in *The Cambridge Illustrated History of the British Empire*, ed. by P.J.Marshall (Cambridge: Cambridge University Press, 1996), pp. 185–223. See also Boehmer, 'Imperialism and Textuality', in *Colonial and Postcolonial Literature*, pp.12–59.

11. David Cannadine, 'Creating a New Penguin History: A Series Introduction' in *The Penguin History of Britain: A Major New Series from Penguin Books* [A Prospectus] (London: Penguin Books, 1996), p. 2.

12. Robert Crawford, 'The Scottish Invention of English Literature', in *Devolving English Literature* (Oxford: Clarendon Press, 1992), pp.16–44.

13. Chris Baldick, 'A Civilizing Subject', in *The Social Mission of English Criticism 1848–1932* (Oxford: Clarendon Press, 1983), pp.59–85; Urvashi Butalia, 'English Textbook, Indian Publisher', in *Rethinking English: Essays in Literature, Language, History*, ed. by Svati Joshi (Delhi: Oxford University Press, 1994), pp. 321–45.

14. A.W.Ward and A.R.Waller, 'Preface', *The Cambridge History of English Literature*, 15 vols (Cambridge: At the University Press, 1907–27), I, p.vii.

15. See for example Firdous Azim, *The Colonial Rise of the Novel* (London: Routledge, 1993). Azim ackowledges a debt to the theoretical writings of Said, Spivak, Bhaba and others (see Section V, above). For criticism of the simplifications etc involved in this approach, 'at least in regard to the sixteenth and early seventeenth centuries', see David Armitage, 'Literature and Empire', in *The Origins of Empire: British Overseas Enterprise to the Close of the Seventeenth Century*, ed N.Canny (Oxford: Oxford University Press, 1998) (*The Oxford History of the British Empire*, ed W.R.Louis, vol 1), pp. 99–123.

16. Nancy Armstrong and Leonard Tennenhouse, 'Why Categories Thrive', in *The Imaginary Puritan: Literature, Intellectual Labor, and the Origins of Personal Life* (Berkeley and Los Angeles: University of California Press, 1992), pp.196–216.

17. Crawford, 'Modernism as Provincialism', 'Barbarians', in *Devolving English Literature*, pp.216–305; Todd, *Consuming Fictions*. See also 'Postmodernism and Post-colonialism', in *The Post-colonial Studies Reader*, ed. by Bill Ashcroft, Gareth Griffiths, and Helen Tiffin (London: Routledge, 1995), pp.115–47.

18. Warner Berthoff, 'Continuity in Discontinuity: Literature in the American Situation', in

American Literature: Volume 9 of the New Pelican Guide to English Literature, ed. by Boris Ford (London: Penguin Books, 1988), p.655.

19. Lawrence Buell, *New England Literary Culture: From Revolution through Renaissance*, (Cambridge: Cambridge University Press, 1986), p.207.

20. Meenakshi Mukherjee, *Realism and Reality: The Novel and Society in India* (Delhi: Oxford University Press, 1985), p.43. For the influence of Scott and the historical romance in general as 'the paradigmatic novel of empire, appealing to nationalist, imperialist, and colonial readers alike', see Katie Trumpener, *Bardic Nationalism: The Romantic Novel and the British Empire* (Princeton: Princeton University Press, 1997)

21. (Ithaca: Cornell University Press, 1984).

22. (Toronto: University of Toronto Press, 1989).

23. Sisir Kumar Das, 'Factors of Change', in *A History of Indian Literature. Volume VIII, 1800–1910: Western Impact – Indian Response*, (New Delhi: Sahitya Akademi, 1991) p.44.

24. Emmanuel Obiechina, 'Background to the West African Novel', in *Culture, Tradition, and Society in the West African Novel* (Cambridge: Cambridge University Press, 1975), pp.12–13.

25. Northrop Frye, *The Secular Scripture: A Study of the Structure of Romance* (Cambridge MA: Harvard University Press, 1976).

26. See for example, 'Hybridity', in *The Post-colonial Studies Reader*, pp.181–209.

27. Boehmer, *Colonial and Postcolonial Literature*, p.245.

28. Boehmer, ibid, p.248.

29. See for example, the remark of Gareth Griffiths in the latest treatment of the field, *New National and Post-colonial Literatures: An Introduction*, ed. by Bruce King (Oxford: Clarendon Press, 1996), p.176: ' . . . recent theory needs to be balanced by more historical and sociological study, concentrating on the issue of who controlled and controls the production and consumption of the literary text; this affects the degree to which the colonial subject is silenced with at least as much force as the philosophic and linguistic issues which have exercised recent criticism'.

In what follows I incorporate aspects of the brief survey of the history of the book in the English-speaking world I made in 'The Role of the History of the Book in the Humanities', in *Zukunftsaspekte der Geisteswissenschaften: Vier Vorträge*, ed. by Bernhard Fabian (Hildesheim: Olms-Weidmann, 1996), pp 91–120.

30. (London: Verso, 1983): rev edn 1991.

31. Harry Huntt Ransom, 'The Collection of Knowledge in Texas', in *The Conscience of the University and Other essays* , ed. by Hazel H.Ransom (Austin TX: University of Texas Press, 1982), pp.72–81.

32. Jane Millgate, 'Publishing Context and Later Influence', in *Scott's Last Edition: A Study in Publishing History* (Edinburgh: At the University Press, 1987), pp.89–90. As her title indicates Professor Millgate concentrates on the other great innovation of Scott and his publishers, 'the idea of a collected edition with authorial revision', followed *inter alia*' by Dickens, James, Hardy and, more recently, Graham Greene ('Conclusion', pp.114–5).

33. Richard H.Brodhead, 'Manufacturing You into a Personage: Hawthorne, the Canon, and the Institutionalization of American Literature', in *The School of Hawthorne* (New York: Oxford University Press, 1986), pp.48–66.

34. William Charvat, *Literary Publishing in America, 1790–1850* (Philadelphia: University of Pennsylvania Press, 1959), and *The Profession of Authorship in America, 1800–1870*, ed. by Matthew J.Bruccoli (Columbus OH, Ohio State University Press, 1968).

35. Ian Willison, *The History of the Book in Twentieth-Century Britain and America: Perspective and Evidence*. The 1992 James Russell Wiggins Lecture (Worcester MA: American Antiquarian Society, 1993).

36. *The Complete Works of George Orwell. Volume Two. Burmese Days: A Novel*, ed. by Peter Davison (London: Secker & Warburg, 1986), p.31.

37. See, for example, V.S.Naipaul's reference to *Nelson's West Indian Reader* in his auto-biographical novel, *The Enigma of Arrival: A Novel in Five Sections* (Harmondsworth: Viking, 1987), p. 156.

38. Crawford, 'Modernism as Provincialism'.

39. Ian Willison, 'Introduction', in *Modernist Writers and the Marketplace*, ed. by Ian Willison, Warwick Gould, and Warren Chernaik (Basingstoke: Macmillan Press, 1996), pp.xii-xviii.

40. David Marr, *Patrick White: A Life* (London: Jonathan Cape, 1991), p.438.

41. Alan Hill, *In Pursuit of Publishing. Foreword by Chinua Achebe* (London: John Murray in Association with Heinemann Educational Books,1988).

42. Willison, 'The Role of the History of the Book in the Humanities', pp.108–10.

43. Gayatri Chakravorty Spivak, 'Three Women's Texts and a Critique of Imperialism', in *"Race", Writing, and Difference*, p.278.

44. Jean-Yves Mollier, 'Histoire de la Lecture, Histoire de l'Édition', in *Histoire de la Lecture: un Bilan des Recherches*, ed. by Roger Chartier (Paris: IMEC Editions, 1995), p.212.

GEORGE SAINTSBURY: CRITICISM AND CONNOISSEURSHIP

ALAN BELL

GEORGE SAINTSBURY SCARCELY needs introducing to an Edinburgh University seminar. The fact that this gathering bears his name is evidence in itself that his memory is still cherished in Edinburgh. The University has named one of its chairs of English literature after him, and half a century ago his admirers (many of them his pupils) founded in his memory a prize for meritorious undergraduate work. The fact that the seminar is sponsored by a Californian winery is proof of a wider fame, and that it is organised jointly by the French and English literature departments is a salutary hint that he should be remembered for his work as a critic of French literature as well as of English.

My own involvement with him goes back to my days at the National Library of Scotland, when as an official of the Department of Manuscripts I found Saintsbury's notoriously difficult handwriting a challenge to palaeographical ingenuity. He himself referred to it as 'an astonishment and a hissing and a curse to all mankind'. Over the years I used to assemble transcripts (often necessarily partial ones) of his many letters. I remember one postcard on which the only readable words appeared to be 'drunken bridesmaids'. On the principle of *lectio difficilior* (though with no second text to compare them with) drunken they turned out to be. However improbable the reading, in the end it proved to be quite plausible when a context had been patiently teased out for an unexpected phrase. I have not been back to the manuscripts recently, and have got out of practice in deciphering a hand that had for so long been the despair of generations of Edinburgh compositors, especially at R. & R. Clark's, who did so much work for Macmillans.

My old friend Augustus Muir, novelist and literary editor and latterly a business historian, was a student of Saintsbury's before the First World War. He collected materials towards a biographical study of the Edinburgh professor he revered above all others. His widow's executors passed them on to me, and they have been a great help in preparing a few reflections on Saintsbury for this seminar. I shall try to keep in mind Professor George Edward Bateman Saintsbury (1845–1933) as a publishing phenomenon in his own right, an outstandingly productive journalist – political as well as literary in his interests – before he became an equally productive professor. His own papers have scarcely survived at all, and even the original of his cellar-book is inaccessible in a private collection. The National Library of Scotland (which holds all his letters to Blackwoods, and some others) does however possess an account book detailing all his literary earnings. He had voluminous correspondences with his publishers (Macmillans as well as Blackwoods, for example), with colleagues like the historian William Hunt, and literary figures like Austin Dobson and his Oxford contemporary Robert Bridges. The letters are lively and informal, less convoluted in style than many of his other writings. One can only wish that they had been rather more *legible*. Still, there is enough to be read there which can fill out the basic biographical record of his life.

Saintsbury was born in 1845 at Southampton, where his father was then manager of the docks. He had a Kensington upbringing, was educated at King's College School, then in the Strand. He received there a good grounding in classics and seems even at that stage to have been a voracious reader. From 1863 to 1868 he was at Merton College, Oxford, holding a classical scholarship. He took a first in Mods, but then over-reached himself by attempting the Greats course in one year rather than the usual two, with a view to going on to the additional final school, then still combined, of Law and History. Alas he achieved only a second class, a disappointment that he felt badly. After he had competed unsuccessfully for five fellowships at various colleges, he developed a sense of rejection by Oxford. But there was no lifelong resentment, and Merton College (which made him an honorary fellow in 1909) retained its place in his affections. From his undergraduate days he gained friendships with Mandell Creighton, the historian of the medieval church and later successively Professor of Ecclesiastical History at Cambridge and Bishop of London, and with Robert Bridges of Corpus Christi, Merton's neighbouring college. If Saintsbury's vagrant reading as an undergraduate had imperilled his degree, it was to be the foundation for his developing career as a literary journalist.

First, not least because he married young and had a wife to support, he had to work his passage as a schoolmaster. From a year at Manchester Grammar School he moved to Elizabeth College, Guernsey (1868–1874) and thence for two years as headmaster of the ill-funded Elgin Educational Institute, a new private school in the north of Scotland. He recalled the schoolmastering experience as penitential, but his six years in the Channel Islands set him up in wide reading in French literature. One can reasonably see the later Saintsbury as one of the great bulk writers of his day, but this is exceeded only by his reputation as one of the great bulk *readers* of all time. He was diligent but relaxed: 'I am afraid I have been all my life a rather unconcentrated reader', he once wrote of himself. He once told his Aberdeen colleague (and later his successor in the Edinburgh chair) H. J. C. Grierson that he never worked after dinner. Grierson replied that he himself often read a good deal of an evening. 'I do not regard reading as work,' was Saintsbury's reply.

This reading was in due course put to service in essays which found a market in London periodicals, especially the *Academy* to start with. Then in October 1875 the *Fortnightly* (edited by John Morley) published a signed essay on Baudelaire. Thirteen guineas he received for it, but the reputation he gained was worth even more. Morley soon commissioned a series of eight further essays on French literature which were the makings of a book. He decided, when the Elgin Institute was obviously failing, to attempt the literary life in London, and to live by his pen.

His fluency and his knowledge rapidly set him up in literary activity. A good deal of work came to him from *London*, edited by W. E. Henley during its brief lifetime from 1877 to 1879. His political opinions and ready pen were also an advantage. The *Saturday Review*, where he became Assistant Editor from 1883 to 1892, used him as a pungent critic of Gladstone's Irish policy, a task he found particularly congenial. He excelled in Toryism 'of an extreme and picturesque type', and he was also a High Churchman who reverenced Dr Pusey. The Toryism showed throughout his life. Comments on wage policy which he published in his *Scrap Books* in the 1920s provoked grudging admiration from George Orwell, who in *The Road to Wigan Pier* remarked of Saintsbury that 'it takes a lot of guts to be openly such a skunk as that'.

His journalism was also a success financially, and by 1880 he was able to save for the first time. Schoolmastering seems to have brought in £348 a year, with some additions for special fees. By 1877 his account book shows £670, and by 1881 he recorded earnings of £1511. Journalism also gave him access to a congenial social and intellectual world which he recalled in a good essay of 1930, 'Journalism fifty years ago', reprinted in the 1946 *Memorial Volume*. It has useful reflections on the increased influence of Oxford and Cambridge on the periodical journalism of the day; the growth of the editorial 'we'; the supply of journalists to meet the needs of an expanding trade; and on anonymity by one who had written 'hundreds of signed and thousands of unsigned articles'. Though only a *feuilleton*, it is a suggestive piece which makes one regret that Saintsbury did not write an autobiography.

In 1880 he produced a *Primer of French Literature* which was followed in 1882 by his better known *Short History* (Clarendon Press); they achieved six and seven editions respectively. Later in life he was to remark, without special boasting, that 'I have never yet given a second-hand opinion of anything, be it book or person', and these works on French literature have a freshness and briskness which bear this out from an early stage in his career. The books are not in the highest sense original, obviously not so to French scholars of the day – though there does not appear to have been much then, even in French, with the same sweep and control of detail. Matthew Arnold and others had emphasised to English readers the importance of French literature. It was Saintsbury's role to give them the *facts*, and he did so in these two books, in three dozen articles for the ninth edition of the *Encyclopaedia Britannica* (which were collected and edited as late as 1946), and in innumerable essays and introductions to individual writers. Oliver Elton referred to this body of work as 'a light to lighten the gentiles'.

The *Short History* was attacked by Edmond Scherer, who made the most of the errors of facts and dates. These were corrigible, and Saintsbury duly corrected them in the successive reprints. He reacted with dignity to Scherer's strong personal attack, and later – magnanimously – translated Scherer's essays on English literature with an approving preface by himself.

The *Short History* is strong on French lyrical poetry, less so on the drama (Racine is coldly treated). It is not a work of intellectual history, and one wouldn't search in it for movements or tendencies. Its strength (and this applies to all his other historical work) is in the assessment of individual authors. This does not make his histories merely annalistic handbooks for students, however.

What gives the *Short Histories*, and much of his other writing, a unity of approach, is their emphasis on literary *form*. He seems never to have attempted a principled defence of his vigorously-practised historical approach, but there is this emphasis on form versus content, and he eschewed theory as far as possible. It would be interesting to see his histories and essays examined by a modern critical theorist – a task I am wholly incompetent to perform. The emphasis on form over content is one of his constants, and he made it a principle that no dislike of a writer's opinions or ideas should influence our view of his art. He remained faithful to this throughout his career, and stressed 'treatment' and execution as separable from the intellectual substance – or 'matter' – of the artistic product. This was an approach which was rigorously applied, and noted by some contemporaries. But it enabled the recorder of whole national literatures to approach them with fairness, and catholicity.

Meanwhile he was also writing voluminously on English literature, not just in reviewing but in essays and books. In 1881 there was *Dryden* for the 'English Men of Letters' series (and this *Dryden* was followed by a long set of reprints of Scott's Dryden edition, with new introductions). To Dryden he remained faithful, as also to Thackeray and Balzac, both of whom were accorded prefaces that were gathered into books later in life. He was a contributor, too, to most of those *series* which are such a phenomenon of English publishing of the late 1870s onwards, and which as a group deserve the attention of publishing historians. 'English Men of Letters' (for the *Dryden*, as mentioned); *Manchester* (where he had taught and had for a short time worked in the *Guardian*) for 'Historic Towns'; *Lord Derby* for 'The Queen's Prime Ministers'; and *Marlborough* for 'English Worthies'.

By the time he published his *History of Elizabethan Literature* (1887) his main interests had turned towards English literature, and as with French there was a comprehensive *Short History* which came in 1898. It would be bibliographically exhausting to try and set out the huge output of anthologies, primers, histories, surveys and introductions to editions, and reprints which came out in the '80s and '90s. The four-volume *Collected Essays* which he published in retirement, and a posthumous gathering of his *Prefaces and Essays*, give an idea of their scope. On the historical side what he was doing met a general need, as English literary history lacked a comprehensive study, and something was needed to consolidate a subject that had been fragmented into miniature biographies (as in 'English Men of Letters') and individual studies. His methods deserve consideration in the light of what was happening in general historical writing at the time. John Richard Green's *A Short History of the English People* was published in 1874 and the compact survey was long fashionable.

Saintsbury's training as a journalist gave him great facility, and he could throw off an article, or a book, with great ease. But often his prose is weighted down with learned allusiveness, and is usually ill-revised (there is a vigorous analytical attack on a *Macmillan's Magazine* article, published in the *Pall Mall Gazette* in 1886 under the heading 'Half Hours with the Worst Authors'; it is plausibly attributed to Oscar Wilde). Some change was needed to ensure that this apparently unlimited literary energy was better channelled and directed, not least after Saintsbury lost his well-paid *Saturday Review* connection following a change of editor, and took on far too many introductions and anthologies. Soon an academic opportunity offered, and he was able to take up a post that would channel his work away from literary journalism into more substantial works of scholarship.

After twenty years of solid work, he gave up reviewing in 1895, picking it up again only in retirement. His essay on 'Twenty years of reviewing', published as a rather regretful *au revoir* in *Blackwood's* in 1895, is still a well-judged introduction to the craft, dealing with aspects like fairness, excessive severity, the importance of the literary editor's judgement, and also the sheer excitement that the task offered to a dedicated professional. He quoted his favourite *Pendennis* as the *locus classicus*: 'As for Pen, he had never been so delighted in his life; his hand trembled as he cut the string of the packet and beheld within a smart new set of neat calico-bound books – novels and travels, and poems.' Saintsbury knew that this remained 'true (except, perhaps, as to the trembling of the hand) of some of us to the last'. Reviewing had given him much pleasure and much learning, and helped him 'to pay double debts, by doing a momentary duty and adding a little to more permanent stores of knowledge and habits of practice'.

In 1895 he secured the Crown appointment to the Regius chair of Rhetoric and English Literature at Edinburgh University. W. E. Henley and Walter

Raleigh were the other front-running candidates, but it was Saintsbury (at the age of 50) who became successor to David Masson. He held the professorship for twenty years. There was some apprehension before his arrival in Edinburgh because one of his more prominent recent contributions to literature had been an essay on 'Cookery of the Grouse' in the *Fur and Feather* series in 1893. Edinburgh need not have worried. The chapter is a good one, wide-ranging and elegantly shaped. It begins with a reference to a French recipe for 'Grouse à la Dundy', which Saintsbury recalled as from 'Dundy . . . not only the gamiest, *la plus giboyeuse*, city of Scotland, but also renowned for every refinement of taste and luxury – superior in short to Peebles itself'. It ended with a fanciful German recipe, remarking that 'after this and other things the mind recoils from these excesses to the elegance of a good roast grouse simple of himself'.

This is not perhaps the time to dwell on his professorial activities, save to mention that he was one of the most prominent figures in the University of his day, not least among the student body who recognised that he was prodigiously a professor, a notable physical and intellectual presence even when confronted with a huge and disorderly First Ordinary class but soon winning their respect. He became a hero to them, with the vagaries of his syntax a special part of the living legend. One of them committed to memory a Saintsbury sentence which went thus: 'But while none, save these, of men living, had done, or could have done, such things, there was much here which – whether either could have done it or not – neither had done.'

The years of the professorship were the time of the big books, at a time when there was a demonstrable market for the comprehensive manual. He had limbered up for the *Short History of English Literature* (Macmillan 1898), similar in approach and structure to the *French Literature* volume the Clarendon Press had first brought out in 1882, with a *History of Nineteenth-Century Literature 1780–1895* which came out from Macmillan in 1896. There were three volumes (Romance, Early Renaissance and Late Nineteenth Century) in the twelve-volume set of 'Periods of European Literature' series for which he acted as General Editor, some taken on when other contributors failed. These were Blackwood's publications, as was the *History of Literary Criticism and Taste in Europe from the Earliest Texts to the Present Day* (1900–1904). Macmillan published his *History of English Prosody* in three volumes 1906–1910, with the one-volume *Historical Manual* afterwards, and in 1912 the pioneering single volume *History of English Prose Rhythm*.

A lot of production and some sales records survive for these substantial volumes. It would be interesting to see how well they sold as well as how they were received. Saintsbury met a need with these substantial contributions, which would make any HEFCE assessment panel gasp and stretch their eyes.

As for their contents, I cannot speak with detailed specialist knowledge.

My impression of the histories, when I have consulted them for particular authors or subjects, is that they are clear and firm in their judgments, sometimes oddly elongated in their expression, and weak in their thematic placing of individual authors and their writings. I have the feeling that that the habits of the journalist-essayist and the well-practised writer of introductions surely over-influenced the historian of English literature. In making such comments on these huge books one is not necessarily being disrespectful of the real foundations of the reputation of one whom Arnold Bennett called (with no respect intended) the 'Albert Memorial of learning'.

Saintsbury was never minutely careful as to dates and details, and his histories both French and English are more reliable in revised editions where he accommodated the corrigenda pointed out by the more assiduous of his readers. Churton Collins had a run-in with him over factual errors, though the case was by no means as serious as Collins's attacks on Gosse round about the same time, and the necessary corrections were made. The first job the young David Nichol Smith, later doyen of eighteenth-century English studies, ever had, was to revise the dates in the index of *Nineteenth-Century Literature*. 'It was then that I began to gather the evidence', Nichol Smith recalled, for a gastronomic audience, 'which in time led me to the conclusion that the only dates in which he could be trusted to be minutely accurate were the dates of vintages. In these I understand he was impeccable.'

The last book he finished in Edinburgh is *The Peace of the Augustans*, subtitled 'a survey of eighteenth century literature as a place of rest and refreshment'. 'Rest and refreshment' was offered to the distressed and febrile world of 1916, when Bell's published it, and it is interesting that it was reprinted in 1946 among the World's Classics which had achieved such notable success with the Trollope revival offering refreshment during the Second World War. When *The Peace of the Augustans* first appeared *The Times Literary Supplement* suggested that Saintsbury might almost be proposing a picnic, and that 'rest and refreshment' phrase has proved an irritant ever since. It is certainly characteristic of his later manner, conversational in tone and allusive in reference, and pungent in its denunciation of bugbears. Critics like Claude Rawson have found it wholly exasperating and liken its 'self-indulgent' manner to 'a long evening with a club bore'. But the notion of an 'Augustan Age', whatever and whenever that may have been, remains as a concept that later commentators have to grapple with, and Pat Rogers, for one, finds Saintsbury's approach less unhelpful than Rawson, and indeed a stimulus to his own good study, *The Augustan Vision* (1974).

It would be interesting some time to pursue Saintsbury's reputation among critics. Not as a *Critical Heritage* study, for that useful series ought to be confined to creative writers, but gathering some of the contradictory reactions. For example, Percy Simpson, working in an Oxford tradition of textual scholarship, had little time for him. He told a pupil 'I was once at a dinner with that man Saintsbury, and he got up and talked in a loud, vulgar way about literature. "I take to literature", he said, "as a working man takes to beer." I was tempted to whisper to my neighbour, 'And with the same equally disastrous results!.' (One is reminded of Saintsbury's remarking, in the *Cellar Book*, that Bass the brewers paid him the greatest compliment of his life when they sent him a barrel inscribed 'George Saintsbury, Esq., Full To The Bung'.)

And yet contrast this Oxonian misliking of Saintsbury's bluff, brisk approach with the praise it elicited from no less a commentator than Edmund Wilson, who saw in an 1892 volume of Saintsbury's *Miscellaneous Essays*: 'his expert analysis of the technique of writing, his unexpected and witty allusions, his warm and luminous glow and his inexhaustible curiosity'. All these are elements that are characteristic of Wilson's own approach.

The best modern discussion of Saintsbury is in John Gross's *The Rise and Fall of the Man of Letters*. Gross is guarded in his praise, finding Saintsbury's political views uncongenial, his style almost unbearable, and his lack of a settled theoretical critical stance also culpable. 'His criticism is full of forth-right judgments and downright opinions,' Gross writes, 'yet ultimately shape-less, a wilderness of signposts.' Nevertheless, he finds himself obliged to con-cede that 'flawed though it is, there is something impressive about the spirit as well as the scale of Saintsbury's labours: a magnanimity, an underlying belief that literature, at least, is a republic where every citizen is entitled to his rights. And he has substance. Even the clumsiest contortions of his prose convey an impression of thwarted power rather than affectation. He is . . . unlike the great majority of his contemporaries, a critic whom one can come back to.'

Gross sees the merits of selecting nuggets of excellent comment from the all-enveloping context of the big books or the often ephemeral circumstances of the periodical articles. One cannot do better in advising selectivity than to follow Sir Herbert Grierson (Saintsbury's successor in the Regius chair) in citing the essay on 'The cookery of the grouse', already mentioned. (In his World's Classics *Peace of the Augustans* preface Grierson cites the bird con-cerned as a ptarmigan rather than a capercailzie, but no matter.) The story goes thus. When on Guernsey as a schoolmaster, Saintsbury saw that a bold butcher had imported a capercailzie. He ordered it, to be hung. This bird, the biggest of Scottish moor game, was then forgotten about both by the game dealer and his customer. When it was rediscovered weeks later, 'parts had to be cut away, but the rest was altogether excellent'. That is probably true not only of *The Peace of the Augustans,* but of all his major works, which never cease to surprise and impress in their individual *aperçus*.

Edmund Wilson singled out for special praise the little studies of minor French writers. Saintsbury's vast range of reading and his capacity for recall were put at the service of his final major contribution to literary history, the two-volume *History of the French Novel*, started in Edinburgh in 1914–15 and finished in Bath three years later: Macmillan published it in 1917–19. Though written afresh it is in subject-matter largely a recapitulation (with some new material – for example, on Rabelais) of his contributions to the subject since the start of his reviewing and critical career, during which he had always been convinced that narrative art is the greatest of French gifts, and that French fiction is fundamentally romantic. This *History* is a further big book, and one that no other Englishman of the time could have written.

It was to be the last wide-ranging general survey of its kind that Saintsbury undertook. There were essays to be written, and many to be gathered, giving a final, permanent form (in *Collected Essays*, four volumes 1922–4) to scattered appreciations which have enduring value. I think, for example, of the 1888 *Macmillan's Magazine* essay on Sydney Smith, which retains its freshness, not least as a strong Tory's assessment of a somewhat less strong Whig. And I noticed that Sir Angus Fraser, the George Borrow expert, recently gave high praise to Saintsbury's essay on Borrow which originally appeared in 1886 (also in *Macmillan's*).

Saintsbury retired from his chair in 1915 and settled in Bath. His years there were not merely for retrospection and selective consolidation of the output of a highly productive lifetime. He kept up his modern reading, noting Compton Mackenzie's *Sinister Street* (1915) as 'a remarkable book, the most remarkable novel I think that I have read for many years' (with its 'odd mixture of childishness and decadence'), and keeping up with his friend Kipling (to whom his *Cellar Book* is dedicated). In 1922 he surprised even himself by contributing to the first number of the *Criterion*, edited by T. S. Eliot. 'You'll laugh' – he wrote to a friend – 'to see my name in a new quarterly of almost the *jeunest* jeunes. It was the doing of the man Eliot to whom I spoke to you.' And in 1926–8 we find him writing for the *Dial* on subjects such as 'Technique', 'Irony', 'Things about Blake', and on Anatole France.

In 1921 he wrote about Norman Douglas: 'I am 75. I have read more novels than a man of 750 ought to have done. For some twenty years I used to review hundreds or thereabouts of English and scores of French as they came out. For about twenty [years], the first of this so-called age, I have come across just two new novelists who have given me something that I can recommend to a friend. The author of *South Wind* is the second in order of time, not rank.'

His retreat to 1 Royal Circus, Bath, where he and his invalid wife had an apartment just off the Crescent, was complete, but he was never entirely out of touch. Of younger writers who got to know him in his retirement, Helen Waddell is the most prominent. He indulged in a whimsical and rather tiresome correspondence with her. Those who know William Nicholson's fine portrait of the eighty-year-old Saintsbury, with his tiny spectacles, ectoplasmic beard, crumpled suit and skull-cap, will understand how his aged figure in the window of his study, reading and still reading, became one of the sights of his adopted city. In old age he came to personify the popular ideal of the 'sage' – a word which doesn't quite get it right, though the never-quite-translatable '*savant*' conveys it better.

He is known to a wider world through his writings about wine, not least through the Saintsbury Club which was founded to honour him in 1931 and which continues to cherish his memory. *Notes on a Cellar Book* was published by Macmillan in 1920 as a little square volume in wine-coloured cloth. It owes its origins to the failure of a society monthly called the *Piccadilly Review*, edited by T. Earle Welby, which had commissioned a series of wine articles from the Professor. The *Piccadilly Review* was not an elevated organ like the *Saturday*, but rather Woosterishly social, with reviews of new London dance halls. Only two Saintsbury articles were published before it went under. Saintsbury had the good journalist's dislike of seeing anything going to waste, and approached Sir Frederick Macmillan to see whether there might be a book in these contributions. 'It wouldn't of course be a History,' he said, 'but I think it might interest people.'

Saintsbury's cash-books show that he had once planned a systematic treatise on wine. In 1895 there is an entry 'Wine book: cookery of hare, etc., jettisoned on appointment to Chair, say £100', included in the 'bad debts, etc.' section. This is struck through, and annotated much later 'But some returned after many years by *Cellar Book*'. It was certainly to become a nice little earner, and helped him towards a *renouveau* in his reputation late in life.

His *Notes*, hung on the peg of a slim exercise book as *aide mémoire*, are just that. Its origins as newspaper articles dictate the form of the book, so claret, on which he could have written at great length, and with much authority and affection, is treated almost perfunctorily, and chapters on the miscellanea are out of proportion. At least the restrictions of article-length chapters stop his discursiveness becoming merely garrulous, for it is a conversational book, and the whimsicality and pathos of its vinous reminiscences are kept well under control.

The *Notes* make a richly nostalgic book, particularly wistful in tone when one remembers that ill-health had enforced virtual abstinence on the old man, who had sold up his cellar, and much of his library, on leaving Edinburgh in 1915. His judgments of vintages venerable even then (and now vanished virtually beyond recall) have been respected as authoritative ever since, though some more austere later wine critics have found his circumstantial accounts of wines he has drunk excessive, and they blame him for the origins of a 'baroque' school of wine writing. But the book was a considerable popular success, with several immediate reprints, and it has been in print well beyond Saintsbury's own lifetime. Its success prompted him to write the three *Scrap Books* (1922–24) which are full of discursive reminiscences, especially on the

Oxford of his youth, and reflections on food almost as evocative as his writings on wine. Saintsbury enjoined his executors not to help any intending biographer, but in the *Scrap Books* he came pretty close to infringing his own ban.

The *Cellar Book* attracted a following in the wine trade and among gastronomic writers. Early in 1931 André Simon, the champagne broker, held a luncheon for five in his offices at Mark Lane in the City, where the assembled company (including Maurice Healy, J. C. Squire and A. J. A. Symons), was emboldened by a succession of fine wines to offer a special dinner to Saintsbury, then believed to be living in wineless seclusion. The professor declined, illegibly but not discourteously, pleading poor health and confinement to his house. Nevertheless, the plotters went ahead and convened the banquet in tribute to him at the Connaught Rooms in May. It was a great success. D. S. MacColl, in the chair, proposed the formation of a dining society, the Saintsbury Club, in his honour. It met on his 86th birthday, 23 October 1931, at the Vintners' Hall, and it has continued to meet there twice yearly ever since. It consists in principle half of 'men of wine' and half 'men of letters', but the membership is much more varied than that would perhaps suggest, with diplomats and doctors as well as those of primarily literary background. The principle throughout has been that members' knowledge and love of wine should be 'catholic and articulate'. Membership is restricted to 50, that being the greatest number that can conveniently be accommodated out of an eight-bottle (6 litre) *impériale*. Incoming members are expected to present 'some good wine', to be laid down as a dowry which will be discussed enthusiastically and critically at a later meeting. There is oratory from time to time, and good fellowship in a congenial sodality. Saintsbury himself was appointed Honorary President, and this was perpetuated after his death in January 1933. He remains the Club's tutelary deity, but is far more than a token patron. The Club enjoys his company through his writings, and endeavours to keep his memory green.

A NOTE ON SOURCES

This introduction to Saintsbury was prepared for informal delivery as an incidental contribution to the 1996 conference. It draws on the main printed biographical sources, notably A. Blyth Webster's memoir in *University of Edinburgh Journal* VI (1933), Oliver Elton's in *Proceedings of the British Academy* XIX (1933), and David Nichol Smith's 'Centenary Tribute' printed by the Saintsbury Club after its autumn 1945 meeting. Blyth Webster and Nichol Smith's essays were included with other biographically useful material respectively in *George Saintsbury, the memorial volume* (1945) and *A last vintage: essays and papers by George Saintsbury* (1950), two volumes edited by his devoted pupil Augustus Muir. Saintsbury forbade any biography of himself, a task that would have been much impeded by his notoriously difficult handwriting. Professor Dorothy Richardson Jones has published 'King of critics': George Saintsbury 1845–1933, critic, journalist, historian, professor (University of Michigan Press 1992), a study deriving from doctoral research in the 1930s, a time when Saintsbury's reputation as a critic remained very high. Long gestation enabled it to take some account of later assessments, including the fourth (later 19th century) volume of René Wellek's A history of modern criticism: 1750–1950 (1965), the spirited chapter on 'the bookmen' in John Gross's The rise and fall of the man of letters (1969), and Harold Orel's chapter on Saintsbury in Victorian literary critics (1984).

The present essay draws on two previous contributions of my own: 'George Saintsbury: Edinburgh and After', in University of Edinburgh Journal XXVI (1973) and a 1979 talk to the Saintsbury Club privately printed in 1991. Saintsbury's own papers have not survived, with only a few exceptions, but several substantial groups of his letters are still extant, notably those to the historian William Hunt (Merton College Library, Oxford) and to Helen Waddell (Queen's University Library, Belfast). Specifically related to the theme of this essay are his letters to Macmillan & Co (British Library, Additional MSS. 55019–20) and to William Blackwood & Sons (National Library of Scotland, MSS. 4001–4940 passim). The National Library of Scotland also possesses Saintsbury's account book of literary earnings, maintained like a barrister's fee-book, which with further decipherment and correlation with W. M. Parker's bibliography (in A last vintage, 1950, mentioned above) would repay further study by a student of literary earnings.

INDEX

Index

INDEX